YOUR
CAREER

Choices and Changes

Sixth Edition

David C. Borchard

John J. Kelly

Nancy-Pat Weaver

KENDALL/HUNT PUBLISHING COMPANY
4050 Westmark Drive Dubuque, Iowa 52002

Contributor
Mary M. Greene

Copyright © 1980, 1982, 1984, 1988, 1992, 1995 by Kendall/Hunt Publishing Company

ISBN 0-8403-9383-0

Printed in the United States of America
10 9 8 7 6 5 4 3 2

Contents

Illustrations

FIGURE

Tables

Acknowledgments

A few individuals have been making significant contributions to the field of Career and Life Planning, and their ideas have served as major contributions to this book. We especially acknowledge the following people: Gordon Porter Miller for decision-making theory and practical application; Richard N. Bolles for transferable skills assessment methods, along with numerous career-planning ideas and materials; John L. Holland for personality style and occupational environments theory; Sidney B. Simon for values clarification ideas; and Ned Herrmann for thinking style theory and assessment model.

We particularly express our gratitude and heartfelt thanks to the following: Mary Multer Greene, our editor, for her endless energy, ideas, and professional assistance. Fontelle Gilbert, and Mary Kaye O'Neill, our spirited colleagues, for creative ideas and insightful critiques. Joe Mayer, our "wild and crazy" artist friend for the cartoons that spice up the book, and to Pat Donohoe, our expert copy editor/proofreader for her work on the 6th edition.

Introduction

Searching for a satisfying career may very well be a source of frustration. You may long for a change, but simultaneously feel overwhelmed by the career-choice process.

Your Career: Choices, Chances, Changes offers a solution to this common dilemma. Using a simple but thorough decision-making model, we show you how to take charge of your life and career. You will progress through the chapters, taking small manageable steps supported by explanation, examples, and practical exercises. You will be examining not only your attitudes toward choosing a career, but also your natural talents, values, personality style, wants, and needs in relation to your career choice. You will be exploring the world of work, developing alternatives, setting goals, and making plans while learning an effective, reusable decision-making process. The exercises will give you a chance to personalize the process, making it relevant to your unique life.

You are likely to find this process helpful if you include yourself in any of the following groups:

1. People entering college who need to clarify their career objectives before choosing their academic program.

2. College students who have become disenchanted with their current academic program and career goals.

3. Women preparing to make a transition from homemaker to college student and/or salaried employee.

4. People preparing for a first career.

5. People dissatisfied with their present type of work or career who wish to make a change for the better.

6. Midlife career changers seeking more satisfaction in their careers.

This workbook is not intended for people under pressure to make an immediate job or career change. You need to be willing to commit a significant amount of time, energy, introspection, and effort to career planning and decision making.

We've selected a workbook format to make this material more readily understandable. Please don't just read the book from cover to cover like a novel. Feel free to make notes in it. For best results, do only a small amount in the workbook at any one sitting. Give yourself plenty of time to think about both the material and yourself. Read some, do some exercises, put it down for awhile, and then come back to it later. Take whatever amount of time you feel is necessary to complete the process and reach decisions that make sense for you.

The workbook may be used by individuals either working alone or working together in a career course or support group. However, we believe that you will obtain maximum benefit from doing the work with others. Many of the exercises work best when they are discussed with others so that you have the opportunity to obtain feedback. If you are unable to join a course, consider starting your own group. Of course, doing the workbook on your own is preferable to doing nothing at all, especially if you are highly motivated.

The primary outcomes you will achieve by completing this workbook are:

1. Gaining familiarity and practice with the skills essential in career/life decision making.
2. Discovering your most fulfilling natural talents and understanding how these are transferable to the world of work.
3. Identifying what it takes for you individually to experience satisfaction in your career.
4. Assessing, in general terms, where in the world of work you would most like to contribute your unique natural talents and skills.
5. Becoming familiar with the primary sources of occupational information and knowing how to use these resources to develop and assess your career alternatives.
6. Developing lifestyle goals with which to guide your career and learning plans.
7. Learning how to develop action plans for achieving your career objectives.
8. Becoming a more perceptive and skillful problem solver in matters affecting your career over the years.

The following additional resources will be helpful as you complete the workbook:

The *Self-Directed Search* (SDS) by John L. Holland, the *Myers-Briggs Type Indicator* (MBTI), *The Strong Interest Inventory* (SII), and a college career center or public library.

The SDS, MBTI and SII can be obtained from most college career centers, and these sources add worthwhile information to the chapter on personality styles. A college career center and/or a public library contain occupational resources helpful in developing your list of alternatives and in researching careers.

Completing this workbook will not automatically get you a job. But you will become a far more effective job seeker by learning how to make decisions, set goals, and make plans. Although the material is presented in the context of a career decision, you can apply much of what you learn to life situations in general.

1 Making Career Decisions in a Changing World

What most people want out of life, more than anything else, is the opportunity to make choices.

DAVID P. CAMPBELL
If You Don't Know Where You're Going,
You'll Probably End Up Somewhere Else

DO YOU KNOW PEOPLE WHO:

➡ Don't know how or refuse to make decisions?

➡ Make small decisions easily but panic over those that affect their careers or lives?

➡ Have gotten into their career more by accident than by planning and preparation?

➡ Hang onto jobs they hate for security rather than risk seeking their real passion?

If so, you know people who have settled for less freedom and a lesser quality of life because they didn't know how to make decisions or because they were unwilling to make difficult choices.

Why Work?

Would you work if you didn't have to? Many people who are asked this question say something like, "Of course not, do you think I'm crazy or something?" Where do we get our attitudes about work, and why are they often negative? Is work really the curse of original sin? If work is just a burden, why do some actually love it? Are they just goofy or is it possible that they have discovered something that the work haters have missed?

Answering questions such as these involves examining our deeply rooted beliefs about work—an important prelude to career-planning. Seeing work in a totally negative light will adversely affect the results of your decision making. Think about it—can you really get very excited about a process involving something that you aren't really very enthusiastic about? If, on the other hand, you are excited about your options and the opportunities they can bring to your life, you are going to be much more invested in your future and the career/life planning process.

We're confident that this book can help you to be enthusiastic about the rewarding role that work can play in your life. Consider, for instance, the possibility that work might represent opportunity. Work might, for example, provide you with a means to test yourself in the world, to find out how good you can really be, to grow and develop in ways you've barely dared to dream about, to make a contribution, or to create and operate your own business. The classic study of work by Friedman and Havighurst identifies five basic roles that work fills in peoples' lives[1]:

1. *Income*—maintaining a minimum sustenance level and achieving some higher standard of living.

2. *Expenditure of time and energy*—providing something to do or a way of passing time.

3. *Identity and status*—a source of self-respect and a way of achieving recognition from others.

4. *Association*—a way of having friendships, peer group relations, and authority relationships.

5. *A source of meaning in life*—a way of obtaining purpose and meaning in life through service to others, creativity, self-expression, and having new experiences.

While Friedman and Havighurst certainly have not covered all the reasons people work, they do show that we work for a variety of reasons. It is important to realize that while there are kinds of work that each of us would dislike and/or not do well, there are also kinds of work that we could fully enjoy and even thrive in. The kind of work that fits us depends upon who we are. We are all different. We have different finger prints and different interests. We are also uniquely talented. Fortunately, there are many different kinds of work available now, and there will be even more in the future.

This is a book about career planning and decision making. Your challenge in the career/life planning process is to discover exactly how you are uniquely gifted and what kinds of work match your particular talents. No small task, but in helping people do this over dozens of years, we've found and designed processes that make this task easier, fruitful, and fun! The first step in this process is to help you become an excellent personal decision maker. That's because the career decisions you make directly affect the quality of your life. Since you probably have to work anyway, why not invest your effort and time in career-related activity that enables you to develop and use your best potentials, to make a contribution, to prosper, and to have some fun in the process? Wouldn't you really want to do that anyway—even if you didn't have to work?

What Is Career/Life Planning?

Many people see career planning as a fairly simple and straightforward choice that leads to a top-paying job, regardless of what that job is. Others equate career planning with the event of choosing a major in school, getting a job, or moving into a different occupation. The prevailing assumption here is that the rest of their work lives will somehow fall into place.

The term, as we define it, actually refers to an on-going and life-long cognitive-affective (intellectual and feeling based) process to help you find, pursue, and generate an interesting career and life. In this regard we concede that any number of circumstances and conditions might appear to limit your options now and at various other stages of your life. But please bear this in mind—the work world is huge, multi-dimensional, and ever changing. There are always more opportunities than any one individual, on his/her own, can possibly know about. No matter what conditions you now face, whether you are currently more motivated by material success than by inner values, your best strategy is to find a career direction and work conditions that you enjoy and enable you to capitalize on and develop your top strengths and personal attributes.

Career planning involves two important dimensions—the inner world of self and the outer world of possibilities. The inner dimension means learning about yourself, particularly those traits, interests, personal values, potentials and skills that you really want to put to work in your life. The outer dimension involves discovering what's out there for you—now and in the future. It's about answering certain questions: what kind of work, job, and life style options will enable me to have the kind of life that I want ideally. What can I do that will enable me to grow and develop in ways that suit me? Where can I make the best contribution? What kind of career direction will enable me to connect the best of my inner world with the options available in the outer world?

As you consider these two dimensions, here is an important fact to keep in mind—the world of work now changes so rapidly that it's impossible to know the future. We can, however, know what we personally want to bring to our future! In this regard, it is probably more useful to concentrate on the kind of future we really want to have and how might we get there than it is to worry about what the best jobs of the future are going to be.

What Is a Career?

Perhaps the idea of career brings a role model to mind. Is there someone who comes to mind when you consider the concept of a career? Is identification with that person primarily positive or negative? Perhaps your career role model is a parent, a spouse, or someone you greatly admire. One of the authors of this text thinks of Swiss psychiatrist Dr. Carl Jung as an ideal career role model while another thinks of the poet Robert Frost, and the third identifies with opera singer Harolyn Blackwell.

Career is a term often misunderstood. Ask ten different people to define *career* and you'll probably get ten different answers. Some think the terms *career* and *job* are synonymous. We don't! Your career is broader and more general than your job. A job is a specific agreement with an employer to perform assigned tasks for pay. Having a career, on the other hand, implies that you have prepared for and are building expertise and experience in a particular field. Your career determines what kinds of work you will do and not do. It serves as a frame of reference for the kinds of jobs you will seek, qualify for and accept. It is also the context in which you will continue to develop new skills and insights.

Most dictionaries define *career* as something like "one's progress through life, or one's advancement or achievement in a particular vocation." In this broad sense, your career begins at birth, could possibly end with retirement, but is over only at death (are their careers in heaven?). From our earliest days, we get career-related messages from our families and environment. As a child we begin developing behavior patterns, personality styles, attitudes, interest patterns, and skills that strongly shape the course of our career. Although these experiences strongly influence the early stages of our career, they do not necessarily "lock us in" it for all of life. People change as they get older. As they develop, people undergo psycho-social changes that influence their needs and career goals. These personal changes, combined with shifts in society and the economy, often lead to unanticipated career changes.

Career and Self-Concept

As we develop, we acquire an image of ourselves, a self-concept. Most of us are not even consciously aware of our self-concept, but it is reflected in our actions. The result is that we unconsciously seek jobs and pursue careers to match our inner "self" image. For example, people who see themselves as being neat, well-organized, and good with numbers may seek careers as accountants or actuarials. Those who see themselves as intellectuals may seek professions featuring mental concentration in an area like law, physics, or philosophy. Those who enjoy nurturing may seek out careers as social workers, nurses—or even parents.

This method of essentially unconscious career selection seems to work fine for some but, unfortunately, not for most. The problem is that our self-concept may be an inaccurate reflection of our real preferences and skills, or we may lack self-confidence. From an early age, self-concepts begin developing in response to what we hear our parents and elders say about us, such as "Isn't she just the perfect little mother," or "He's just like his father" (when Father is a lawyer), or "He's going to be a super athlete," or "She has the mind of a wizard." When people around us make such biased observations, either negative or positive, they influence the shaping of our self-image.

How Seymore's father saw him   *How Seymore's mother saw him*   *Seymore's mother and father*

A poor self-concept undermines your career development as well as your life satisfaction. Fortunately, your self-concept can change over time and through attention. By taking a more deliberate and systematic approach to determining your skills, personal traits, preferences, needs, and values, you can bring your self-image into line with your true abilities and desires. You can also greatly enhance your self-confidence by knowing what you are particularly good at and what you can achieve with your talents and abilities. The payoffs for generating an accurate self-concept can be tremendous. This kind of self knowledge can guide you through appropriate job and career changes, make you more resilient in dealing with life's challenges, and guide you in finding a sense of security in yourself.

Career Impact on Life

Your career will have a huge impact on your life and your lifestyle. Your career determines and influences things like:

- Your sense of esteem and self-worth
- Which of your abilities and talents will be used
- Which of your interests will find expression in work
- How much money you will earn
- What kinds of clothes you will wear
- What kinds of benefits your job will provide
- What kinds of organizations you will work for
- The locations and environments you will be working in
- What kinds of people you will associate with
- What kinds of activities will fill your working hours
- How much time you'll have for home, family, and leisure
- How much of your time you will spend working

- What kinds and levels of responsibilities you will have
- What kinds of things you will be learning
- What kind of a lifestyle you will have
- How healthy you will be and how long you will live

Obviously, this list can go on and on. It is difficult to identify anything in your life that is not affected directly or indirectly by your career. Your career has and will exert a powerful influence on your self-image and your sense of esteem and self-worth. It will even influence your love life, your family life, and life energy.

Career Decision Making

In spite of the critically important role that career plays in life, most people slip into careers with little forethought or preparation. In fact, most people spend more time selecting new clothes or a new car than they do in deciding upon their career. Based on dozens of years of experience in assisting career seekers and job hunters, career planning specialists Richard Bolles and John Crystal have concluded that most people choose their occupation absent mindedly, and they make their career decisions in haphazard fashion—without awareness that there are real alternatives or possibilities from which they may choose.[2]

Making a choice is required whenever people are faced with more than one alternative or have unsettled questions. Whether we rationally or intuitively settle these questions and whether we reach a conclusion consciously or unconsciously, we have made our decision. Many of us are afraid of decision making. Actually, we are afraid of making a wrong choice or, perhaps, a less-than-perfect one. That may be because we confuse the outcome of the decision with the decision itself. For these reasons, some of us look for others to tell us what to do, while some of us procrastinate, sometimes putting off the decision indefinitely.

Unfortunately, avoiding decisions does not result in eliminating risks and unwanted outcomes. At best, not making a decision results in keeping things the way they are and feeling more dissatisfied. This is true even with everyday decisions. For example, if you stay at home on a Saturday evening because you can't decide whether to go to the movies, see a play, go bowling, or visit a friend, the result is the same as deciding to stay at home. Incidentally, staying at home by choice feels much better than staying at home because you couldn't make up your mind.

Similarly, what happens when you are in a job you hate or when you lack enthusiasm about your academic program, and you do nothing to change? The result of indecision is predictable. You are, in effect, deciding to stay in that academic program, job, or life situation. By not deciding, you forfeit the opportunity of achieving a better outcome.[3] Since your performance, self-confidence, and attitude are likely to decline as a result, you are increasing the risk of your most feared outcome—failure.

TABLE 1.1 Reminders on Decision Making

- Successful career/life decision making originates in self understanding.
- Decision making is a developed skill rather than a genetic endowment.
- To feel and be more competent, you must become a better decision-maker.
- Failing to decide forfeits the opportunity to control your future.
- Personal freedom is a function of decision-making.
- Hate your career? Who chose it? Who is responsible for it?

Steps to Career-Planning Success

Breaking down your career/life planning process into smaller steps will make the choices seem much less overwhelming. Each step of the way, you will be gaining knowledge to help you make a decision about your next career goal and to help you make plans to achieve that goal. The following diagram shows the six steps used in this book to assist you in making your career/life decision.

FIGURE 1.1 Career/Life Decision Making Sequence

1. **Transferable skill identification**
2. **Clarifying personal preference and assets**
3. **Finding interesting possibilities**
4. **Analyzing the choices and choosing**
5. **Future directions: goals and plans**
6. **Career implementing and job marketing**

Step #1, identifying skills, is accomplished by examining talents and competencies. Chapter 2 shows how many skills are revealed by the everyday activities you have performed well at home, in school, and in voluntary and paid jobs. Most important, you will discover the patterns or relationships revealed by seemingly trivial skills and accomplishments. These skill patterns show whether your talents are primarily related to working with people, data, or things. You will also determine which of your personal traits are likely to contribute to your success.

Step #2, clarifying personal preferences, is accomplished by discovering your natural traits and interests so you can determine which careers best match your style. Chapter 3 helps you to do this by exploring your thinking style—the way you prefer to process information of all kinds. Chapter 4 explores your personality-related interest patterns. Chapter 6 helps clarify your true needs and values—your "deep-core" motivators.

Step #3, Finding interesting options, gives you a chance to use the self-knowledge acquired in the earlier steps to identify careers of potential interest. At this point, you will be compiling a master list of your better options. Chapters 5 and 7 will show you ways to discover and explore your occupational alternatives.

Step #4, making a choice, involves narrowing your alternatives and making a career choice that is appropriate to your current situation. Chapter 7 will help you evaluate these career alternatives in terms of your skills and preferences and occupational outlook. *You can return to this chapter any time over the course of your life to help you refocus and make good decisions.*

Step #5, setting goals and making plans, involves developing the specific goals and plans needed to translate your career decision into action steps. Chapter 8 shows how to design meaningful goals and plans for a career that will fit into the life you want to have.

Step #6, implementing your career, is designed to help you turn hopes and plans into reality. Chapter 9 shows how to overcome mental and situational blocks that can disrupt your best-laid plans. Chapter 10 helps generate ideas and actions to successfully finance your goals. Chapter 11 summarizes an effective process for getting the right kind of career-related jobs.

Changing Workplace, Changing Careers

Over the past twenty years, dramatic changes have been taking place in every aspect of careers as we have know them. These changes result from massive transformations in society, the economy, and the corporate world. Several complex factors are driving these changes: the shift from a nation-based to a world economy; accelerating technology that continually makes some work obsolete and generates other; a major shift in the nature of work, from primarily manufacturing based to service and information oriented; and a changing population with increasing numbers of older Americans and greater numbers of females and minorities (many of whom are entering the workplace and moving into positions formerly dominated by white males). The results have produced massive restructurings of those organizations that were the mainstay of the industrial-age job market. These large, manufacturing based industries were the places most people pursued their careers.

Most of what we have believed about careers, in fact, comes from the culture of these industrial giants and the corporate world. But since the 1980's we have seen these organizations transform their nature as they struggle to remain afloat in an era of massive change. Corporations such as General Motors, IBM, and Bethlehem Steel have found it necessary to reinvent themselves to keep from being bowled over by competition from places like Japan, Taiwan, Singapore, Germany, and the European Community. From the outside these transformations appear in the form of downsizing, re-engineering and corporate mergers that continue to eliminate the traditional jobs of millions of workers. On the inside, these organizations are transforming themselves from large, hierarchical structures comprised of many rungs of management, administrative support, and assembly-line production into smaller, less structured, and more flexible entities that change and reorganize quickly. Not even the Federal Government, that bastion of secure employment, is immune from the forces of change as this massive bureaucracy responds to the imperatives to consume less of the nation's limited budgetary resources, to become more productive, and to shrink to more manageable proportions.

In addition to the changes occurring within the traditional organizations of the past, we see thousands of new industries with names like Apple Computer, Microsoft Corporation, Novell, Comsat, and Gentech popping up like mushrooms on a decaying haystack. We're also seeing the first stages of a new wave of change spurred by the prospects of the super-information highway with interactive and virtual-reality applications. This technology is changing the way we work, learn, and live.

What does all this mean for people choosing their careers for the first time or needing to make career changes? It essentially means that just about everything we thought we knew about career choice and career development is obsolete. We must now reinvent our thinking about occupational choice, career development, how we get jobs and implement careers, and even our old view about retirement.

A Changing View of Career Development

The conventional wisdom of the industrial age suggested that it was rather simple-minded to assume that common people (i.e., middle-class Americans) might actually exercise much personal autonomy over their careers. In fact, the conditions of that era actually provided rather limited opportunities for most individuals to manage their own careers. A primary orientation of industrial era work life was to get a job with a Fortune 500 company. Thereafter, one's career development was determined almost exclusively by the individual's sex, educational preparation (blue or white collar tracks), the employing organization, and on-the-job performance. People (men) were expected to get a job, to provide for themselves and their families, without particular regard to their interests, skills or potential. Work was not supposed to be fun, and the organization called the shots. A primary employment goal was to work your way up the corporate ladder and hang in there until retirement. It was only in the retirement phase of life that people could actually begin to exercise control over their lives. But even that newly available freedom was often overshadowed by a self-limiting viewpoint: "I've worked hard for the right to never have to work again, and I don't intend to." But things are different now!

The mass production job mentality no longer holds much relevance in a globally-oriented, knowledge based, and fluid economy. For over two decades now the Fortune 500's have been laying off workers and thinning out those heavy middle-management and hierarchical structures. More and more people are being forced to change jobs and careers as the types of work they have been doing simply fade away, a consequence of corporate America's late 20th-century struggle to adjust to rapidly changing and vastly different new realities. Totally new dynamics in almost every realm (economics, politics, the sciences, education, the environment, communications, culture, health, and psychology) now force us to re-examine our long held ideas, assumptions, and myths about job, career, and lifestyle. The following table summarizes some of the major structural contrasts between career development in the mass production era and that of the rapidly evolving new reality.

Industrial-age notions of a limited number of stable and well defined career paths within the structure of giant corporations has become more memory than fact. How relevant now are the once-prized values of corporate loyalty and promotions up hierarchical structures? The last vestiges of guaranteed corporate commitment to career-long employment may have vanished in 1993 when IBM was forced to publicly concede that it could no longer honor such a policy.

Where does all this leave us career-wise? One thing is certain—we can no longer assume that we can simply work hard, do what we're told, and leave our future in the hands of the company. Like it or not, our personal futures and our career development have become our individual responsibility. Furthermore, we can no longer look to a secure career path with a single employer.

The New Reality

Because today's job market is amorphous, unstable, non-hierarchical, non-traditional, and uncertain, we can expect to be changing jobs and making career transitions frequently. This leads to one inescapable conclusion—we had better become proficient career developers and life transition managers for ourselves. This will require new perspectives and new approaches if we are to thrive in a new reality.

Death and Rebirth

An unwelcome job dissolution announcement can be to a career what an unexpected terminal medical diagnosis is to a life—a devastating shock. But both kinds of notices can also serve as wake-up calls. In either case, denial tends to be the first predictable reaction, followed by anger and grief. A rapidly growing body of literature on the subject suggests that those who are able to move through these emotional stages and accept death's inevitability are able to let go of their attachments to the past and then move through life's final transition—often in an apparent state of bliss. In similar manner, the death and dying of a lifestyle or career can awaken us to the inevitability of life-affirming change and transition.

While impending physical death signals an ending to the reality we have known in this dimension, career death can actually awaken us to intriguing new possibilities and a rebirth experience in the here and now. Many who have gone through major career transitions report that their job loss was actually a blessing in disguise. It forced them to discover something better than what they had.

Career Development in Paradigm Shifting Times

We can't always avoid unexpected shocks like losing a job, but we can be better prepared for change by viewing career decision-making as a continuing, life-long process rather than as an occasional event. We can do this by integrating the two separate but intimately related dimensions of reality: the evolving inner world of self and the rapidly changing outer world. The following diagram of a new career development model depicts this relationship between the two simultaneous spheres of human existence.

TABLE 1.2 Career Development: Then and Now

Characteristics	Mass Production Era (1865*–1980's**)	Knowledge-Service Era (1980's–?)
The primary sources of employment	Huge manufacturing industries oriented to the national economy	Knowledge-service enterprises, competing in a global market
The nature of the job market	Two-tiered factory: • blue collar (B/C) • white collar (W/C)	Multi-tiered (no tiered) mixed technical, service, professional, executive
Occupational characteristics	A few stable, clearly classifiable types	Many rapidly evolving and amorphous types
Career preparation	Complete your education and then get a job	Continual working-learning, keeping pace with information and technology growth
Career choice: how you enter and pursue a career	Luck, happenstance, what you happened to know about or fall into	Decision-making aided by a professional, and ongoing attention
Job-acquisition strategy: how you get a job	B/C: family work ties W/C: resumes, classified ads, placement services	Skills/competencies based on self-definition through networking
Primary employment targets	Fortune 500 corporations	Smaller companies, skill contracting agencies, self-employment
Locus of control: career determiner	The organization	The individual (with the aid of professionals)
Career development objective	Climbing prescribed organizational ladders	Personal development in areas of expertise
Employment source	One organization for entire career	Series of organizations and contracting agents
Primary employment concerns (rewards)	Salary, benefits, leave, promotions, titles	Developing potentials, pursuing life interests
Major career limitations	Restrictions based on sex, race, age, religion	Skills, knowledge, and job development savvy
Retirement financing	Company retirement and Social Security	Portable, personal retirement programs
Retirement considerations	40 years—gold watch, and no work ever again; relax, play, travel, die	On-going balance in self developing work, leisure, learning

* In his book *The Third Wave*, Alvin Toffler defines the industrialized North's Civil War victory over the agricultural South as the final stage in the full-blown emergence of the "Second Wave" (industrial era) in the USA.

** It wasn't until the 1980s that American corporations really appear to have understood that a new era had arrived, requiring totally new approaches (total quality control, employee input, consumer satisfaction, etc.) if they were to survive in the face of unprecedented new challenges. The resulting massive organizational restructuring now revolutionizes our thinking about the fundamental nature of work, job, career, retirement, and even life itself.

FIGURE 1.2 Career Development Cycle

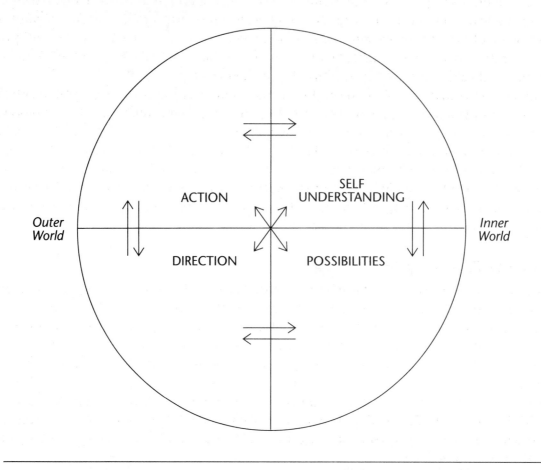

This diagram helps to point out that there are always a variety of dynamic forces acting upon us as we evolve in our careers and that these forces are generated both from the outer and inner worlds. A major change in either realm upsets a pre-existing equilibrium and initiates an inner drive to regain a personal comfort zone. This process works much as thermostats regulate room temperature. We all possess a thermostatic-like regulating mechanism that operates to keep our systems at a self-determined, albeit unconscious, comfort zone. When anything upsets this idiosyncratic setting, our system reacts by attempting to return things to normal.

For example, a great many of those who lost tenured track positions, such as middle managers with General Motors, aeronautical engineers with Lockheed, and blue collar workers with Bethlehem Steel, suffered serious psychic consequences. Emotional trauma is experienced not only from the actual loss of salary and benefits but even more so from the perceived loss of status and sense of self-worth related to intangible factors such as job status, title, position, or organizational association. The reaction to such a traumatic event can rob us of hope and leave us not only frightened and reeling, but unsure of who we are or the meaning of our life and work. Concentrating our problem-solving and decision-making solely on getting another job won't necessarily re-establish homeostasis, that is, return us to our old personal comfort zone. In terms of the career process model, such effort would make no more sense than merely repairing the body of a car damaged in a head-on collision without attending to the engine. When the world dramatically changes around us, we need to change ourselves in appropriate ways. An important aspect of this change must address the human engine—the self.

A major change within the inner realm of the self (physical, psychological, spiritual) can also upset a psychic equilibrium and produce career ramifications. Dramatic and unforeseen changes, such as the loss of a dearly loved one or a traumatic deterioration in one's own health, are sure to disrupt an established sense of personal order. But there are other and less apparent dynamics that can generate perplexities for the inner world—confrontations with one's aging, emotional burn-out, personal meaning crises, personal values shifts, spiritual awakening, existential angst, etc.

The model shows that our attention continually moves from a focus in one quadrant to another as we respond to the dynamics of inner and outer forces. There is no sequential order to this process; we just might jump from any quadrant to another at any time. Expanding personal insight may lead us to ACTION, and some actions may force unpredictable SELF-UNDERSTANDING or create interesting new DIRECTIONS. New POSSIBILITIES may occur to us at any time—even in the shower, driving to work, or over a beer with a friend. It should be noted that we begin this cycle in our early formative years, with the evolution of our self-concept, and that there is no end to this process. We are continually engaged in the cycle of life, enmeshed in two ever-changing worlds.

Paula and the Career Cycle

At the mid-point of what seemed to have been a secure career track, Paula's position as an accountant with a Washington, D.C., commercial real estate firm abruptly ended with a job-termination notice. Like thousands of others in the finance industry, Paula was the victim of a tidal wave of mergers, consolidations, and "right-sizing." Yet, even though she had been successful as an accountant, she had never fully enjoyed this kind of work. However, since she was unsure what else might be better and because she was fully supporting herself with a nice salary and benefits, she had stayed with the job, giving little consideration to her future. But then, at the age of forty-six, the job termination convinced her that the time had come for a major career change. She was forced to concede that since seeking job security would be a blind alley anyway, she might as well invest the time and energy necessary to find out what she really wanted to do.

Until receiving her job termination Paula had been preoccupied with the outer-world dynamics of her career. Now she was shocked by the unexpected job loss and forced into reassessing what to do next. In terms of the career development cycle, she was catapulted from the ACTION quadrant into the SELF-UNDERSTANDING quadrant. She realized she could not go back to what she had; those kinds of positions were melting like old snow in warm spring showers. But after long tenure in one industry, she felt unprepared to deal with her major predicament—what did she want and what was available?

Paula decided to engage the services of both a professional therapist and a career counselor to obtain deeper self-awareness and to help clarify her personal interests and career possibilities. Her self inquiry focused around questions such as who am I now, what I truly value, what my core personal assets are, what I really want to do, and what new possibilities are available or could I create.

With new insights to these kinds of questions, she moved on to the POSSIBILITIES quadrant of the model. At this stage she developed a lengthy list of options that would capitalize on her top talents and engage her strongest interests. In this phase of the process, counselors often encourage clients to develop forty of more possibilities without being too concerned about the practicalities of actually pursuing a particular career. The most important thing here is to tap creative ideas, particularly those that connect with personal potentials and passions. Even though Paula was initially able to identify a few interesting possibilities, her counselor kept pushing her for more, with the emphasis on quantity rather than quality—the rationale being that you can't get to real quality without first generating powerful ideas. Such ideas tend to originate intuitively and creatively rather than deductively and analytically. Analysis is called for later in the decision-making when the wheat (brilliant ideas) must be separated from the chaff (unworkable ideas).

Paula identified and explored her most promising options and chose a new career direction. Self-assessment helped uncover a creative bent (new awareness after concentrating on her analytical skills for so many years) in the form of love for art and aesthetic appreciation of old buildings. Through information interviews with people in the arts, architecture, and related fields, she discovered the historical preservation field and learned that some colleges offer degrees in that specialty. She went on to obtain a bachelor of science degree at one of these colleges, doing so well that she went on to obtain a master's degree in the field. Currently she is working with an architectural firm involved in the restoration of historical buildings and the regeneration of old and deteriorated downtown centers.

Paula recognized that this transition will probably not be her last. Yet in spite of the temporality of today's career situation, she has a sense of security that comes from preparation for the reality of the changing world in which she lives. She has a much clearer knowledge of who she is, what she wants in her life and career, and how to market her strengths. Although she doesn't know how long her current employment situation will last, she feels confident in her ability to market herself and get jobs and to create income-generating work as a consultant. She no longer intends to find job security with a Fortune 500 corporation but is much more content to work in smaller organizations where she can make a difference and have some fun in the process.

Critical Issues and New Realities

Paradigm shifts bring both negative and positive outcomes. The bad news is that little remains of our once relatively stable and predictable occupational world. The good news is that the new era has opened up unprecedented opportunities for just about everyone willing to take advantage of them. Doing so, however, necessitates far more creative decision-making and assertive transition management than we have been accustomed to. It also requires replacing outmoded mindsets about work and career development with those that work in a new and very different reality.

It's no longer realistic to concentrate our career efforts on positions offering permanent employment and linear progression. While we can't know what the future will bring, we can determine what we will bring to the future. It makes sense, therefore, to award "self-development" a priority. Self knowledge is, in fact, the only available "given" in the futures planning equation.

The emergence of a new era forces us to examine old assumptions and to formulate new concepts about life and career. One such concept has to do with the role of fun and personal passion in work. Personal passions, in this context, may be thought of as strong interests, core values, or ardently felt causes. While neither fun nor passion were afforded much credibility as a career planning orientation in the past, that is changing in the new paradigm. Because there are far more choices available to more individuals than ever before, we can discover ways for expressing our personal passions through our work. Since we have to choose from such a variety of options anyway, we may as well go for what's enjoyable.

Stress is another factor that changes our perspectives about career planning. The uncertainties of these times provoke anxiety. Our current stress levels are undoubtedly elevated by decades of conditioning to seek job security and avoid risk. Pursuing a personal passion may well be the best antidote to "new age" stress.

In this regard, passion is directly related to energy and inversely related to stress. Unremitting stress robs us of energy, enthusiasm, and hope. These, conversely, are just the ingredients that personal passion generates. Both stress and passion involve fantasy in a process of visualizing future scenarios. But personal energy becomes directed, concentrated, and action-focused when we visualize ourselves achieving interesting goals. We motivate ourselves from the inside out—a highly self-empowering process. Stress, on the other hand, involves preoccupation with frightening possibilities, draining away energy into deceptive fantasies—a self-victimizing activity. Defining personal passion goals is far more productive as a personal management and career development strategy than is lapsing into stress-evoking anxieties.

Conclusions

The career transition experiences of thousands of people like Paula suggest at least three strategies for personal career management in the rapidly evolving realities of the knowledge service era:

1. No longer can we trust any exterior agent, whether it be a corporation, the union, government, or luck, to tend our career. In today's reality we have little choice other than to personally manage our lives and careers. That requires letting go of outmoded mass production era mindsets about what careers are supposed to be and becoming far more creative, savvy, and self-directing than we individually and collectively have ever before needed to be.

2. Career development has become so complex that it is difficult to successfully undertake alone. The good news is that there are more services becoming available all the time. Many corporations have either created or contracted for human resource development (HRD) services that include career development assistance. The Federal Government is in the process of creating agency-based skill clinics that provide career counseling. A growing number of community centers, schools, colleges, and individuals offer professional career counseling; and increasing competition means better and more cost-effective service.

3. Career developers in the new paradigm recognize the market value of an individual's unique attributes and styles. When it comes to occupational choice, our personal profiles of uniqueness blend in nicely with some types of careers but poorly with others. While the "cookie cutter" mentality of the mass production era provided little opportunity for pursuing individual differences, that is no longer the case. Now our future satisfaction and success requires ongoing, intelligent, self-aware decision-making.

For those who fail to take advantage of the opportunities for self-development and self-direction that the knowledge service era increasingly provides, the future may look dismal. Their best hope may be to hit the lottery big or to squeak into a cushy retirement. For those recognizing the opportunities available in the new era and willing to take full advantage of them, the future has never been brighter. It is a perceptual difference! Viewing the future through the eyes of fear results in becoming victims of our feelings. Seeing the promise of the future generates hope, energy, and enthusiasm.

Supplemental Exercises

1. In almost every high-school scene, you can observe numerous unofficial groupings of students, such as the athletes (jocks), the scholars (brains), the leaders, the losers, the punks, the preppies, the squares, the hippies, the neat dressers, etc. Make a list of all of the groups you can recall from your own high-school days, using your own labels.

2. It is possible to see the various types of self-concepts in a high-school setting by observing the differences in these unofficial groupings of students. Describe some of the attributes that you remember from the groupings you identified in item 1.

   Group   *Attributes*

3. Which group from item I did you most identify with? Describe the attributes (self-concepts) of that group.

4. Which of those attributes you identified in item 3 do you see as being similar to your view of yourself? If you are aware of any other individual attributes, add these to the list.

5. Review the attributes of your self-concept above. Can you see how your self-concept might have influenced your life or choices?

6. How might your self-concept influence your career in the future?

Exercise 1-B. YOUR CAREER/LIFE DECISIONS OF THE PAST

A career/life decision is one that has had a significant effect on your career and your life. In the spaces provided below, list several of the most significant career/life choices you have made so far in your life. Examples: first work experience, summer job, selection of high school courses, decision to attend college, first job, job change, getting married, having children, leaving home, moving, joining the service.

Start by listing the earliest decision you can recall and then record each subsequent major career/life choice in chronological order to the present time. Enter your decisions to the right of the numbers below, leaving the box to the left blank for now.

Note: If you are having a difficult time recalling the career/life decisions you consciously made in the past, then fill in with significant career/life choices that you faced in the past.

My Career/Life Shaping Decisions of the Past and How I Made Them

☐ 1. _____

☐ 2. _____

☐ 3. _____

☐ 4. _____

☐ 5. _____

☐ 6. _____

☐ 7. _____

☐ 8. _____

☐ 9. _____

☐ 10. _____

Exercise 1-C. ASSESSING YOUR DECISION-MAKING STYLE

From the list below, select the best description(s) of how you made your choices in Exercise 1-B above. Fill in the boxes to the left of each decision in 1-B with the appropriate letter(s) from the following list:

A. Took the safest way.

B. Took the easiest way.

C. Let someone else decide for me.

D. Did what I thought others expected me to do.

E. Did what I had been taught that I should do.

F. Did the first thing that came to my mind.

G. Did nothing.

H. Chose what I felt was intuitively right.

I. Consciously weighed all of the alternatives available and then chose the best one.

J. Used some other approach _____

QUESTIONS TO CONSIDER:

1. From the exercises above, what did you learn about the way you have made your career/life decisions in the past?

2. What effects have your past career/life choices had on your life? How do the outcomes of these decisions affect you now?

3. Based on what you learned about your past career/life decision-making style and the effect of these choices on your life, what changes would you like to make?

Exercise 1-D. YOUR MAJOR DECISION

You are unlikely to solve problems or to make decisions that could enhance the quality of your career and life if you are unaware that you are in a decision-making situation or unclear about what it is. Focus on an important career/life choice you are facing now. Describe a situation that requires a major career-related decision. If none comes to mind, list a major choice you expect to face in the future.

Some typical examples:

- I am just beginning college and do not know what to pursue.
- I am almost finished with my college but don't know what career to pursue.
- My kids will soon be on their own, and I need to develop new life directions.
- I am forty plus and in a dead-end position. I want to move into a more satisfying new career where I can get ahead and use my best skills.
- I love working with people, but my present job involves working with machines. I must get into a career that involves more personal contact.
- I like my work, but I am likely to be laid off. I need to prepare for a new job.
- I like my job, but I am not making enough money to survive. I need to get a new position that I enjoy as much but that pays better.
- I need to begin planning for retirement. I want to prepare for a new lifestyle that includes interesting activities and rewarding part-time work.

MY CRITICAL CHOICE ISSUE

Some Additional References

ARTICLES

Church, G. J. "Jobs in an Age of Insecurity." *Time*, November 22, 1993, pp. 32–39.

Richman, L. S. "When Will the Layoffs End?" *Fortune*, September 20, 1993, pp. 54–56.

Richman, L.S. "How to Get Ahead in America." *Fortune*, May 16, 1994, pp. 46–54.

Lee Smith, "Landing That First Real Job." *Fortune*, May 16, 1944, pp. 58–60.

BOOKS

Caroline Bird, *Second Careers, New Ways to Work After 50*. New York: Little Brown & Co., 1992.

Charles Handy, *The Age of Unreason*. Boston, Mass.: Harvard Business School Press, 1989.

Marsha Sinetar, *Developing A 21st Century Mind*. New York: Villard Books, 1991.

Kate Wendleton, *Through the Brick Wall*. New York: Villard Books, 1992.

VIDEOS

The Business of Paradigms and *Paradigm Pioneers Discovering the Future Series*, Joel Arthur Barker, ChartHouse International Learning Corporation, 221 River Ridge Circle, Burnsville, MN 55337 (telephone: 1-800-328-3789)

Up Is Not the Only Way, Barr Films, 12801 Schabarum, P.O. Box 7878, Irwindale, CA 91706-7878 (telephone: 818-338-7878)

NOTES

1. Friedman and R. J. Havighurst, *The Meaning of Work and Retirement* (Chicago: University Press, 1954.)
2. John C. Crystal and Richard N. Bolles, *Where Do I Go From Here With My Life?* (Berkeley, California: Ten Speed Press, 1978)
3. Gordon Porter Miller, *Life Choices* (New York: Thomas Y. Crowell, 1978), p. 4.

2 Your Skills in Action

"But I don't have many skills . . ."
"I've just been a housewife all my adult life."
"I've only had unskilled jobs."
"I just graduated from high school."

ANONYMOUS STUDENTS

DO YOU KNOW PEOPLE:

- ➤ Who believe that they don't have skills?

- ➤ Who aren't aware of whether they prefer working with data, people, or things?

- ➤ Who feel that they have skills but don't realize how these can transfer from one job or career to another?

- ➤ Who are reluctant to change careers because they feel they don't have the right skills for the new career?

- ➤ With highly developed talents who have difficulty finding and keeping jobs?

If so, then you know people who share common misconceptions about their personal skills. The truth is that all of us have a great many skills, and we are all highly talented in our own ways.

Abundant Skills

Although almost everyone is uniquely talented, most of us have only a vague awareness of what our skills really are. It's unlikely that we will realize our unique potentials unless we are clear about what skills we possess. Understanding our unique skills can help us choose a career or see how our skills might transfer from one field, occupation, or job to another.

The word *skills,* as used here, refers to competencies or developed abilities needed to achieve a desired outcome or to make something happen. Skills are the foundation of all human achievement. Your skills continuously come into play in all your activities, from leisure to learning to work-related tasks, from routine actions to complex projects. It takes some blending of skills to do anything, even routine functions like talking, writing, walking the dog, taking out the garbage or teaching your canary to talk.

As you study this chapter and perform the various exercises, we encourage you to keep two important ideas in mind. The first is that you can acquire skills in almost any area you choose. The second is that because each of us possesses unique genetic endowments and life programming, some types of skills will be easier and much more enjoyable to develop than others. Therefore, we encourage you not to underestimate your ability to acquire whatever skills are needed for your career and education. We do recommend, however, that you pay special attention to your natural endowments or your preferred skills. These are the skills that are the most likely to be the keys to your success. These are the skills that you will be motivated to use and to develop. Take your preferred skills into account as you make your career and life goals. Look for ways to capitalize on them; they are your unique gifts. The assessment activities of chapters one through six are designed to help you clarify just what your unique "gifts" are. Exercises contained in chapters seven through eleven will assist you in setting goals to capitalize on your particular interests and potential.

The Types of Skills

Three types of skills are discussed in this chapter: functional, self-management, and special knowledge. Functional skills are abilities or talents that are inherited at birth and developed through experience and learning. They are aptitude related and determine your proficiency with data, people, and things. Self-management skills are the behaviors you have developed in learning to cope with your environment and the people and conditions in it. Special-knowledge skills are those having to do with mastering a specific body of information related to a particular type of work, profession, occupation, educational or leisure activity. Special-knowledges are what you have learned and committed to memory. The following table provides examples of the three different types of skills.

TABLE 2.1 Three Types of Skills

Functional	Self-Management	Special-Knowledge
Starting new ventures	Energetic	Financial planning
Negotiating contracts	Determined	Real estate brokering
Creating new services	Resourceful	Catering
Diagnosing interpersonal problems	Insightful	Group dynamics
Repairing machines	Dependable	Brake systems (on cars)
Calculating taxes	Ethical	Accounting
Coaching athletes	Enthusiastic	Basketball strategy
Making decisions	Responsible	Career planning
Analyzing samples	Methodical	Chemical laboratory techniques
Advising clients	Tactful	Divorce law

Your Functional Skills

Functional skills are natural abilities or talents that are acquired through heredity. Actually you acquire the potential for certain types of abilities genetically. These potentials are then either developed through your life experiences or remain dormant. If, for example, you inherited an aptitude for analytical problem solving, writing poetry, or persuading others, you may have developed this functional skill through school course work and/or practical application. Then again, you may possess a real potential for these skills but just never developed them for one reason or another. Perhaps you neglected to exercise these potentials because your life circumstances hindered their development, or perhaps you accepted a prevailing myth that people like you (or your sex, race, nationality, etc.) aren't good at this kind of thing—for example, women aren't good at solving math problems or men aren't good at nursing or nurturing others. There is also the possibility that you may have inherited a limited potential for these specific aptitudes and are unlikely to develop them into highly proficient functional skills no matter how diligently you apply yourself. The following relationships summarize these principles:

Potential plus development	=	Functional skill
Potential plus non-development	=	Latent functional skill
Potential life barrier	=	Erroneous conclusion that you have no skill in this area
Lack of potential plus effort	=	Frustration (and perhaps a modest skill development)

Having a functional skill means that you are able to perform some specific type of activity, action, or operation with a good deal of proficiency. Simply put, it means that you can do a specific thing well. To have a functional skill one must first begin with the potential to develop a certain ability such as selling, shooting baskets, singing, solving complex mathematical problems, or envisioning how an object would look from many different perspectives. This potential must then be developed through experience, education, practice, play, work, etc.

Incidentally, functional skills are as likely to be developed in everyday activities as they are in the classroom. For example, do you remember the kid on your block who could sell anything, including his rusty old roller skates, to anyone, or the kid who could make the whole gang laugh anytime she wanted? These are examples of well developed functional skills in the early formative stages of life. These people today still retain these abilities. The first kid may now be a very successful salesperson and the second a comedian (if they were astute enough to capitalize on their natural endowments). On the other hand, if they didn't, you might find them languishing around in a job and a lifestyle they hate. They may even think that they don't have much to offer and that life's not a whole lot of fun. If you were good at drawing as a child, you undoubtedly retain that potential today regardless of whether you have developed it into a well used functional skill. If you were the leader of your neighborhood gang as an adolescent, you have that same potential to lead today, whether you are currently practicing leadership or are even aware of it.

The Value of Your Functional Skills

Your functional skills are perhaps the most valuable assets you have in life. Youthful good looks are great, but they fade with age while functional skills stay with you over a lifetime. Well developed functional skills are truly more valuable than money. While money spent unwisely disappears quickly, functional skills actually increase through expenditure. And, even better, your functional skills represent the resources you need to earn money whenever you want. Beyond that, productively using your functional skills feels good. Both financial and psychic reward are attainable to those who intelligently use their functional skills. One of life's greatest satisfactions comes from fully utilizing your talents towards personally meaningful ends. And, conversely, one of the greatest causes of dissatisfaction in life is the realization that one's best talents are not being fully used and developed.

In today's world there is a particularly compelling reason for knowing what our best functional skills are. The world around us is changing at a rapid pace. Technology brings new advances daily. Unskilled jobs are decreasing while more demanding and technologically advanced jobs are increasing. Most career specialists predict that in our rapidly changing world, younger workers may need or want to change jobs as often as every three to five years and undergo significant career changes every decade or so. In our unstable world, older workers also are not spared from the need to make job and career changes.

In today's world there is a natural tendency to search for a constant, stabilizing factor, the "for-certain" element in life. The only real constant, however, lies within us, in the form of our personal attributes and talents. Your skills remain with you regardless of the job, occupation, or field in which you might be involved. As long as you know what your functional skills are, rapid change does not have to be a serious threat to you occupationally. If your job is phased out or taken over by a computer, you have the resources needed to make a successful job or career change because your functional skills are transferable. Your transferable skills allow you to move easily from one job to another where similar aptitudes are required. If you have been feeling trapped in a job that no longer energizes you, it may well be time to transport your transferable skills into a more challenging situation. In fact, when you know exactly what your functional skills are, it is even possible to make changes without extensive retraining.

Skill identification can help you clarify what you have to contribute to a particular type of work and provide clues for suggesting where to go with your career. If, for example, you realize that you are talented at communicating, establishing rapport, and advising others, you may want to explore people-oriented occupations like teaching, counseling, nursing, or selling. Or let's say you know that you prefer hands-on activities with equipment, tools, or machines: you might consider a job in computer repair, medical technology, auto mechanics, robotic technology, electronic engineering, industrial arts, or aeronautics/astronautics.

Everyone Has Functional Skills

Perhaps you've said to yourself, "Well, I don't have many skills." If so, you are not alone in this misconception. People often come into the Career Center feeling depressed and lamenting their lack of skills. These blues quickly vanish when they discover how traits or accomplishments they have taken for granted point to valuable skills. Experienced career planning specialists like Richard Bolles and the late John Crystal, through years of experience, have observed that people completing a thorough skills identification process discover 200 to 500 or more skills.[1]

The problem is not that you lack skills. Instead, you have so many individual skills that it's probably hard to recognize them. You also might not recognize them because you have used them so long and so well that they have become automatic and unconscious. Or you might discount your skills, erroneously assuming that anyone can perform those things that you can do well. Functional skills are a bit like icebergs in that the greater portion of them lie hidden below the surface of our everyday awareness. Even people who recognize their basic skills are often amazed to discover just how many specific skills the functional skills identification process can reveal.

Because people usually enjoy activities that they perform well, your first exercise involves recalling activities which gave you positive feelings. These feelings may come from within and/or may come from other people's favorable responses.

Exercise 2-A. REFLECTIONS ON THE PAST AND PRESENT _____

Reflect on the following questions, writing your responses in the spaces provided. Write whatever comes to your mind instead of trying to narrow your responses.

1. What compliments or other positive feedback have you received for particular activities? (Example: praise for organizing my art club's successful fund raising activity.) Positive feedback may be as

simple as a smile or as significant as a meritorious pay increase. Write down at least 5 different compliments, briefly explaining the situation.

2. When have you felt the most alive and energetic? List at least five specific situations. (Examples: jogging two miles daily, planning and preparing food and decorations for a dinner party, building a model airplane, thinking of ways to improve store displays at your first job.)

3. When have you felt the most confident and capable? List at least five situations. (Examples: giving a presentation and getting rave reviews, getting an "A" on a major exam in your toughest subject, having someone ask for your ideas/advice about carpentry work.)

4. What are you discovering about yourself? Are there any similarities in your responses? Make some notes here to help you remember your thoughts.

5. Review your responses to 1 through 4 above. What skills do you think you used in these various examples? List at least 10 of them in the space provided. You may want to ask a friend or family member to listen as you describe some of the things you have listed and see if they can help you find skills or abilities that you used.

Here is another chance to look at skills. This exercise involves describing successful experiences you have had in order to identify the skills you were using in the process. This is one of the best ways to become aware of and clarify your top skills. Once you know what skills you have used successfully in the past, you can make plans to capitalize on these same skills in the future.

Make a list of 15 achievements, large or small, from your past. These should be descriptive phrases of memorable activities or events where *you* contributed to a satisfying, but not necessarily perfect, outcome. The satisfaction may have come from improvement in a particular activity. Try to list particular events rather than general situations. For example, if getting good grades is one of your achievements, list the most satisfying "A" you've ever obtained, or if traveling is one of your achievements, indicate one particularly significant travel experience you had. The following is a list of some sample achievements to help you start thinking about your own achievements.

Assembling telephone equipment
Cooking a gourmet meal (cordon bleu, for example)
Training a horse
Playing basketball (learning to play, or a particular game)
Enforcing regulations in a particular situation
Typing a report with complex tables
Playing a computer game well
Persuading someone to buy something
Managing people to reach a fund raising goal
Playing guitar for an audience
Writing a feature story for a community newspaper
Teaching your child to read
Helping a neighbor cope with her husband's death
Figuring out a new approach for an office project
Decorating the community center for Christmas
Writing song lyrics
Structuring a research project
Analyzing people's needs for improved computer equipment
Classifying information for a biology experiment
Repairing an auto engine
Refinishing a valuable old piece of furniture
Designing a prize winning Halloween costume
Writing a piece of poetry

Your List of Achievements: (Keep in mind that achievements can be simple everyday things, but the requirement is that you had to put forth effort or work to make them happen).

1.

2.

3.

4.

5.

6.

7.

8.

9.

10.

11.

12.

13.

14.

15.

From your list of 15, select the five achievements that made you feel the happiest, most satisfied, or most energetic. You may want to choose achievements that resulted in positive reactions from someone else, although this is not essential. Copy each of these descriptive phrases at the top of a blank sheet of paper. Next, write a paragraph or two describing each achievement. Start at the beginning and say it simply. Don't worry about grammar, organization, or any fine points of writing. Just tell what happened, describing exactly what you did to contribute to the satisfying outcome. Choose action words to tell what you did and include as much relevant detail as you can recall. The following examples show how a satisfying achievement can be elaborated upon in preparation for identifying skills.

Example 1: Doing a Bass Fish Mounting

Because I enjoy fishing a lot, I decided that I wanted to learn how to do fish mounting. The first step I took to achieve my goal was going to the library and checking out books about fish mounting. There I got some pretty good ideas of the types of mounts and procedures involved. Then I got in touch with a taxidermist who agreed to train me. I went to the taxidermist once a week for about three months. I would always bring a fish I had just caught to practice with. He showed me, step-by-step, how to clean and skin the fish and how to dry and preserve it. He also taught me how to put the finishing touches on a fish and then how to mount it in the desired position. I worked with him for about three months until he felt the work I was doing was of professional quality.

Shortly after I finished my training, I caught a large bass and decided to try out my skills. I cleaned the fish carefully, not leaving any meat behind that would spoil. Then I salted the skin and braced the fins in the positions that I wanted them in. Next I put a filler in the bass to give it its original shape back. I mounted the fish in an open-mouthed position in order to give it a fierce look, as if it were feeding. After a few weeks of drying, my bass was ready to paint. I selected colors to bring back the original look and then give it a coat of shellac to seal the paint and give the fish a wet look and the life-like appearance. I think my final product is very professional; it's hanging on a wall in my house.

Example 2: Buying a Townhouse

I decided that I wanted to buy a nice place to live after my husband and I divorced. I dreamed of a place that would be attractive and located in a pleasant neighborhood where I could go to bed in the evening and hear the sounds of the wind in the trees and awake in the morning to the music of birds singing. I also envisioned a place that would not require much yard work and would be within a half hour commute to work.

First I analyzed how much I could afford for a place and what my monthly payments ought to be. In considering the options within my price range, I figured out that a townhouse would be my best buy. Next, I began exploring the area to see what was available. Initially I thought I would like to buy in the Crofton area and found a realtor to work with. I looked at several places there but didn't find exactly what I wanted within my price range. Then I learned that there were some nice townhouses being built along the golf course in Upper Marlboro, so I drove out and took a look. I loved the location and the models.

It didn't require much consideration to decide that this was where I wanted to live. I selected the lot and the model I wanted and signed a contract. I was concerned that my monthly payments would be more than I could afford but trusted that it would be possible to rent out the spare bedroom for about $400.00 per month.

I am now in my new townhouse and decorating it with a modest budget to make it feel like home. I was able to rent out my room by placing an ad in the *Post*. With this additional income I have been able to make my monthly payments by sticking closely to a budget. While things are currently a bit tight financially, I am confident that I will be able to make it.

What Kinds of Skills Do You Have?

As you were writing down responses for Exercise 2-A and B, did you notice that various action words described your skills? If these words reveal your involvement in accomplishing something or making something happen, they are directly describing a functional skill you possess. Maybe you *organized* a team, *composed* correspondence, *operated* equipment, *balanced* a ledger, *prepared* a speech, *repaired* a radio. These kinds of skills are called functional skills because you can apply them to (make them function in) various situations.

Your paragraphs may also contain words that suggest other types of skills, those that describe your behavioral traits. Descriptive words like *neat, punctual, curious, easygoing, good judgment, honest, resourceful, self-confident, reliable,* and *decisive* reveal your self-management skills.

Exercise 2-C. IDENTIFYING FUNCTIONAL SKILLS FROM YOUR ACCOMPLISHMENTS

FUNCTIONAL SKILL ASSESSMENT SURVEY

This survey is designed to help you assess your functional skills and decide what specific skills you prefer to use in your career. To make the survey easier, quicker, and more fun to complete, you may want to assemble some pens or markers with different colored inks.

Directions

1. First copy the title from each of your five achievement paragraphs above into the five spaces provided for that purpose at the top of the skill assessment grid.

2. Next, determine which skills you used in each of your five achievements. Choose one color of ink to check or color in the boxes for all of the skills you used for each of your five achievements. If you did not use a skill for a particular achievement, leave that box blank.

3. If for your five achievements there are skills you used but that are not listed, write in these skills in the spaces labeled "Other" at the bottom of each cluster or group of skills. Try to match the skills you are listing with the appropriate cluster or group of skills on the grid. Then, using the same ink color that you did before, check or fill in the boxes for these "Other" skills under the achievements in which you used them.

4. Now, from the skills that you have used, determine which skills you most prefer to use. In making this determination, consider what skills you enjoy using the most and want to use in your new career. Using a different ink color, check or color in the box in the "Preferences" column for each skill for which you have a definite preference.

| Functional Skills Assessment Grid | Achievements | | | | | Pref- |
A. Manual/Technical	1	2	3	4	5	erences
Assembling/installing (putting things together according to directions)						
Constructing/building (using tools/materials, blueprints to build something)						
Fixing/repairing (cars, machines, broken objects, etc.)						
Manual dexterity (skill in performing hand movements quickly and accurately)						
Mechanical reasoning (understanding how to operate machines and tools)						
Hand, eye, foot coordination (basketball, football, soccer, etc.)						
Physical agility (moving your body quickly and easily)						
Physical stamina (overcoming fatigue from physical activity)						
Using hand tools (hammer, screwdriver, wrench, etc.)						
Operating machinery or equipment (chain saw, forklift, rototiller, etc.)						
Driving vehicles (cars, trucks, tractors, etc.)						
Moving materials by hand (bricks, lumber, shingles, etc.)						
Landscaping, groundskeeping, horticultural skills (planting trees, designing gardens, growing and caring for plants)						
Reading, understanding technical manuals (figuring out how to put in a garage door opener or fix a bike)						
Other _____ _____ _____ _____						

Functional Skills	Achievements					Pref-
B. Analytical/Problem Solving	1	2	3	4	5	erences
Analyzing/diagnosing (separating into parts for study/examining to determine the problem)						
Researching/investigating (studying thoroughly by gathering information, searching for facts)						
Interpreting data (explaining the meaning of words, numbers, symbols)						
Classifying/organizing/systematizing (placing information into categories)						
Evaluating/assessing (carefully examining information)						
Scientific/technical writing (technical manuals, specifications, scientific reports, etc.)						
Logical decision making/analytical problem solving (choosing/solving problems based on a rational process)						
Financial analysis (examining financial and numerical data for possible trends)						
Mathematical reasoning (using logical thinking in performing mathematical computations)						
Measuring (using instruments to obtain accurate scientific or numerical data)						
Separating important from unimportant facts (Making decision, gathering evidence, taking tests, etc.)						
Putting facts, figures or information into logical order (writing reports, making graphs, preparing presentations, etc.)						
Scientific curiosity (asking questions about natural phenomena in order to understand)						
Estimating (projecting the cost or amount of materials needed)						
Other _____						
_____						
_____						
_____						

Functional Skills Assessment Grid	Achievements					Pref-
C. Innovative/Original	1	2	3	4	5	erences
Using your imagination to create (making a movie, acting a role, choreographing a dance, etc.)						
Graphic designing (posters, logos, advertising pieces, etc.)						
Using intuition (perceiving information via the "sixth sense")						
Designing programs, events, activities (political rallies, block parties, fund raisers, etc.)						
Originating ideas (dreaming up novel concepts)						
Creative showmanship/acting/performing (juggling, making up jokes, singing, etc.)						
Creative writing, self-expression (poetry, short fiction, drama, etc.)						
Possibility thinking (being open to new and different ideas and ways of doing things)						
Artistic sense/aesthetics (appreciating beauty whether natural or manufactured)						
Drawing/artistic designing (cartoons, collages, prints, etc.)						
Creative movement/dancing/miming (folk dance, clowning, figure skating, etc.)						
Synthesizing (putting facts and ideas together in new, creative ways)						
Being innovative (developing something new and different from the conventional)						
Composing music, songs, lyrics (writing, arranging, or playing music)						
Other _____						
_____						
_____						
_____						

Functional Skills	Achievements					Pref-
D. Social/Interpersonal	1	2	3	4	5	erences
Listening skillfully/hearing (really listening to both the verbal message and its accompanying feelings)						
Developing rapport/understanding (connecting with others)						
Counseling/helping/guiding/mentoring (assisting others through listening, communicating acceptance, modeling behavior)						
Drawing people out/interviewing (being skillful at obtaining information from people)						
Instructing/training/educating (coaching sports, training animals, teaching crafts, etc.)						
Putting others at ease/social grace (meeting new people, making introductions, smoothing awkward situations, etc.)						
Group facilitating (being skillful at helping groups to work together)						
Being diplomatic (saying the right words in delicate or potentially volatile situations)						
Being of service/responding (acting appropriately upon requests made by others)						
Providing information/advising (giving helpful information to others who request or need it)						
Cooperating with others (working together to accomplish something)						
Showing warmth and caring (expressing concern for the welfare of another/others)						
Being supportive (giving aid or assistance to another/others in need)						
Healing/nursing/nurturing/curing (caring for the sick, injured or suffering)						
Other _____						
_____						
_____						
_____						

Functional Skills	Achievements					Pref-
E. Detail/Data	1	2	3	4	5	erences
Working with numerical data (bills, accounts, statements, etc.)						
Proofreading/editing (memos, manuscripts, advertising copy, etc.)						
Inspecting/examining/inventorying (carefully observing records/things to determine if they meet standards)						
Word processing/keyboarding (letters, records, forms, etc.)						
Following directions/procedures accurately (programming, office procedures, etc.)						
Maintaining records (handling data and records according to definite specifications)						
Doing basic arithmetic quickly and accurately (calculating change, handling accounts, bookkeeping, etc.)						
Scheduling/organizing events or activities (being responsible for making arrangements and handling details)						
Compiling details on schedule (getting assigned tasks done on time)						
Monitoring (keeping track of data, information or numbers)						
Categorizing/sorting (placing like items in the right places)						
Remembering numbers or specific facts (having a good memory for data and information)						
Attending to details (handling routine tasks on a regular basis)						
Filing, classifying, recording, retrieving (entering data into and obtaining data from records, files, data bases)						
Other _____ _____ _____ _____						

Functional Skills	Achievements					Pref-
F. Managing/Influencing	*1*	*2*	*3*	*4*	*5*	*erences*
Administering a program or resources (being responsible for people, materials, activities)						
Directing/supervising (being in charge of the work of others)						
Making business-related decisions (hiring, firing, downsizing operations, etc.)						
Negotiating contracts, deals, or transactions (obtaining the best conditions possible in transactions with others)						
Selling, persuading, influencing (convincing others of the worth of your ideas, products, services)						
Convincing others through the force of personality (being a charismatic leader)						
Overseeing programs/projects/activities (monitoring to determine progress towards objectives)						
Organizational/group goal setting/planning (reaching agreement upon what to do and how to do it)						
Undertaking entrepreneurial activities (starting new ventures)						
Organizing and managing an activity, task or project (being responsible for the order and completion of activities)						
Exercising leadership in a group (convincing a group to proceed in a particular direction)						
Taking risks (venturing into the unknown)						
Budgeting (developing and following a fiscal plan)						
Coordinating people and activities to work together (bringing human and material resources and events together in time sequence)						
Other _____ _____ _____ _____						

Your Priority Skills

After completing the Functional Skill Assessment Grid, identify those skills you have checked or colored in both for consistent use and for preference. These are your priority skills. Are there many? Do they tend to fall within one or two groups or clusters of skills? Any surprises?

Make a list of your top ten priority skills and prioritize them by listing the most important one first, the second most important one next, etc.

My top ten priority skills are:

Functional Skills

1.

2.

3.

4.

5.

6.

7.

8.

9.

10.

Now consider your least used and least preferred skills. As you've probably already determined, these are the ones you have not checked or colored in any boxes for. Identifying and prioritizing these can help you be clear on what you do not want to do in your future career. List the five skills that are your least used and least preferred skills. Prioritize the list by putting first the skill you most definitely do not want to use in the future, then the skill you rate as your second least desirable, etc.

My least used and least preferred skills are:

1.

2.

3.

4.

5.

Your Preferred Family of Skills

You have probably already noticed that your priority skills tend to fall within certain groups or clusters of skills. You may, for instance, have many skills checked off or colored in for use and for preference under the group or cluster labeled *Social/Interpersonal*. And, conversely, you may have hardly any skills checked off or colored in for use and for preference under *Detail/Data*. We call these clusters or groups of skills *families*. It is natural to have a stronger base of experience with and inclination for some families of skills than others. Look over your grid and determine which families you have the most and least preference for. Prioritize the list of six families below by numbering them in order of your preference, with the most preferred being #1 and the least preferred being #6.

Skill Family	Preference Ranking
A. Manual/Technical	_____
B. Analytical/Problem Solving	_____
C. Innovative/Original	_____
D. Social/Interpersonal	_____
E. Detail/Data	_____
F. Managing/Influencing	_____

Using Your Top Skills Groups to Choose a Career

How does ranking your top skills get you any closer to making a career decision? Knowing your preferred skills gives you a starting point from which to begin identifying career options suited to your unique blend of skills. The task is to learn what kinds of careers and what particular jobs require your combination of preferred skills. Library reference books such as *The Guide To Occupational Exploration* (GOE) and *The Dictionary of Occupational Titles* (DOT) will be helpful in showing you that. It is also useful to be aware of your least preferred skills, or poorest skills, so that you stay away from career options where these types of skills would be called for. Chapter 7 covers occupational research in detail.

Researching also means asking people (i.e., neighbors, relatives, friends, classmates, etc.) for their ideas and advice about careers requiring your particular skills. Often a casual conversation can uncover an exciting option that you would not have considered or known about.

Work and Data, People, Things

Figure 2.1, the Functional Skills Hierarchy[2], illustrates the relationship of skills to data, people, and things as well as the different levels of these skills. These various ways of working with data, people, and things can occur in many work settings. For example, analyzing reports (data) is done in health clinics, environmental agencies, schools, and company offices. Operating copying machines (things) is done in space transport companies, department stores, computer assembly companies, and museums. Instructing (people) is done in homes, churches, schools, government offices, and health spas. The service or product at the work site may change, but the basic function—what you do with data, people, and things—does not.

The performance requirements for skills related to data, people, and things range in degree of ability from lesser, at the bottom of the diagram, to greater, at the top of the diagram. Successfully moving up from a lower-level skill to a higher-level skill requires increasing ability as the complexity of the skills increases.

For instance, in the data column on the diagram, the lowest skill, "comparing," is a fairly simple task involving examining two or more items for similarities or dissimilarities. The highest skill, "synthesizing," on the other hand, is very complex and involves combining diverse concepts into a coherent whole. The skill of synthesizing is a complex and high-level skill because it incorporates all of the skills that precede it in the data column.

The diagram shows that the lower the skill level required in a job, the more the work duties are prescribed by someone else. What that means is that people performing jobs using only lower-level skills will have very little discretion in determining what they do and little chance to use their own

FIGURE 2.1 Functional Skills Hierarchy

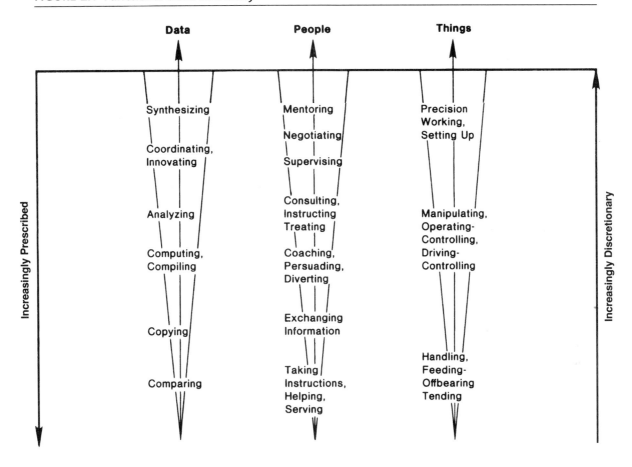

judgment and creativity. People who feel more secure when the procedures and duties are well defined and predictable might be more comfortable working at the lower-skill levels. Entry level jobs often begin at the lower skill levels but provide opportunity for advancing to the higher-skill levels with experience.

The higher the skill level involved in a job, the fewer the duties and regulations that are prescribed by someone else. This affords employees more freedom to decide how they are going to spend their time. Far more is left to employees' judgment, creativity, and decision making. Of course, along with greater self-determination comes greater responsibility in ensuring that an organization's goals are met. Higher level skills jobs tend to pay higher level salaries.

Defining Data, People, and Things

Data skills always involve interaction with some types of symbols, details, or information. Data are related to numbers, words (anything you can read or write), facts, or ideas (any creative work that goes on in your head). People skills category may include working with various kinds of people or with a specific group of people. It is important to note that information, facts, and statistics about people are data-related functional skills and should not be confused with people-related skills. The people-related skills involve actual interaction with people.

Skills related to things involve interaction with objects, tools, machines, and/or materials. Such things may include desktop items such as telephones, calculators, computers, etc. Skills associated with things may also involve spaces, buildings, and all manual labor.

Skills involved in working with animals may be classified under the "things" column when the work-related function is strictly utilitarian, as in producing cattle for beef. Working with animals may also be included as a people skill when the work involved is in a helping or caring role. The veterinarian, for example, interacts with animals in a helping role, and the skill orientation would therefore be classified under the "people" category for functional skill identification purposes. In contrast, medical lab technicians may need to relate to animals as objects of medical science research, which would be a "data" orientation.

Exercise 2-D. DATA-PEOPLE-THINGS PREFERENCE

The following exercise will show you how your functional skill preferences are distributed under the data-people-thing categories.

1. Place your #1 functional skill, from Exercise 2-C, under the appropriate heading below. If you are unsure where to list a skill, ask yourself, "Whom or what would these skills be used with—data, people, or things?" Continue filling in the table with all ten of your preferred functional skills.

Data	People	Things

2. After you have listed your "top ten" preferred skills on the table, add your least preferred functional skills to the same table. When you do this, be sure to use a different color ink for these skills so that you won't confuse them with your preferred skills. The contrast between your "most" and "least" preferred skills may begin to give you a picture of what types of careers fit and don't fit your particular profile.

3. Assessing your data-people-thing preferences:

   a. Under which heading(s) are your preferred functional skills listed?

   b. Under which heading(s) do your least preferred skills cluster?

c. Based on this exercise begin making a list of the kinds of careers that might be associated with your "preferred" skills and also list a few to stay away from—those associated with your least preferred skills.

Careers Associated with Your Most
Preferred Functional Skills

Careers Associated with Your Least
Preferred Skills

Functional Skills versus Self-Management Skills

Self-management skills are your specific behavior responses or character traits. They describe the way in which you manage yourself and relate to others. Along with functional skills, self-managment skills are important components of what people have to contribute in the world or work. Of the two, self-management skills are more widely recognized because they are often easier to observe and identify in work settings. Functional skills, however, are more basic to the actual performance of work tasks.

Knowing your specific functional skills can help you determine how qualified you are to perform the actual tasks of a particular job. Being clear about your self-management skills can suggest how adaptable you would be to the working conditions of a specific job.

The Importance of Self-Management Skills

According to John Crystal, functional skills are usually the personal attributes that get us hired, and self-management skills are those that get us fired.[3] This is true, of course, only when our self-management skills do not fit well with the conditions associated with a particular work setting. For example, the artist's or creative thinker's emotional self-expression and spontaneity might cause conflicts in a business office where working conditions involve highly structured activities, orderly task performance, and an emotional climate of relative calm. It is important, therefore, to really understand your self-management skills and assess how well they might fit with a particular job or work situation that you might be considering.

The importance of self-management skills for job survival can clearly be seen from glancing at any supervisory evaluation form. The majority of evaluation criteria measure self-management skills. Self-management skills that many employers or supervisors particularly value include initiative, resourcefulness, cooperation, dependability, flexibility, and loyalty. A deficiency in one or more of these skill areas will probably cause poor performance evaluations. Consistently low periodic evaluations can lead to a failure to be promoted, a demotion, or even an outright dismissal by an employer.

Self-management skills alone will not qualify you for any positions, except possibly the lower skill-level jobs. Usually people qualify for certain jobs or occupations primarily because they possess certain required functional skills and special knowledges and have relevant work experience. However, in addition to reviewing your written qualifications, a prospective employer or employer's representative will interview you. This interview or series of interviews allows you to display self-management skills to advantage. Your self-management skills or deficiencies are also important aspects of references from former employers or associates. If the self-management skills you display and your employment references emphasize are particularly valued in the new work setting, you might be hired over any number of equally or even more qualified candidates. Conversely, just one serious self-management deficiency can knock you out of the running. For example, an employer who is seeking a counselor generally requires the functional skills of listening and speaking effectively, sensitivity to others' emotional needs, and ability to analyze an individual's practical needs and offer appropriate advice. Job applicants who, in addition, display complementary self-management skills such as friendliness, sincerity, warm humor, and cheerfulness will have an edge on their competition, all other qualifications being equal. Notice that in people-oriented occupations, self-management skills are often part of the actual job requirements. In other words, they overlap with functional skills in some careers.

Here's another real-life example to stress just how important it is to match the unique blend of an individual's skills to what's required for a job. To function effectively as a public relations (P.R.) manager, you would need to possess a number of excellent skills, including the functional skills of creative writing and public speaking and the self-management skills of gregariousness, tact, and flexibility. We know of an individual who was hired as a P.R. manager at a fairly large organization because of her excellent knowledge of P.R. work, her impressive functional skills, and the self-management skills she demonstrated impressively during the interview process. What the hiring process could not reveal, however, was an inability on her part to work compatibly and cooperatively with her staff and associates. On the job, she turned out to be a disaster. She was constantly squabbling with someone over minor issues that any effective P.R. manager should have easily been able to handle. After putting up with her poor self-management skills for about a year, the organization was eventually forced to fire this talented and hardworking woman. In retrospect, she should have either recognized this self-management deficiency and corrected it or obtained a job where she could have put her best skills to productive use in a setting where getting along with staff and peers was not a critical requirement of the job.

Observing Self-Management Skills

Self-management skills are the first skills that an employer can observe when initially meeting job applicants in face-to-face interviews. Imagine, for example, that you are a job seeker and have arranged an interview with a potential employer. Here are some of the opportunities that employer has to observe your self-management skills.

You have arranged your appointment at 9 A.M., but you arrive at 8:45 A.M. The potential employer already has learned something about your *punctuality, dependability,* and perhaps *eagerness.*

Upon greeting the interviewer you step forward *confidently* and greet the person *warmly,* at the same time expressing your *enthusiasm* at this opportunity to convince the interviewer of your potential worth to the organization. You have taken care that your *dress* and *grooming* are neat and appropriate for the occasion. In addition, you have taken the *initiative* to research carefully the potential employer's company or organization and have used your *resourcefulness* to identify a special problem within that organization that you feel capable of resolving. All these actions can be planned to convey to the prospective employer your interest in and suitability for the position.

Thus, in the course of perhaps an hour's interview, you have demonstrated to this prospective employer a number of self-management skills. (The *italicized* words in the above paragraph are self-management skill words.)

Not all self-management skills are so readily observable in an interview situation. Some, like loyalty, reliability, and resilience, can be assessed only after a substantial period of time on the job. Because they are so personal, most people have trouble accurately assessing their self-management skills. It is particularly difficult to evaluate self-management deficiencies without being defensive when they are associated with negative or painful experiences. Rely on other people's observations to learn more about your self-management skills, but always look for consistent observations. Get feedback from a variety of people or at least from the types of people likely to be your employers or co-workers.

1. From the following partial list of self-management skills, circle those that you think of and that others have consistently mentioned as being most characteristic of you. Keep in mind that while a given self-management skill may be characteristic of you, it does not mean necessarily that you are that way in every situation. Add to the end of the list any self-management skills you have that are not included.

Self-Management Skills

Adventuresome	Empathetic	Precise
Alert	Enthusiastic	Punctual
Assertive	Energetic	Quiet
Astute	Ethical	Reliable
Attentive	Expressive	Resilient
Authentic	Firm	Resourceful
Aware	Flexible	Respectful
Calm	Focused	Responsible
Candid	Friendly	Risk-taking
Cheerful	Generous	Self-confident
Collected	Helpful	Self-controlled
Committed	Honest	Self-reliant
Composed	Initiative	Sensitive
Concentration	Insightful	Sincere
Concerned	Integrity	Spontaneous
Conscientious	Kind	Steadfast
Cooperative	Loyal	Sympathetic
Courageous	Methodical	Tactful
Courteous	Openminded	Thorough
Curious	Optimistic	Thrifty
Decisive	Orderly	Tolerant
Dependable	Outgoing	Trustworthy
Diplomatic	Patient	Unique
Discerning	Perceptive	Versatile
Discreet	Persistent	Vigorous
Dynamic	Playful	
Eager	Poised	
Easygoing	Polite	

2. Prioritize your top ten self-management skills from those that you have identified as most characteristic of you. Place them in order of preference below.

    My top ten (most characteristic) self-management skills are:

    1. _____

    2. _____

    3. _____

    4. _____

5. _____

6. _____

7. _____

8. _____

9. _____

10. _____

Relating Self-Management Skills to Work Settings

Some self-management skills are advantageous in almost any work setting. For instance, cheerfulness, cooperation, enthusiasm, friendliness, good judgment, honesty, kindness, and sincerity are universally appreciated attributes. It is possible, however, for some positive self-management skills to be inappropriate or misunderstood in some kinds of job situations. For example, although cheerful, joking behavior by an employee could be taken as a lack of sensitivity in the office of a funeral director, a very serious and sober demeanor in a counselor might be considered cold and unresponsive in a therapy center. Different work settings require different combinations of self-management skills. For instance, assertiveness, adventurousness, ambition, enthusiasm, and dynamism are important skills for salespeople to possess. Concentration, astuteness, curiosity, deliberateness, and precision are traits more likely to be found in the work setting of engineers or researchers. Knowledge of your unique combinations of self-management skills can help you reach an appropriate career decision.

Exercise 2-F. SELF-MANAGEMENT SKILLS AND WORK SITES

Review your list of self-management skills and make some assessments on how to capitalize on those most characteristic of you and also those least characteristic of you.

1. How might you capitalize on your most preferred self-management skills in the workplace? How could you use them to help yourself and others?

2. Review the list of self-management skills on page 39 and identify the five least characteristic of you. List them below.

_____

_____

_____

_____

_____

3. Indicate some things that you might wish to keep in mind about your least preferred self-management skills both in terms of career choice and on-the-job behavior.

Distinguishing the Three Types of Skills

	Functional Skills	*Self-Management*	*Special Knowledges*
How they are acquired:	As natural talents or aptitudes we possess from birth.	As basic abilities we learn by relating to significant people early in our development. Acquired later in life only through great effort.	Learning.
How they develop:	Through practice and further refinement at any time in our lives.	Through responses we make to the conditions imposed on us by significant people (parents, peers, etc.) and social institutions (schools, church, etc.)	Repetition and memory.
What they are related to:	People, data, and things.	Life environments (family, school, work) and their conditions that force us to adapt.	Specific work situations.

Assessing Your Special Knowledge Skills

We all have acquired mastery of certain kinds of knowledge over the years. Perhaps you are acquainted with someone who knows a lot about certain kinds of sports such as football or tennis (special knowledges) even though that person may or may not be able to play them well (functional skills). As you begin identifying your list of possible career options, it's a good idea to take stock of your favorite special knowledges to see how important it might be to pursue a career that would enable you to apply a favorite body of knowledge.

One career changer, for example, had developed a great deal of knowledge about art and also about marketing (special knowledges), was good at selling (functional skill), and had a strong love of art (strong personal interest). He realized, however, that he was not an artist himself. After carefully considering his interests and assets, he decided to pursue a career as an art merchandiser. He is now making a very nice living as an art consultant for organizations looking to enhance the aesthetic appeal of their business offices. His role is to help his clients identify what kind of art would enhance a particular work setting and then negotiate with artists to purchase or obtain on consignment the needed artwork. As you can see, this individual was clever at seeing how to capitalize on his assets and interests. You too may be able to discover clever ways of combining your unique assets in a career in which you can earn a good living.

Do the following exercise to help identify the special knowledges you have acquired over the years and to determine if there are any particular ones that you might wish to pursue in your career. This exercise is generally more helpful for mature adults who have acquired substantial bodies of special knowledges over the years than for younger individuals seeking their first career.

However, we recommend that you give the exercise a try even if you are a younger student, for you could discover an important piece of self-knowledge that might suggest a career path for you when considered with the other assessment data you will be acquiring. As you do this exercise, it can be useful to survey the entire spectrum of your life's history in search of special knowledge skills. Perhaps you will find a clue from childhood that will help put you on the road to a new career. We know of one person, for instance, who loved fairy tales as a child and could recite many of them by heart as an adult. She is now pursing a career as a Jungian therapist, specializing in using fairy tales to identify archetypal myths that have a role in influencing major life decisions.

Exercise 2-G. DISCOVERING YOUR SPECIAL KNOWLEDGES

1. Divide a piece of paper into three columns headed Work, Learning, and Leisure. Then begin listing all of the special knowledges you have acquired over the years in each of these three categories. Be as thorough as you can, keeping in mind that some of your special knowledges may not be readily apparent. You may have to do some mental digging to uncover these. You might even need to do a careful memory search to recall that you learned a lot about gas combustion engines while working on your car as a teenager or that you found out how to conduct formal meetings while serving as a class officer in school.

   Other special knowledges are less subtle. You might, for example, have learned a lot about computer operations through taking formal courses, or you may have picked up a great deal of knowledge on your own through trial and error in working with your own computer. Special knowledges are often acquired by attending classes or workshops, reading books or manuals, or watching how someone else does something. Remember, you were not born with these kinds of skills: you acquired them through learning.

2. After identifying your own list of special knowledges, go back over your lists and circle your favorite knowledges. Work with this list until you have narrowed it down to the ten that seem most important to you, the ten that you might want to use in the next phase of your career.

3. Prioritize your list of ten, using the prioritizing process described in Appendix B of the book. As you go through the prioritization process, ask yourself "How much do I value this special knowledge and how important might it be for me to use it in my career?"

4. List your top five special knowledge skills below, then list some career options in which you might put your knowledge to use:

Your Top Special Knowledge Skills	Possible Career Options
1. _____	_____
2. _____	_____
3. _____	_____
4. _____	_____
5. _____	_____

Summary

Everyone has unique talents and skills. Our skills can be categorized into three groups—functional, self-management, and special knowledge. Functional skills are aptitude-related and are transferable from one job, career, or profession to another. Your abilities to work with data, people, and things are defined by your functional skills. By identifying your top functional skills and by knowing your preference for working with data, people, and things, you can both discover and then effectively communicate what you have to contribute to a job or a career. Self-management skills relate to how we cope with or relate to people, conditions, and situations in our world, including our work. Our special knowledge skills are what we have learned and what we know.

Knowing what level of skills you possess and prefer is helpful in understanding yourself and identifying suitable career options. The more you know about your skills, the better decisions you can make in your career, educational, and job choices. In this regard, the more you know about yourself, the better you can capitalize on your unique assets as a person and prevent your shortcomings from becoming major obstacles.

Case Study of Cynthia

Cynthia is an example of someone who used her transferable functional, self-management, and special knowledge skills to change from one career to another. Tired of her secretarial job, Cynthia decided to look for a new position where she would have more responsibility and opportunity to make decisions. She undertook a systematic inventory of the skills she used in her job. In addition to her typing and shorthand transcription skills, she found that her boss frequently asked her to compose correspondence and memos as well as schedule and arrange meetings with other management staff.

Cynthia was popular among the other secretaries because of her functional and self-management skills. She was such a good listener, negotiator, communicator, and advisor that sometimes she was called on, informally, to arbitrate an office disagreement. She was very effective at summarizing each side's views, helping them to resolve their differences, and helping them to reach a compromise satisfactory to all. They considered Cynthia honest and fair.

More and more, Cynthia was dissatisfied with her primary duties of typing and answering the phone. She was spending too much time working with machines rather than with people. After she had assessed her skills, Cynthia realized that she had high-level human relations skills that could be transferred to other fields without extensive retraining. She narrowed down her alternatives to several good possibilities: an office manager, an Equal Employment Opportunities (EEO) personnnel specialist, a labor relations assistant, a program coordinator for a convention center, a hotel public relations director, and a travel industry representative.

After doing extensive research on these careers and on actual opportunities in her own city, Cynthia decided that a position in hotel public relations was her most interesting and potentially satisfying option. She investigated five large hotels and discovered that two of them were lacking in strong, dynamic public relations programs. Using what she knew about her skills and the knowledge she had acquired in her research, she prepared a proposal outlining what she thought she could do to meet a hotel's needs.

Cynthia obtained interviews at those two particular hotels and was very excited to be offered positions at both. Today Cynthia is challenged by her job and much more satisfied with her new position as the hotel's assistant coordinator of public relations. She is using most of the functional and self-management skills that she identified in her old secretarial job. She is also applying some of the special knowledges she acquired in her previous position (such as wordprocessing, telephone answering techniques, and correspondence and office procedures) while learning new ones associated with the hotel business and public relations.

Assignments

1. Brainstorm with your family and/or friends to find names of people they know who use preferred skills similar to yours in their work. If they don't know anyone personally, perhaps they might refer you to someone else who does.

2. Begin talking with people who use the kinds of skills in their work that you prefer using.

3. Think back to some of the jobs you've had in the past (volunteer or paying jobs) and answer the following questions:

    a. What were some conditions of the work environments to which you were required to adapt?

    b. Were your self-management skills compatible with the conditions of the work environments?

    c. If they were not compatible, did that incompatibility contribute to your quitting or leaving?

    d. If they were not compatible but you stayed on the job, what adjustments did you make in order to be more compatible?

Additional Resources for Skill Identification

Eureka Skill Inventory
The California Career Information System
Room 408
130 33rd Street
Richmond, California 94804
Tele #(415)235-3883

The Job Hunting Map by Dick Bolles
Ten Speed Press
900 MODOC
Berkeley, California 94707

Motivated Skill Card Sort
Career Research and Testing
2005 Hamilton Ave.
San Jose, California 95125
Tele #(408)559-4945

Skill Sort Cards
(See Appendix E)

Notes

1. John C. Crystal and Richard N. Bolles, *Where Do I Go from Here with My Life?* (Berkeley, California: Ten Speed Press, 1978), p. 70.
2. Adapted from Richard N. Bolles, *The Three Boxes of Life and How to Get Out of Them* (Berkeley, California: Ten Speed Press, 1978), p. 146.
3. John C. Crystal, Career Planning Workshop, Prince George's Community College, Largo, Maryland, Spring, 1979.

3 Understanding Your Mental Powers

How we think influences how we communicate, solve problems, deal with relationships and make decisions.

NED HERRMANN

DO YOU KNOW PEOPLE WHO:

➥ Are great at analyzing facts and coming to logical conclusions?

➥ Think best when thinking aloud while interacting with others?

➥ Are brilliant at coming up with unique ideas and new ways of doing things?

➥ Approach problems in a structured way and "follow the book" in making predictable decisions?

If so, you know people who process information and experiences in uniquely different ways because of their different thinking styles.

Traditional Measures of Intelligence

What is your I.Q.? Do you think of yourself as a genius, highly intelligent, about average or not too smart? Most people decide how smart they are when they are young and spend the rest of their lives, consciously or unconsciously, making their achievements conform to this imagined potential. Your concept of your abilities probably came from early interactions with significant people like parents, family, teachers and friends. Rarely do children base their self-concept on their own observations.

Next, your concept of your intellectual abilities probably was changed or reinforced by various I.Q. tests of general abilities and other tests of general knowledge. Do you remember tests like the Iowa tests or California Test of Achievement? Or the SAT, ACT, or GRE exams? These tests may be a more objective measuring tool of intelligence, but are they the true indicators of personal ability and human potential? The problem with I.Q. tests and general knowledge tests is that they turn out to be fair predictors of only one thing—academic success—for only one "standard population."

The truth is that I.Q. scores are not a measure of true human potential. High I.Q. scores are not a guarantee of material success. But this is not surprising since many people with high I.Q. scores may be motivated by values other than wealth. It's more surprising that people with the highest I.Q. scores often fail to meet their intellectual potential as well. The issue is further clouded by stories of "retarded" children or adults with very low I.Q. scores who turned out to be unusually gifted in one specialized area. Clearly, other elements are involved in human potential.

In fact, no one really knows what an I.Q. is. Mind power is more than a matter of the natural abilities you have at birth. Your concept of your intelligence and the ways you learn how to use your mind are equally important influences—positive or negative. Recent research on brain injuries has shown that people use only a small portion of their brain. Research also shows that latent brain cells can take over the functions of damaged brain cells. Unless your brain is either physically impaired or psychologically damaged beyond correction, you have the capacity for intellectual accomplishment beyond anything you have demonstrated so far in your life. Consider the possibility that you just might be more intelligent and creative than you have ever dared to imagine.

But what does this have to do with career planning and success? A great deal! First, doesn't it make sense to understand the way you think—your thinking style—to become a more successful learner? After all, this is the information age, where learning and creative problem-solving have become a way of life and a life-long activity. Also, if you want to choose an occupation that will put your best abilities to use, doesn't it make sense to explore how your mind works the best? The content and exercises in this chapter will help you to do just that.

> *Effective thinking, creativity and intellectual success are held prisoner by negative expectations. Open your mind, and let out your full human potential.*

The Influences on Your Thinking

Becoming your intelligent best requires several types of awareness. First, you should become aware how pressing needs and values can have a major but hidden influence on your thinking and decision making. It's helpful to understand this influence, so it has a positive rather than negative effect on your career decision. Needs and values are especially relevant as you decide what particular work or academic environment is the best place for you to implement your career. Accordingly, needs and values are covered before you explore your career alternatives in Chapter 6, "Discovering What Motivates You."

It's also useful to understand how negative attitudes hinder clear thinking as people try to carry out perfectly appropriate career decisions and plans. Some people turn totally passive, waiting for the world to come to them. Others get sidetracked easily and frequently, never committing to the decision, goals, and plans they have on paper. Still others resort to unnecessarily extreme or premature changes trying to reach their goals. This topic will be addressed fully in Chapter 9, "Hurdling Your Barriers."

The third influence on your thinking is called your thinking or learning style. This influence can be tested, and the result is considerably more useful to career planning than traditional I.Q. tests. Simply defined, your thinking style is the general approach you prefer in trying to understand information or experience. This chapter is designed to help you determine and understand your own primary thinking and learning style. By choosing a career involving primary activities that require your dominant thinking style, you will refine and expand your mental powers. You will also be able to perform the tasks involved more easily than someone of equal or higher I.Q. who is intellectually mismatched to the job.

Recent Research on the Brain

Researchers like Nobel Prize winner Roger Sperry and his associates studying "the split brain" and Carl Pribram on the holographic brain have produced startling new insights into how the human brain works. Psychologist Howard Gardner at Harvard has used brain research to prove that human intelligence is far broader than the simple verbal, linear, and sequential activities measured by I.Q. tests. Educational researchers have applied this research by discovering ways to enhance learning by gearing educational content to individual learning styles. Bulgarian psychotherapist Gregory Lozonov has demonstrated new learning approaches involving "whole brain" activities which accelerate learning performance and tap into little used creative abilities.

These discoveries about the human mind can be summarized by one insight. All people have learned to access their brain in characteristic ways. In other words, you have acquired "favorite" ways of thinking. Since people's unique approaches to thinking share common characteristics, various researchers have classified the approaches into thinking or learning styles. Ned Herrmann's model of thinking styles based on recent brain research has been particularly accurate in predicting which occupational tasks will be easier to perform for any individual. *The Herrmann Brain Dominance Survey* (HBDS) tests your preferred thinking styles and divides them into four categories. Many of the exercises in this chapter are adapted from Herrmann's work.[1]

Complete Exercise 3-A now before reading further, since the information might influence your responses. The more accurately your responses reflect your actual way of thinking, the more quickly and decisively you can identify your best assets. There are no "bad" outcomes or "bad" thinking styles that can result from this exercise. You are simply discovering your preferred mode of thinking.

Exercise 3-A. ASSESSING YOUR THINKING STYLE

PART 1. COMPARISONS

Use this scale to rate how well the traits listed below describe you.

Rating Scale	
4	Most like me
3	Next most like me
2	Somewhat like me
1	Least like me

Directions

1. Read the table across from left to right for each of the ten rows. In row #1, decide which of the four words appearing across in Column A, B, C or D best describes you. Assign 4 points to that word by writing "4" in the box preceding it. Then decide which word is the next best description, and give that word 3 points by writing "3" in the preceding box. Repeat this ranking, assigning "2" points to the next closest description and finally "1" point to the word that is the least descriptive word in that row.

    Example: For row #1, Ben decides that "Dreamer" best describes him, "Sociable" next most, and "Logical" the next most, and "Doer" the least. He assigns scores for row #1 as follows:

A	B	C	D
1. 2 Logical	1 Doer	3 Sociable	4 Dreamer

Rank and score the words in the following summary table in the same manner to indicate how closely they describe you. Consider each row separately. Then add up the totals for each column, and fill in the totals boxes with pencil.

If you are not sure how some of the terms in the table are meant, check the Definition of Terms after the table.

Part 1. Summary Table

	A	B	C	D
1.	logical	doer	sociable	dreamer
2.	analytical	detail-oriented	cooperative	intuitive
3.	factually precise	orderly	tender hearted	original
4.	critical	conventional	spiritual	imaginative
5.	reserved	practical	warm hearted	creative
6.	verbally accurate	straight forward	genuine	individualistic
7.	exact	cautious	tactful	big picture thinker
8.	studious	efficient	outgoing	innovative
9.	rational	systematic	sympathetic	futuristic
10.	questioning	planner	accepting	possibility thinking
	A Total	B Total	C Total	D Total

Your total scores for box A+B+C+D should equal 100.

DEFINITION OF TERMS

Analytical: Mentally breaking things or ideas into parts and examining them to see how they fit together.

Conceptual: Ability to mentally conceive designs, ideas, plans, programs.

Conventional: Abiding by the usual or standard way of doing things.

Critical: Judging the value of an idea or product, discriminating, fault finding.

Doer: Being able to carry out and complete activities.

Entrepreneurial: Undertaking a business venture, assuming the risk for the sake of profit. An intuitive sense about a product or service that would be a good investment risk.

Evaluative: Examining the known facts to make a logical conclusion.

Futuristic: Able to think about future possibilities. Comfortable in thinking about what might be in the future.

Ingenious: Clever, resourceful, original or inventive.

Impartial: Favoring no one side or party more than another. Being fair or just.

Innovative: Able to come up with new or novel ideas, methods, actions, or devices.

Intuitive: The immediate knowing of something without the conscious use of reasoning. Instantaneous knowing. Flash of insight.

Investigative: Seeking after the facts, examining them in detail.

Rational: The ability to think clearly and draw reasonable conclusions from the facts without feeling or emotion.

Resourceful: Ability to deal effectively with problems.

Sequential: Dealing with things and ideas one after another or in numerical order.

Spiritual: Pertaining to divinity or soul as opposed to the body or material.

Systematic: Following an orderly plan. Doing things one step at a time.

Further Directions

2. Now that you have rated the descriptive words above, review each row to find the items you have assigned a score of "4" because they were most self-descriptive. Decide which one word best describes you, and change the score of "4" to "10" for that description. Then decide which of the remaining words next best describes you, and change that description's number from a "4" to an "8." Finally, decide which characteristic next best describes you, and change that number from a "4" to a "6."

3. After completing step #1 on previous page, re-total the columns. Your new grand total for columns A+B+C+D should equal 112.

PART 2. RANKING YOUR PREFERENCES

Directions

1. In the following list of twenty traits, circle the ten (10) which you think best describe you.

Part 2. Traits Table

	Trait	Ranked Value		Trait	Ranked Value
1.	Investigative		11.	Deliberate	
2.	Conceptual		12.	Controlled	
3.	Risk Taking		13.	Impartial	
4.	Evaluative		14.	Patient	
5.	Conservative		15.	Analytical	
6.	Objective		16.	Musical	
7.	Organized		17.	Entrepreneurial	
8.	Harmonizing		18.	Ingenious	
9.	Helping		19.	Resourceful	
10.	Personal		20.	Spiritual	

Further Directions

2. Now rank the ten traits you have circled from 1–10 in numerical order, assigning the highest number ("10") to that trait which is most like you, on down to "1" to the trait that is relatively the least like you.

3. After completing your rankings, place your "Ranked Value" numbers in the boxes of the "Part 2. Your Ranked Value Summary Table." Place your "Ranked Value" for each number item in the unshaded box. Place a "0" in the boxes for those items which were not among your top ten ranked value traits.

Example

Ben assigned his highest ranking ("10") to "risk taking" and his next highest ranking value ("9") to "harmonizing." His Summary Table would look like this:

Part 2. Sample Summary Table

Item #	Trait	Ranked Value			
		A	B	C	D
1.	Investigative	0	/ / / / / / / /	/ / / / / / / /	/ / / / / / / /
2.	Conceptual	/ / / / / / / /	/ / / / / / / /	/ / / / / / / /	0
3.	Risk Taking	/ / / / / / / /	/ / / / / / / /	/ / / / / / / /	10
4.	Evaluative	0	/ / / / / / / /	/ / / / / / / /	/ / / / / / / /
5.	Conservative	/ / / / / / / /	0	/ / / / / / / /	/ / / / / / / /
6.	Objective	0	/ / / / / / / /	/ / / / / / / /	/ / / / / / / /
7.	Organized	/ / / / / / / /	0	/ / / / / / / /	/ / / / / / / /
8.	Harmonizing	/ / / / / / / /	/ / / / / / / /	9	/ / / / / / / /

4. After completing your Summary Table below, add up the totals for each of the four columns.

Part 2. Your Ranked Value Summary Table

Item #	Trait	A	B	C	D
1.	Investigative		/ / / / / /	/ / / / / /	/ / / / / /
2.	Conceptual	/ / / / / /	/ / / / / /	/ / / / / /	
3.	Risk Taking	/ / / / / /	/ / / / / /	/ / / / / /	
4.	Evaluative		/ / / / / /	/ / / / / /	/ / / / / /
5.	Conservative	/ / / / / /		/ / / / / /	/ / / / / /
6.	Objective		/ / / / / /	/ / / / / /	/ / / / / /
7.	Organized	/ / / / / /		/ / / / / /	/ / / / / /
8.	Harmonizing	/ / / / / /	/ / / / / /		/ / / / / /
9.	Helping	/ / / / / /	/ / / / / /		/ / / / / /
10.	Personal	/ / / / / /	/ / / / / /		/ / / / / /
11.	Deliberate	/ / / / / /		/ / / / / /	/ / / / / /
12.	Controlled	/ / / / / /		/ / / / / /	/ / / / / /
13.	Impartial		/ / / / / /	/ / / / / /	/ / / / / /
14.	Patient	/ / / / / /		/ / / / / /	/ / / / / /
15.	Analytical		/ / / / / /	/ / / / / /	/ / / / / /
16.	Musical	/ / / / / /	/ / / / / /		/ / / / / /

Item #	Trait	A	B	C	D
17.	Entrepreneurial	/ / / / / /	/ / / / / /	/ / / / / /	
18.	Ingenious	/ / / / / /	/ / / / / /	/ / / / / /	
19.	Resourceful	/ / / / / /	/ / / / / /	/ / / / / /	
20.	Spiritual	/ / / / / /	/ / / / / /		/ / / / / /
	Totals				

Note: Your totals for columns A+B+C+D should add up to 55 points.

PART 3. WORK ACTIVITIES

Directions

Using the same scale as in Part 1 above, decide for each of the following situations which type of work activity is of greatest interest to you (your preferred activity). Then assign the highest score to that situation by filling in its box with "4." Then decide what your next preferred work activity is, and assign that a score of "3." Decide which is your least preferred activity, and award that a "1." The remaining item then gets a "2."

1. Working with people as a:
   - A. ☐ financial planner
   - B. ☐ supervisor
   - C. ☐ teacher or counselor
   - D. ☐ creativity consultant

2. Working primarily with:
   - A. ☐ facts and information
   - B. ☐ plans and procedures
   - C. ☐ emotions and feelings
   - D. ☐ ideas and possibilities

3. If working with a large plant nursery, I would prefer to be:
   - A. ☐ business manager/accountant
   - B. ☐ plant and garden supervisor
   - C. ☐ customer assistant
   - D. ☐ plant and flower arranger

4. If I were the manager of a company, I would be most concerned about:
   - A. ☐ making decisions logically based on hard data
   - B. ☐ establishing clear and efficient procedures
   - C. ☐ the employees getting along well and feeling good about their work
   - D. ☐ the future possibilities of the company

5. In my work setting, I would like:
   A. ☐ a private office with a computer and data base
   B. ☐ a good planning calendar and other aids for organizing my daily activities
   C. ☐ some friendly co-workers around and pleasant background music
   D. ☐ a private office with a window view and plenty of time to think and dream

6. If I had to use a computer, I would like to use it to:
   A. ☐ perform complex analytical functions
   B. ☐ increase office efficiency
   C. ☐ communicate with others via electronic mail
   D. ☐ create graphic design possibilities or write up ideas for new programs

7. I would prefer to be:
   A. ☐ a scientist or technical specialist
   B. ☐ a mid-level manager or supervisor
   C. ☐ a counselor or radio talk show host
   D. ☐ a "think tank" specialist or fiction writer

8. I would rather:
   A. ☐ analyze technical data
   B. ☐ get the bugs out of computer programs
   C. ☐ give talks and presentations
   D. ☐ develop innovative concept papers (idea papers)

9. If in the military, I would rather be:
   A. ☐ an intelligence expert
   B. ☐ a highly decorated top sergeant
   C. ☐ a chaplain or medical support assistant
   D. ☐ a strategic campaign planner

10. If you were to be assigned to a large, inhabited, orbiting space station, would you prefer to be:
    A. ☐ a nutrition scientist whose job involved conducting careful research to determine the food value of colony grown foods
    B. ☐ a space colony events manager, involved with the planning, scheduling and overseeing of the various events and activities
    C. ☐ a space station psychologist involved with helping people to adjust to space colony life
    D. ☐ an entrepreneur who designed and developed a business that sells products and/or services to meet the needs of the colony residents.

Note: After completing items #1–10 above, tally up all of your scores on the "Part 3. Summary Table"

Part 3. Summary Table

Question	Points Awarded for item			
	A	B	C	D
1.				
2.				
3.				
4.				
5.				
6.				
7.				
8.				
9.				
10.				
Totals				

Note: Your totals for Column A+B+C+D should equal 100.

PART 4. DEVELOPING YOUR THINKING STYLE PROFILE
Directions

1. After completing Parts 1, 2, and 3 above, summarize your scores for Exercise 3-A below using the Combined Summary Scores Table. Fill in the rows for Parts 1, 2, and 3 by entering the subtotal scores for each choice. Then add up grand totals for each column.

   Example: Ben's total "A" score from the Part 1 Summary Table was "20." Accordingly, Ben looks for the Part 1 row on the Combined Summary Table , and enters "20" under the column "Choice A."

Combined Summary Scores for Exercise 3-A, Parts 1, 2, and 3				
My summary score from	Choice A	Choice B	Choice C	Choice D
Part 1				
Part 2				
Part 3				
Grand Total*				

*Use these scores to plot your thinking style profile.

2. Use the combined totals for your Choice A, B, C and D scores to plot your "thinking style profile." To do that, first mark your combined "A" score on the A diagonal of the profile. Then mark your combined "B," "C" and "D" scores on the corresponding diagonals.

3. Draw your profile by connecting your plotted marks on the "A," "B," "C" and "D" profiles. The resulting profile represents a graphic visualization of your thinking style profile.

4. Read on further now to learn what your thinking style profile tells you.

Your Thinking Style Profile

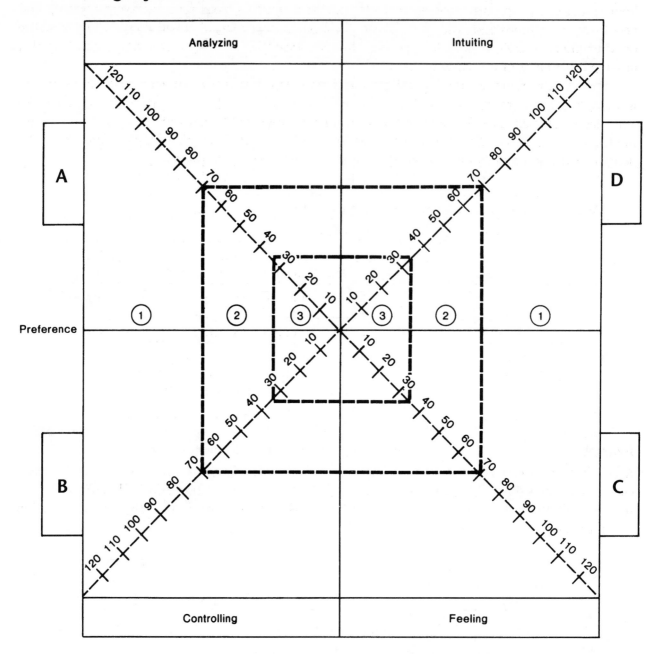

The Three Thinking Predilections

Number	Biases	Range of Scores
1	Prefer	70 and over
2	Use	35–69
3	Avoid	0–34

Identifying Your Profile

Your thinking style profile provides valuable insights concerning your unique way of thinking and perceiving. This information can be helpful in identifying occupations that will allow you to capitalize on your preferred style of thinking. You will also see exactly what kinds of activity would help you develop other kinds of thinking styles further.

Your profile provides you with both a visual representation of your orientation to the four styles of thinking/perceiving represented and also a four digit-numerical code. The numerical code identifies your degree of preference for each of the four different kinds of thinking adapted from Herrmann's model. Table 3.1 defines the degrees of preference represented in your thinking style code. Table 3.2 describes the four unique different kinds of thinking represented by this model.

TABLE 3.1 Thinking Style Degrees of Preference Codes

Code	Degree of Preference	Description
1	Prefer	A strong preference. This code indicates you would favor this kind of thinking whenever and wherever possible.
2	Use	A comfort zone. This code means you would use this kind of thinking whenever you need to, but would have no particularly strong positive or negative bias concerning it.
3	Avoid	This code represents a clear avoidance bias for activities involving this kind of mental process. You would use this kind of thinking only when required and would experience resistance in so doing.

EXAMPLE

A 1232 profile indicates a person who strongly favors logical thinking, has some "safekeeping" tendencies towards control and efficiency, mistrusts human emotions when reaching conclusions, and gives some consideration to more simultaneous intuitive thinking to grasp the "big picture" of the situation or information being considered.

Diagram of a 1232 Profile

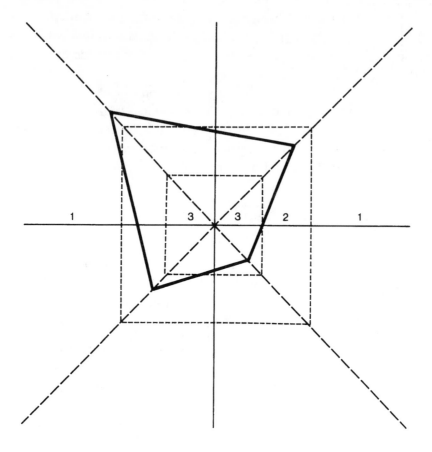

Question: What kind of occupations might be appropriate for a person with this kind of profile? What kind of learning activities and/or subject matter would he/she favor? Avoid?

Exercise 3-B. WHAT'S YOUR NUMBER?

Using the numbering system from Table 3.1 above and the combined scores that you plotted on "Your Thinking Style Profile" on page 54, complete the table below. Note the correct score ranges for degree of preference (prefer, use, avoid) at the bottom of the "Thinking Style Profile."[2]

My Four-Digit Thinking Style Code

Hermann Model Quadrant	A	B	C	D
Thinking Style	Analyzing	Controlling	Feeling	Intuiting
My four degrees of preference codes (1, 2, or 3)				
My degree of preference (prefer, use or avoid)				

TABLE 3.2 Characteristics of the Four Styles of Thinking

Quadrant	A Analyzing	B Controlling	C Feeling	D Intuiting
Thinking process	Logical analysis of facts to form rational conclusions	Step-by-step sequential conventional procedural	Inner awareness reacting to the inner state	Simultaneous intuitive futuristic holistic envisioning
Traits most valued	intelligence logic rationality factual analytical reason	form and structure the conventional security efficiency control	harmony empathy communicating touching personal love and caring	ideas and concepts vision risk-taking possibilities creativity
Traits least valued	feelings emotions subjectivity	intuition abstract futuristic	detached rationality "cold facts"	conventional procedural sequential
Some favorite leisure activities	chess computers building models	cards fishing bowling spectator-sports	clubs music cooking dancing social events	art creative-writing science-fiction
Some favorites subjects	history mathematics economics physics science	business-management computer-programming accounting	humanities drama music religion psychology	art literature design philosophy metaphysics
Some preferred skills	examine data scrutinize observe research read for information evaluate test analyze quantify logical problem solving estimate evaluate assess critique	budget make arrangements plan organize schedule maintain records monitor proofread implement plan follow-through expedite classify supervise	act as liaison counsel communicate entertain perform interview for information host/hostess deal with feelings mediate motivate promote teach, train negotiate treat, nurse sell	design conceptualize generate ideas compose music, poetry, etc. imaging possibilities integrate portray images prognosticate initiate change synthesize visualize write

The Four Styles of Thinking

Have you already noticed how differently various people think? You are probably aware of certain predictable behavior or responses in your friends and associates. Perhaps you know someone who is highly creative or someone who always seems to be very organized. After years of research and observation, Ned Herrmann concluded that just four different styles are associated with brain functioning or how people access their brains. You have already been introduced to Herrmann's thinking styles through the previous exercises.

Herrmann uses the names of physical regions of the brain to name his thinking styles. These regions are the left and right sides of the outer "cerebral" brain and the inner, "limbic" brain. His model is based on research showing that specific areas of the brain are associated with specific kinds of thinking activities. The limbic system appears to specialize in fundamental thinking activities associated with bonding and taking care of ourselves. The cerebral system is associated with higher level, abstract thinking. The codes being used in this chapter are adapted from Herrmann's work. These codes are related to Herrmann's four styles of thinking as follows:

TABLE 3.3 The Brain and Four Styles of Thinking

A	Left Cerebral Analytical	Right Cerebral Intuiting	D
B	Left Limbic Controlling	Right Limbic Feeling	C

THE ANALYTICAL THINKER

ANALYTICAL/LEFT CEREBRAL. This style of thinking is characterized by a careful, logical analysis of all available facts and information to produce answers or insights. This is the kind of thinking that I.Q. tests like SAT's, ACT's and Graduate Record Examinations (GRE's) measure. Those who favor this kind of thinking conclude that logical observation is the only way to determine reality, so truth cannot be determined until the "facts prove it so." This thinking style relies on a rigorous and critical thought process.

Analytical thinkers are inclined to question everything until they are convinced through careful examination of the available evidence. They are not swayed by emotional arguments or unexamined "good" ideas. They want the "cold, hard facts," and they want to know cause and effect. This approach is effective with problems and decision-making situations that can be resolved by finding the "one best answer" and where all the required facts are available for analysis. As an example of thinking style in action, visualize a detective putting all the pieces together to determine "who done it" or an M.D. weighing the data to diagnose a medical condition and diagnose the likely outcome. Much of our scientific and technological advances have evolved out of this kind of thinking.

However, strong dominant analytical thinkers tend to be stymied by circumstances where not enough facts are available and in situations needing original ideas or an understanding of the human emotions involved in an issue. Predominantly analytical thinkers tend to favor subjects and occupations like accounting and certain specialties of medicine and law where they can put their preferred thinking styles to the best use.

THE CONTROLLED THINKER

CONTROLLING/LEFT LIMBIC. This kind of thinking is characterized by a one-step-at-a-time or sequential process. Those who favor this kind of thinking prevent problems through careful organization and planning. The controlled thinker avoids risks wherever and whenever possible. This style of thinking concentrates on details, dominance, and managing events through planning.

Controlled thinkers tend to be conservative in outlook and efficient and reliable in their daily activities. They like to have specific tasks to perform and a time frame for completing the job. Any kind of ambiguity or formlessness is annoying. Since this kind of thinker proceeds with tasks in an organized and planned way, time is well managed and things get done step-by-step on schedule. To get a better picture of this kind of thinking in action, imagine a person "debugging" a computer program, a highway patrolman determining who was "at fault" in a traffic accident based on the relevant traffic laws, or a manager working out a plan to control employee pay, vacation, and benefit policies. Left limbic oriented thinkers are great at getting things done in an efficient, timely manner.

Like predominantly analytical thinkers, the predominantly controlled thinkers do not see themselves as creative and don't trust emotions or intuition in making decisions. Controlled thinkers can be overly conventional and rigid or "tight" in their thinking. Occupations that require this kind of thinking style include many supervisory or middle management positions, police, secretarial, and many computer specialist positions.

THE FEELING THINKER

FEELING/RIGHT LIMBIC. This thinking approach involves paying attention to emotions, feelings and the spiritual self. Feeling individuals tend to be empathetic, charitable, personable and conversational. In problem solving and decision making situations, they work best in interacting with others, "talking out" a problem. These thinkers want to get in touch with any emotions involved and to understand the situation through verbal interaction. Right limbic thinkers also tend to be in touch with their spirituality and to be highly responsive to music. They may look for "inner guidance" as well as to "outer discussion" in their thought process.

For examples of this kind of thinking in action, visualize a counselor assisting a client in a problem-solving situation through the process of "talking about it" and being attuned to the non-verbal communications. Or imagine a teacher who is able to influence and motivate a student through patient understanding and caring interaction. Right limbic dominant individuals tend to excel in thinking that involves awareness of feelings and emotions. They are responsive to people and to the "inner world" and excellent at establishing rapport through communications.

Feeling thinkers are inclined to trust their feelings over facts. For that reason, they can tend to be overly "soft" or uncritical, unsystematic thinkers or even "bleeding hearts." Occupations that require feeling-oriented approaches include counseling, social work, teaching, nursing, human resource development, and music.

THE INTUITIVE THINKER

INTUITING/RIGHT CEREBRAL. Right cerebral thinking is characterized by possibility thinking and creativity. Intuitive insights are often portrayed as a sudden flash of light. The thought process leading to that apparently sudden insight is not fully understood. Intuitive thinking tends to be "big picture" or holistic thinking, where different elements from various sources are synthesized or brought together more simultaneously than step by step to reach conclusions.

Intuitive thinkers often have grand ideas about innovative new ways of doing things or creative redesigns of old methods, products, or services. Intuitives are visionaries, who see the possibilities in situations and get excited about their ideas for the future. To visualize right cerebral thinking in action, imagine an artist conceiving of an idea and bringing it to completion on canvas, or Beethoven evolving his "Fifth Symphony," or a manager coming up with a new employee development program or simultaneously seeing a creative, flexible solution to a longstanding problem. Intuitive thinkers are great at

What happens when you put an intuitive right cerebral person in an analytical left cerebral job.

coming up with ideas, insights, and possible solutions to problems. They often get their best ideas in unstructured situations and places like reading, dreaming, walking, driving, listening to music, etc.

However, purely intuitive thinkers tend to work on their own inner time frame and don't work well on regular schedules. They tend to approach problem solving in an unstructured way and let their brain incubate on a problem until they have a flash of ideas. Intuitives are inclined to come up with many ideas, of varying quality. Intuitive thinkers are not inclined to prove their ideas through a careful consideration of the facts. Instead, they are usually anxious to try them out or get on to the next challenge. People with primarily right cerebral thinking styles do well as artists, creative writers, entrepreneurs, or program developers.

Your Thinking Style Profile

Your own thinking style profile consists of some degree of preference (or avoidance) for all four thinking styles described above. There are a total of 71 different four-digit code possibilities. Perhaps you are uncomfortable labeling your mind with a single "four-digit" code. If so, we don't blame you. But this simplified code is a useful tool for helping you develop a list of occupational alternatives.

By helping you understand what thinking styles are dominant in your own mind, your code also helps you capitalize on your best assets and understand what thinking styles could be developed further. Having the versatility to use different thinking styles for different situations is a great asset to most people. It's true that some conflicts may be encountered by the rare people who have 1111 thinking style codes, with strong preferences for all approaches. But such versatility will be a strength in any high-level occupation, as long as the individual can use the different thinking styles appropriately for different problems. What conclusions can you draw from your own profile? Figure 3.1 illustrates five different thinking style profiles and summarizes how these varying preferences are likely to work together.

FIGURE 3.1 Sample Thinking Style Profiles

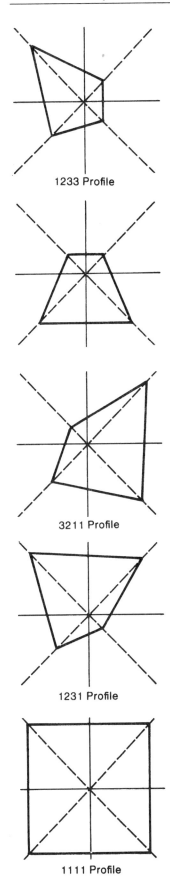

1233 Profile

3211 Profile

1231 Profile

1111 Profile

1233 Profile. "The Technician"

The initial "1" indicates strong left-cerebral, analytical thinking with a preference for logical problem solving. The "2" score in controlled thinking indicates the capacity for organization, planning, and efficiency, when needed. The "3" in the feeling sector and intuitive sector shows this person avoids feelings, interpersonal interactions, and creative, big picture ideas. Individuals with this profile work well with problems requiring a step-by-step analysis of the facts.

3113 Profile. "The Organized Friend"

This profile with "1" in both the controlled thinking and feeling sector shows a strong preference for order, planning, and control as well as strong preference for interpersonal relationships and a trust for feelings. Prefers planned activities with others. A reliable worker and a caring friend. Avoids analytical and intuitive activities.

3211 Profile. "The Creative Helper"

This profile with a "1" in both right brain sectors (feeling thinker and intuitive thinker) shows a possibility thinker and creative problem solver. Loves to help people and enjoys interactive communication. The "2" in the controlled thinking sector shows the capacity for organization and planning when needed. Individuals with this profile avoid analytical thinking.

1231 Profile. "The Abstract Thinker"

This profile featuring a "1" in both cerebral sectors shows a thinker who loves to hypothesize based on facts, devise ideas, designs, strategies and then analyze them for logical consistency. The "2" score in controlled thinking shows the capacity for planning and efficiency, if required. Individuals with this profile avoid personal feelings and close personal interactions.

1111 Profile. "The Chief Executive Officer"

A multi-dominant profile, showing an individual who enjoys all kinds of activities and thinking. Can experience conflict between analyzing and feeling and risk taking and safe keeping. Relates well with different thinking styles. With the right skills, can become an effective leader if able to match up or balance different thinking styles appropriately to different situations. Must also be able to delegate thinking tasks to others to take maximum advantage of the profile.

Putting Your Profile to Work

At this point, the relationship between thinking style and career should be clearer. Herrmann concludes that competence in your career depends upon performing activities that fully involve your most preferred thinking style(s). When you do that, you are likely to enjoy your work and be productive at it, a good combination for success at work. Without this compatibility, both employer and employee are likely to suffer. Herrmann's research suggests that one of the main causes of drug and alcohol problems on the job is the failure to match personal thinking style preferences with job activities.

To help you find occupations requiring thinking styles compatible with your own profile, Table 3.4 contains a listing of sample occupations reflective of the four modes of thinking. Any occupation, however, is likely to involve all four of the thinking styles in varying proportions. What is important to note are your *dominate* thinking styles. The occupations in Table 3.4 (pp. 64–65) are placed in categories on the basis of the most dominant thinking styles.

As you do the following exercise, it is important to remember that there is no single perfect way to find the best career for you. Thinking style is just one of several tools used in the book to help you identify a fairly lengthy list of career possibilities that are "right for you." Later in Chapter 7 we will show you how to narrow down your list and to select your best choice. For now however, begin the process of identifying career possibilities by going on to Exercise 3-C.

Exercise 3-C. SELF-INSIGHTS AND CAREER PROSPECTS

1. Review your thinking style profile and your four-digit code, and then list personal insights acquired. Be as specific as you can about what you prefer and what you should avoid in your work, education, relationships, and life. List a few words on Appendix A[1] that will serve as a reminder to you of the most important aspects of your thinking style.

2. Using Table 3.4, identify those occupations that fall within your preferred mode(s) of thinking. Circle any that are of interest and involve skills you have identified in Chapter 2.

     First, go through the list corresponding to your strongest preference. If your code is a 1232, for example, you would look for occupations in the "Analyzing" column. Circle any occupations of interest to you. Then go back to the individual columns corresponding to the next strongest preferences and circle occupations of interest there.

     After you have circled a number of occupations, narrow that number down to the 10 or 12 that you like best and that probably require some of your best skills. Transfer these to the "occupations of interest" section of Appendix A[2].

     (*Note*: Leave the Holland code column blank; you'll find out how to obtain that in Chapter 5.)

Being Your Successful Best

If you truly want to develop your total mind power, you will not only capitalize on your best assets, but you will also effectively "manage your deficits." In this regard, you might think of your avoidances and deficits. Your thinking deficits are not necessarily "ability" deficits. If you have a fully functioning brain, you can develop your ability in all four styles of thinking. It is difficult, however, to develop a competence in an area in which you lack interest. It's a bit like learning how to swim when you dislike or fear the water. It is possible for people who fear the water, however, to overcome their bias and to learn how to swim—even well.

You are going to be the most successful when you are engaged in activities that fully utilize and develop your preferred skills, thinking preferences and personal interests in pursuit of what you truly value. Generally, people are far more successful in activities that fully use their preferred thinking style and require little or nothing of their least preferred style. It makes sense, therefore, to effectively put your preferences to productive work. Table 3.5 lists some suggestions for activities that capitalize on the strengths within each of the four areas.

How do you overcome mental biases? Hate mathematics, for instance? Stop saying you can't do it, and consider that you are dealing with a mental preference, which probably has little to do with the functioning capabilities of your brain. Believe you are not creative or can't get along with people? Remember, that these attitudes are learned, often from isolated experiences that left a deep impression.

A good reason to develop your "least preferred" thinking skills is that multi-dimensional or whole-brain thinking is simply more powerful than one-track thinking. Whole-brain thinkers can do more things well than those who use only a small portion of their brain power potential. Think, for example, of the analytical thinker trying to solve a problem when only limited facts are available and many solutions are possible, each controversial to some people in the organization. Many problems in business and in life are like that. It's really only in rare situations where all the facts are available and where there is only one right answer.

Or what if you are a great intuitive thinker who is always coming up with terrific ideas but can't get any of them off the drawing board into action? Wouldn't it be nice to be able to tap into the left limbic controlling portion of your brain for some productive planning, organizing, and structuring? Consult Table 3.5 for ideas on how to develop your preferences in the four areas. Sometimes you can change an avoidance area to one of relatively more comfort by experimenting with the activities associated with your non-dominant quadrants. And you can upgrade your limited thinking style preferences in the same way.

TABLE 3.4 Occupations Grouped by Thinking Style

Left Brain Dominant Occupations

A Analyzing	B Controlling
Accountant	Air traffic controller
Biologist	Automobile dealer
Computer scientist or engineer	Auto mechanic
Computer systems analyst	Administrative assistant
Criminal investigator/detective	Bookkeeper
Dentist	Bank manager
Economist	Bookstore manager
Engineer (agricultural, automobile, aeronautical, electronics, etc.)	Bureaucrat
Financial analysts, administrator or planner	Computer technician
Geologist	Computer programmer
Horticulturist	Credit advisor
Lawyer	Data base manager
Market researcher	Driver (bus, taxi, train)
Mathematician, math instructor	Electronics technician
Mechanical diagnostician	Emergency medical technician
Medical researcher	Factory supervisor
Meteorologist	Fire fighter
Military strategist	Hotel/motel manager
Neurologist, neural surgeon	Health care manager
Nutritionist	Insurance agent
Optometrist	Law enforcement officer
Orthodontist	Librarian
Orthopedic surgeon	Marketing manager
Osteopath	Manufacturing manager
Pathologist	Military line and technical officer, enlisted, petty officer
Physician (medical doctor)	Medical records technician
Pharmacist	Merchant mariner
Physicist	Office manager
Printer technician	Paralegal
Psychologist (research)	Pilot
Radiologist	Proofreader
Researcher (technical)	Purchasing agent
Scientist, science teacher	Real estate agent
Scientific research	Research assistant
Statistician	Restaurant manager
Stockbroker	Retail manager
Strategic planner	Robotics technician
Veterinarian	School administrator
	Technical writer
	Telemarketer
	Travel agency route planner, manager
	Warden

TABLE 3.4 Occupations Grouped by Thinking Style *(continued)*

Right Brain Dominant Occupations

C Feeling	D Intuiting
Actor, performer	Architect
Humanities teacher, instructor	Advertising designer
Child care provider	Art administrator
Chiropractor	Art museum curator
Coach (athletic, speech, drama, etc.)	Artist
Communications specialist	Cartoonist
Comedian	Choreographer
Cosmetologist, hair dresser	Creativity consultant
Counselor	Culinary experimenter
Customer service representative	Designer (creative, non-technical)
Dancer	Editor (book, journalist)
Funeral counselor, director	Entrepreneur
Human resource development (HRD) specialist	Fashion designer
Hospice counselor, manager	Film maker, producer
Massage therapist	Floral arranger
Mediator, arbitrator, conflict resolution specialist	Futurist (non-technical, theoretical)
Minister, priest, rabbi	Graphics designer
Musician, music teacher	Humorist
Newscaster	Interior designer
Nurse	Landscape architect
Occupational therapist	Literary agent
Ombudsman	Manager of creative and/or intuitive
Organizational development consultant	enterprises
Parole officer	Musical composer
Performer	Playwright
Pediatrician	Philosopher (theoretical: abstract as
Physical therapist	opposed to logical-analytical)
Psychologist (counseling, school)	Novelist
Psychotherapist	Movie set designer
Public relations specialist	Mythologist
Roman Catholic nun	Poet
Recreational therapist	Psychiatrist
Sales (not technical)	Physicist (theoretical)
Social worker	Strategic designer, theorist
Sociologist	Theorist (creative, non-technical)
Special education teacher, consultant	Toy designer
Teacher (elementary, special ed.)	Writer (non-technical, science-fiction,
Therapist (art, music, dance)	creative)
Vocational rehabilitation specialist	

Note: Individual occupations are placed into categories based on the predominant style of thinking most often required in the work place. The groupings should be thought of as approximations rather than absolutes because in actual practice: (1) most occupations use all of the thinking styles to varying degrees, and (2) the nature of work activity can vary a great deal from one work setting to another.

TABLE 3.5 Capitalizing Thinking Style Attributes

Analyzing	Intuiting
Get the real facts.	Be attuned to signs of change.
Analyze the issues.	Look for ideas and associations.
Problem solve logically.	Read widely and randomly and let your brain play with the material to form unique and novel associations.
Look for proof in the facts.	
Question all assertions and conclusions.	
Quantify facts where possible.	Focus on a task or problem, and let your creative mind play with various possibilities.
Use the computer.	
Play devil's advocate.	Be prepared to capture your insights and intuitions.
Argue rationally.	
Be verbally accurate.	Use intuition to solve problems.
Be exact and precise in communications.	Trust your instincts.
Treat others fairly and justly.	Draw, paint, sculpt, play, dance and meditate to stimulate your creativity.
	Work in bursts of energy.
	Use mental imagery, fantasy, dreams.
	Expect flashes of insight.
Look for standard ways to solve problems.	Get input from others in decision making.
Appreciate procedures.	Appreciate feelings and trust them.
Be self-disciplined.	Look for insights in feelings.
Reach conclusions in an orderly step-by-step process.	Go with your "inner flow."
	Listen to music for mood and harmony.
Use time management techniques.	Use feelings and emotions to understand others.
Work precisely.	
Break tasks down into parts, decide on the order to accomplish the parts, and schedule time to do them.	Listen and communicate with self and others.
	Care about others and express feelings verbally and nonverbally.
Prioritize tasks, and do the most important first.	
Keep "to do" lists.	Work with others, associate with team and group activities.
Be organized, punctual, and reliable.	
Plan time carefully.	Talk about problems, tasks, and assignments.
Keep a schedule calendar.	

Controlling	Feeling

> *A brain strained by a new idea never returns to its original shape.*
>
> Oliver Wendall Holmes

Summary

Old ideas about intelligence and creativity are being altered by modern brain research. It is now clear that most individuals have considerably more potential than formerly realized. One way to develop that potential is to discover and develop your preferred thinking style. A thinking style is a favorite way of thinking or processing information and experience.

Ned Herrmann has devised one thinking style model that identifies four types of thinking—analytical, controlling, feeling, and intuiting. This is valuable input for career planning because various occupations emphasize various thinking styles. If you want to be both motivated and successful in your career, it's important to select an occupation involving activities that use your dominant thinking style preference or preferences. Knowledge of thinking styles can also help you develop your total "whole brain" potential.

Assignment

1. Read the description of ten occupations that interest you in the *Dictionary of Occupational Titles* or *The Occupational Outlook Handbook.* Attempt to identify the four-digit thinking style profile code of these occupations, using the model explained in this chapter. Compare your thinking style profile code with these other codes. How would they appear to fit your thinking style preferences?

2. Conduct information interviews with two or three people in careers of possible interest to you. Ask them questions about the nature of their problem solving and information processing activities to learn about the thinking styles their professions require. Compare your own thinking style profile with these, and make assessments about any possible match.

Notes

1. Adapted from Ned Herrmann, *The Herrmann Brain Dominance Survey* and *The Creative Brain* (Lake Lure, North Carolina: Brain Books, 1987).
2. Adapted from Ned Herrmann, *The Herrmann Brain Dominance Survey* and *The Creative Brain.* This book can be ordered from Brain Books, c/o Applied Creative Services, 2075 Buffalo Creek Road, Lake Lure, N.C. 28746.

   Herrmann publishes other findings in the *International Brain Dominance Review,* a semi-annual publication providing brain dominance information and research. This periodical can be ordered from the Brain Dominance Institute, 2075 Buffalo Creek Road, Lake Lure, N.C. 28746.

Seeking Your Personal Match

The degree of satisfaction which you get from your work directly affects the degree of health and vitality in the rest of your life.

TOM JACKSON
Guerrilla Tactics in the Job Market

DO YOU KNOW:

➡ People who like working with their hands but dislike socializing?

➡ Inquisitive people who enjoy solving abstract problems that require investigating and researching?

➡ Highly creative people who express themselves in original and artistic ways?

➡ Social people who are particularly good at listening to others and who enjoy serving and assisting other people?

➡ Gregarious and friendly people who are very effective at persuading or influencing others?

➡ Neat, organized people who can be counted on to take care of details?

If so, you know people whose personalities and interest patterns characterize six personality styles.

Thinking Style versus Personality Style

Chapter 3 explored the significance of people's different styles of thinking or processing information. This chapter explores the significance of different personal styles and interest patterns. Chapter 3 dealt with your mind, while this chapter deals more with your personality. In both cases, you can examine your ingrained preferences to discover revealing patterns of behavior. These preference patterns are just as important as skills in finding a compatible career.

Do Opposites Attract?

You have probably noticed that people associate with those who appear to share similar interests. Or maybe you accept the commonly held belief that opposites attract. If you think opposites attract, you can easily test the validity of that belief. How enjoyable is it for you to be around people who don't care about the things that interest you?

When they have a choice, people either consciously or unconsciously seek out others who share at least some of their interests. In contrast, you may notice that you pull away from people who don't respond to your interests.

The belief that opposites attract is true for magnets, but the dynamics are more complex for people. People's values or needs may motivate initial attraction to their opposites. However, when people's interest patterns are truly opposite rather than complementary, an unusual amount of conflict and alienation results. The same problem is experienced internally when an individual is motivated by two or more opposing interest patterns.

Personality and Career Choice

How does this relate to career/life planning? During your formative years, you develop unique interest patterns. Once these patterns crystallize, they determine your particular likes and dislikes. For example, some people love scientific investigation while others hate it. Others prefer unstructured creativity such as daydreaming while others are attracted to structured activities like record keeping. Some people enjoy social activities while others prefer more solitary ones. Some prefer working with their hands repairing machines or gardening while others are far more excited by intellectually challenging work. These interest patterns that develop as we mature actually define our personalities.

Because your personality reflects your interests, you feel energetic and enthusiastic when doing your favorite activities. Just discussing your favorite interests with others who share them can be very pleasurable. Many people overlook these personal preferences in career planning, looking instead for their "practical" skills to ensure success. The problem with this approach is that success is unlikely unless you are using skills you naturally enjoy in a compatible work environment. Have you ever noticed how hard it is just to get out of bed in the morning when you have nothing interesting to look forward to? You need exciting work, leisure, or learning activities to stay motivated.

Having an opportunity to identify and assess your interests allows you to plan a career that is realistic, enjoyable, and rewarding. The additional advantage in developing a career based on interests is the health benefit. People who enjoy their work tend to be healthier, both physically and emotionally, than those who view work as a "rat race."

> - *To make getting out of bed on Monday mornings pleasurable, arrange to have interesting work activities.*
>
> - *To live a long, healthy, satisfying life, choose a career that allows you to express your personal preferences fully.*

Identifying Your Personality Style

At this point you are ready to learn more about your own personality style. While there are several methods for assessing and clarifying personality styles, we recommend four well-known inventories— the *Myers-Briggs Type Indicator* (MBTI), the *Strong Interest Inventory* (SII), the *Holland Self-Directed Search* (SDS) and the *Campbell Interests and Skills Survey* (CISS). These inventories are available in most college career development centers. If you plan to take these inventories, however, review them with a counselor who has training and experience with the instruments.

Whether or not you choose to take the SII, SDS or CISS, you will find the following exercises extremely helpful in evaluating your personality related interests. Do Exercises 4-A, B, C, and D before skipping ahead to further reading. Reading ahead may alter the way you respond to the questions and give inaccurate results. In doing these exercises, be as frank and honest with yourself as you possibly can. Respond to each item the way it really is for you rather than the way you would like it to be or the way you think it should be.

For this exercise, imagine that you are flying your airplane, taking off alone for a day's excursion. After flying a long distance, you find yourself hovering over six remote islands. Suddenly, your plane develops engine trouble, and you are being forced to land on one of the islands.

Imagine that the diagram below is an aerial view of these islands. From the information available, you know that each island is populated by highly civilized and advanced people who have moved to these locations to associate with other compatible people and to enjoy the balmy climate.

The people on each island have the characteristics described in the diagram. You know that you will be on the island for a long time since ships make only infrequent visits. You also know that transportation between these six islands is nonexistent. Where you land, therefore, determines what kind of people you will be staying with for a long while. Accordingly, you will choose your landing target island very carefully.

Which group of people would you prefer as companions for a significant amount of time? Write the letter for that island in the box below marked *first choice.* Then assume that for some reason you cannot land on your preferred island. Which group of people would be your *second choice* as companions? *Third choice? Fourth choice?* Write the letter of the island for each choice in the boxes below:

☐ First choice   ☐ Third choice

☐ Second choice   ☐ Fourth choice

FIGURE 4.1 Fantasy South Sea Islands

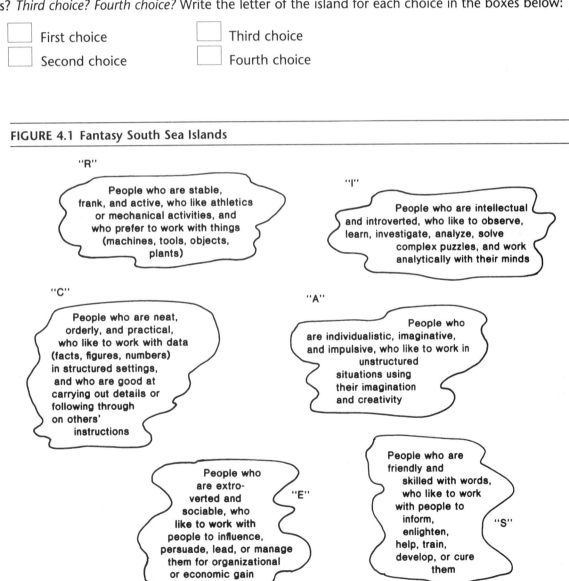

"R"
People who are stable, frank, and active, who like athletics or mechanical activities, and who prefer to work with things (machines, tools, objects, plants)

"I"
People who are intellectual and introverted, who like to observe, learn, investigate, analyze, solve complex puzzles, and work analytically with their minds

"C"
People who are neat, orderly, and practical, who like to work with data (facts, figures, numbers) in structured settings, and who are good at carrying out details or following through on others' instructions

"A"
People who are individualistic, imaginative, and impulsive, who like to work in unstructured situations using their imagination and creativity

"E"
People who are extroverted and sociable, who like to work with people to influence, persuade, lead, or manage them for organizational or economic gain

"S"
People who are friendly and skilled with words, who like to work with people to inform, enlighten, help, train, develop, or cure them

Problem solving can be stimulating, but different people have different preferences in the types of problems they enjoy considering. The following exercise describes six kinds of problems. Assume that you have a job involving 100 hours of your time. You have the option of spending those 100 hours working with any of the six kinds of problems.

You might, for example, decide that you would prefer to spend 50 hours of time working with the "A" types of problems, 30 hours with the "S" types, and 20 hours with the "I" types. In that case, you would mark 50 in the "A" box, 30 in the "S" box, 20 in the "I" box, and 0 in the "E," "C," and "R" boxes. You are free to choose to spend all of your time working with just one instead of several kinds of problems.

This exercise works best if you don't place the same amount of time in more than one box. Take a moment to decide which one you really want to spend at least a little more time doing. Make sure that your combined score for the six boxes adds up to 100. I prefer to spend my 100 hours of time working with and solving the following kinds of problems:

R   Problems that involve using my hands to resolve mental challenges like getting a machine working again, repairing a piece of equipment, building something correctly, or configuring a personal computer.

I   Problems of a scientific or mathematical nature that require primarily mental concentration, fact finding, and logical thinking.

A   Problems that can be solved or partly resolved by combining various concepts or artistic elements to create new approaches, methods, programs, art forms or literature.

S   Problems that involve situations where you are looking for ways to assist others in solving their personal problems and/or getting their lives to work better.

E   Problems associated with persuading and/or motivating others to accomplish the objectives of an organization or business.

C   Problems that can be solved through organization and orderly use of data (information, words, records, numbers, etc.).

Total Score (This total must equal 100.)

Let's continue the process of identifying personality-related preferences. Decide whether you like or dislike each of the listed activities. Using the following scale, assign a numerical value to your like or dislike for each activity. The greater your like or dislike is, the higher the number.

LIKE	DISLIKE
1–2 like a little	1–2 dislike a little
3–6 like considerably	3–6 dislike considerably
7–10 love it	7–10 hate it

Example

If your reaction to "home repairs like carpentry, plumbing, etc." is that you definitely already enjoy or would likely enjoy the activity, then place a number between 7 and 10 in the LIKE box for "Home repairs," depending upon the intensity of your preference towards this or similar activity.

If you know or are fairly certain that you would dislike "designing your own computer program," you would place a number between 1 and 6 in the DISLIKE box, depending upon the strength of your dislike or your probable dislike based on experience with similar activities.

LIKE   DISLIKE

R_1 Home repairs like carpentry, plumbing, etc.

I_1 Designing my own computer program

A_1 Playing a musical instrument

S_1 Going to dinner parties or social events

E_1 Organizing a club, conference, or business meeting

C_1 Keeping a detailed account of personal expenses

R_2 Reading magazines like *Popular Mechanics* and *Hot Rod* or *Aviation Week* and *Space Technology*

I_2 Studying the stars through a telescope

A_2 Writing a novel or a piece of music

S_2 Meeting new people

E_2 Influencing others to buy something or accept your view

C_2 Following procedures and instructions carefully

R_3 Repairing an instrument or machine

I_3 Reading science magazines like *American Scientist, OMNI* or *Discover*

□ □ A₃   Acting or singing in a play or musical

□ □ S₃   Assisting a scouting or sports group

□ □ E₃   Getting acquainted with influential people

□ □ C₃   Keyboarding, using an adding machine or calculator

□ □ A₄   Reading poetry, philosophy, or fiction

□ □ S₄   Serving on a social events committee

□ □ E₄   Debating or giving a presentation

□ □ R₄   Working in a garden or plant nursery

□ □ I₄   Solving math or logic puzzles

□ □ C₄   Taking a bookkeeping, keyboarding or accounting course

□ □ A₅   Drawing, painting, or working with clay

□ □ S₅   Teaching games to children

□ □ E₅   Following politics and engaging in political discussions

□ □ R₅   Tuning an engine

□ □ I₅   Taking a science course like geology, astronomy, or biology

□ □ C₅   Playing bingo

□ □ A₆   Decorating the interior of a house

□ □ S₆   Helping someone with a personal problem

□ □ E₆   Discussing financial investments or business possibilities

□ □ C₆   Working in a neat, organized, and structured setting

□ □ I₆   Collecting rocks and minerals

□ □ R₆   Operating machinery or using hand tools

□ □ A₇   Coming up with new ways of doing things

□ □ S₇   Taking a course in psychology, religion, or sociology

□ □ E₇   Managing a group or supervising others

□ □ C₇   Sorting and categorizing data, records, or files

		I_7	Designing and testing out a model rocket
		R_7	Building models (cars, ships, airplanes, etc.)
		A_8	Creating unique flower arrangements
		S_8	Reading about human behavior or personal development
		I_8	Doing work with a microscope
		E_8	Reading the *Wall Street Journal* or magazines like *Fortune, Money* or *Success*
		C_8	Keeping an accurate appointment book
		R_8	Taking a shop or car repair course
		A_9	Taking an art, music, or philosophy course
		S_9	Participating in meetings and group discussions
		I_9	Playing chess and/or doing crossword puzzles
		E_9	Taking a business, management, or sales class
		C_9	Proofreading
		R_9	Backpacking, horseback riding, or canoeing alone

After you have assigned numbers to each of the above items, use the following table to record and add up your total LIKE and DISLIKE scores for each of the six letters. The code numbers on the left of this table correspond to the numbers found beside each of the six letters in the exercise. For example, if you put a 7 in the LIKE box for home repairs (R1), you would put a 7 in the "L" column directly under R in row labeled "1."

L = LIKE, D = DISLIKE

	R		I		A		S		E		C	
	L	D	L	D	L	D	L	D	L	D	L	D
1												
2												
3												
4												
5												
6												
7												
8												
9												
Total												

Exercise 4-D. IDENTIFYING INTERESTS FROM SKILLS

This exercise is based on the Skill Assessment Survey in Chapter 2, and as such is independent of Exercises 4-A, B, & C in this chapter. Refer to Chapter 2, page 34, where you placed your Preferred Families of Skills in priority order. Based on the column entitled My Preference Ranking, decide what percentage of time you would like to spend using each of your preferred Families of Skills in your work. Make sure that your percentages add up to 100.

My Top Five Skills Family Percentages

_____   R   The percentage of time I prefer to use my Manual/Technical skills in my work.

_____   I   The percentage of time I prefer to use my Analytical/Problem Solving skills in my work.

_____   A   The percentage of time I prefer to use my Innovative/Original skills in my work.

_____   S   The percentage of time I prefer to use my Social/Interpersonal skills in my work.

_____   E   The percentage of time I prefer to use my Detail/Data skills in my work.

_____   C   The percentage of time I prefer to use my Managing/Influencing skills in my work.

Compiling Your Personality Style Profile

Having completed four exercises that explore the concept of personal preference patterns, you can now compile your own Personality Style profile. This profile will help highlight your unique interest patterns and provide valuable career and life planning insights. To develop your profile, complete the following steps:

1. From Exercise 4-A, list the letters for your first four choices below:

	Island Letter	Points
The island of my first choice	_____	20
The island of my second choice	_____	15
The island of my third choice	_____	10
The island of my fourth choice	_____	5

Notice that each letter you have listed above has a corresponding point value. After you rank the Island Letters, put the point value for each of the Island Letters in the designated space on the "Combined Scores Table" below.

Example

If the island corresponding to your first choice was "R" and your second, third, and fourth choices were "I," "C," and "E," you would write the number 20 in the "R" Column of the "Combined Scores Table" on the Exercise 4-A line or row. You would also write a 15 under the "I," a 10 under the "C," and a 5 under the "E." You would leave blank spaces on this line for the other two letters you did not select.

2. Transfer the scores you listed in each of the six problem boxes to the Exercise 4-B line of the "Combined Scores Table." Be sure to place all six scores on the Exercise 4-B line, each in the appropriate column.

3. In Exercise 4-C you added up the totals for all the scores you listed under the LIKE and DISLIKE boxes in the table provided. Transfer your LIKE scores for each of the six letters to the "Combined Scores Table." Do nothing with your DISLIKE scores for now; we will discuss those later.

4. Record your scores for Exercise 4-D on the "Combined Scores Table."

5. After recording all your scores in the "Combined Scores Table," total each column, and record the sums of all in the last row entitled "Total Score."

Combined Scores Table						
	R	I	A	S	E	C
Exercise 4-A Island Fantasy Scores						
Exercise 4-B Favorite Problem Scores						
Exercise 4-C Activity Preference Scores						
Exercise 4-D Preferred Skills Scores						
Total Score						

6. After you have determined your total scores, you can use these to form a bar graph on the "My Personality Style Profile" grid. To do that, first find the number corresponding to your total "R" score along the side of the grid. Then form a bar in the "R" column by filling in with your pen or colored marker from the bottom of the grid up to your total "R" score. Do the same thing for each of the remaining scores. When you have completed this grid, you will have developed a bar graph chart to represent your personality style.

My Personality Style Profile

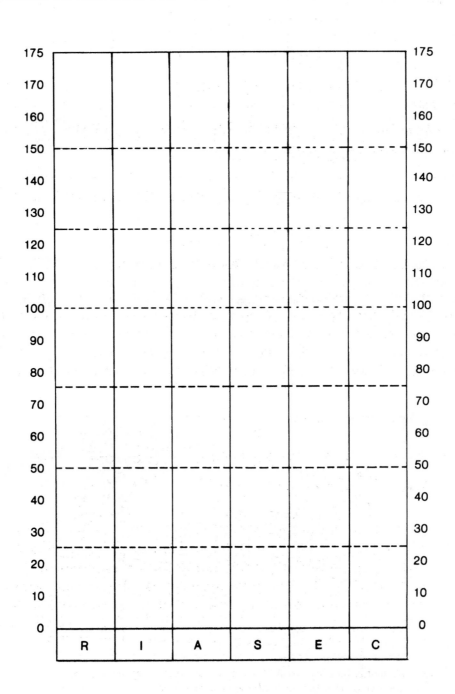

What Your Profile Shows

Now that you have completed the preceding exercise, you probably see that there are some common bonds among the various kinds of interests. In fact, six categories or groups of frequently related interests have been identified through research. Dr. John L. Holland has discovered that in their formative years people develop preferences for certain groups of related activities. These preferences largely dictate likes and dislikes throughout life.

Since your own preferences essentially determine who you are, what you are inclined to do, and how you do it, they are called personality styles. Holland identifies six personality styles, giving them the following labels:[2]

R Realistic

I Investigative

A Artistic

S Social

E Enterprising

C Conventional

To appreciate more fully your own personality style, review your personality style profile on page 78. Indicate below the letters associated with your three highest scores.

	My Score	The Associated Letter	The Holland Name
Highest	_____	_____	_____
2nd Highest	_____	_____	_____
3rd Highest	_____	_____	_____

Clearly, each individual's personality is unique and is made up of more than one of Holland's personality styles. Yet, as Holland has shown, people tend to express certain characteristics and interests in repeated, related preference patterns and in one personality style more than in others. Depending on the strength of interests and characteristics, everyone has a primary interest, a secondary interest, etc. You listed your top three interest types above to indicate your preference priority—your personality style.

No matter how hard Louise tried to be a successful programmer, she knew inside that she would always be a wild flower.

The labels Holland assigns to each personality style may not particularly appeal or make complete sense to you. Don't worry if this is the case, since you will be learning much more about the descriptions and relevance of Holland's important personality style research. For now, look at the short description of each of the six personality styles below. In the box to the left of the appropriate description, place the number "1" next to the letter with the highest score on your personality style profile.

Then read that description and evaluate how well it fits you. Place the number "2" in the box corresponding to your second highest personality style score. Then read and assess this description. Do this process for each of your six scores from the personality style profile.

R   You enjoy physical activity and working outdoors with your hands. You like working with tools and machines and creating things with your hands.

I   Intellectual things turn you on. You prefer to analyze situations and solve problems. You prefer to work alone and are attracted to scientific pursuits.

A   Creative modes of self-expression suit you. You enjoy unstructured and free-flowing environments.

S   You like to work with people, helping, teaching, or training them. You prefer to resolve problems through discussion.

E   You enjoy persuading people and feel comfortable in leadership positions. Economic objectives are important to you.

C   You like to know exactly what is expected of you and prefer to do well-defined tasks. You are probably efficient, practical, and precise in doing things.

> *Did you notice that the description for the letter corresponding to your highest score, your #1 letter, sounds the most like you, and your #2 letter the next most like you? And conversely, did you notice that the description corresponding to your lowest score, your #6 letter, was the least like you?*

Study Table 4.1, Comparison of the Personality Types, on page 82 to learn more about the six interest-based personality types.

In Exercise 4-C you identified a profile of your likes and dislikes, useful information in career and life planning. You can use your top interests to choose compatible careers, jobs, and goals, just as you can use your dislikes to determine what activities you will not choose in your work, leisure, and learning. Review Exercise 4-C on page 73, and record below your insights from that exercise.

My favorite LIKES were:

My major DISLIKES were:

I can use that information in planning to:

I can use that information to avoid doing:

TABLE 4.1 Comparison of the Personality Types

	Realistic	Investigative	Artistic	Social	Enterprising	Conventional
Charac-teristics	Stable Physical Practical Frank Self-reliant	Analytical Independent Curious Intellectual Precise	Imaginative Idealistic Original Expressive Impulsive	Cooperative Understanding Helpful Tactful Sociable	Persuasive Domineering Energetic Ambitious Flirtatious	Conscientious Orderly Persistent Conforming Efficient

Likes	Outdoor work
	Mechanics
	Athletics
	Working with
	  plants, tools,
	  and animals
		Abstract
		  problems
		Science
		Investigation
		Unstructured
		  situations
		Working alone
			Ideas
			Self-expression
			Creativity
			Unstructured
			  situations
			Working alone
				People
				Attention
				Discussion
				Helping
				Socializing
					Power
					People
					Status
					Influencing
					Managing
						Order
						Carrying out
						  details
						Organizing
						Structure
						Working with
						  data

Dislikes	Educational
	  activities
	Self-expression
	Working with
	  people
		Repetitive
		  activities
		Rules
		Working with
		  people
			Structure
			Rules
			Physical work
			Details
			Repetitive
			  activities
				Physical work
				Working with
				  tools
				Working
				  outdoors
					Systematic
					  activities
					Precise work
					Concentrated
					  intellectual
					  work
						Unsystematized
						  activities
						Lack of structure
						Ambiguity

Orienta-tion	Hands-on
	  activities
		Problem solving	Idea creating	People assisting	People
					  influencing
						Detail and data

Preferred Skills	Building
	Repairing
	Making and
	  growing
	  things
		Problem solving
		Analytical
		  reasoning
		Developing
		  models and
		  systems
			Creating
			Visualizing
			Unstructured
			  tasks
			Imagining
				Interpersonal
				  activities
				Establishing
				  rapport
				Communicating
				Helping
					Leading
					Managing
					Persuading
					Motivating
					  others
						Detailed tasks
						Following
						  directions
						  precisely
						Repetitive tasks

People Who Charac-terize the Styles	Thomas Edison
	The Wright
	  Brothers
	Antonio
	  Stradivari
	Chris Evert Lloyd
	Johannes
	  Gutenberg
	Neil Armstrong
	Amelia Earhart
	Arthur Ashe
	Michael Jordan
	Jackie Joyner-
	  Kersee
	Nancy Lopez
		Albert Einstein
		Sherlock Holmes
		George Washing-
		  ton Carver
		Madam Curie
		Sigmund Freud
		Charles Darwin
		Admiral Grace
		  Hopper
		Charles Drew
		W.E.B.Dubois
		Thurgood
		  Marshall
		Dr. Taylor G.
		  Wang
			Alex Haley
			Beverly Sills
			Ludwig von
			  Beethoven
			Michelangelo
			  Buonarroti
			William
			  Shakespeare
			Mikhail
			  Baryshnikov
			Emily Dickinson
			Frank Lloyd
			  Wright
			Mya Angelou
			Emilio Estevez
			Duke Ellington
			Janet Jackson
			Sinbad
				Helen Keller
				Joyce Brothers
				Carl Menninger
				Kenneth Clark
				Florence
				  Nightingale
				Mother Teresa
				Mahatma
				  Gandhi
				Albert Schweitzer
				Jaime Escalante
				Jocelyn Elders
				Coretta Scott
				  King
				Desmond Tutu
					Henry Ford
					Winston
					  Churchill
					Martin Luther
					  King
					Margaret
					  Thatcher
					Lee Iacocca
					Laura Ashley
					Golda Meir
					Cesar Chavez
					Connie Chung
					Barbara Jordan
					Nelson Mandela
						E. F. Hutton
						Dr. Watson
						  (Sherlock
						  Holmes'
						  assistant)
						Noah Webster
						  (dictionary)
						Melvil Dewey
						  (Dewey
						  decimal
						  system)
						Herman Hollerith
						  (keypunch
						  card)
						Carolus Linnaeus
						  (botanist)
						Clarence Thomas

Assessing Famous Personality Profiles

The accompanying figure shows caricatures of the personality styles. Imagine that some of these figures represent famous people. Their actual profiles are illustrated by the bar graphs in Figure 4.2. The Thomas Edison ("RIA") profile, for example, shows Edison at his workbench pursuing interest patterns Edison expressed in his career. Edison's "RIA" code represents a career pattern predominating in working with one's hands to build or create things. We know that Edison almost lived in his laboratory creating countless inventions such as the phonograph and light bulb. But Edison was also an idea person, creating a stream of ideas for new technology ("A" activity). Since ideas must be analyzed and tested for results, Edison could not have developed his ideas beyond the thought stage without good investigative ability and rational problem-solving ("I" activity).

FIGURE 4.2 Famous Personality Profiles

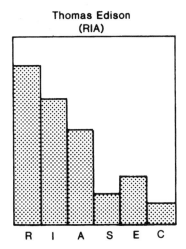

Thomas Edison
(RIA)

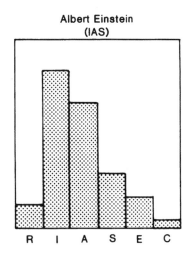

Albert Einstein
(IAS)

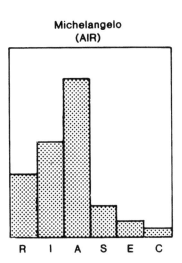

Michelangelo
(AIR)

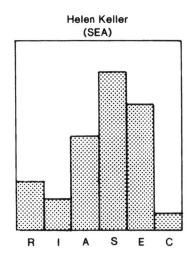

Helen Keller
(SEA)

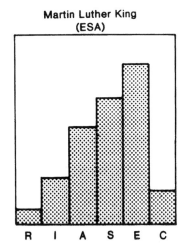

Martin Luther King
(ESA)

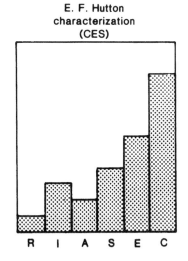

E. F. Hutton
characterization
(CES)

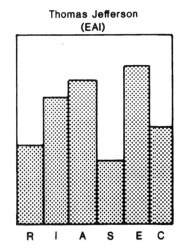

Thomas Jefferson
(EAI)

The Michelangelo ("AIR") profile portrays this magnificent artist as first and foremost a creative genius ("A"). Secondly, he was an analytical problem-solver in many respects, portraying abstract ideas in marble and paint, and complex architectural designs (both "A" and "I" activity). Michelangelo is assigned an "R" to reflect the hands-on type of activity that was involved in actually sculpting a David or painting the Sistine Chapel.

Some famous people are represented by nearly all the styles because they were such multi-faceted personalities. Take Thomas Jefferson, for example. Jefferson is classified "EAI" on the assumption of a dominant "E" as President of the United States. He was also an architect, talented writer, and music lover ("A" activities), as well as a scientific thinker ("I"), a cataloger of data ("C"), a gardener ("R"), and a humanitarian ("S").

Career/life planning is much easier for those who have only one or two peaks from which to make career decisions. A profile like Jefferson's is a great natural gift. But multi-interest people find planning more difficult, since so many interests seek expression. If all these interests do not find an outlet, conflict and frustration result. However, intelligent career/life planning can balance the range of favorite interests in a combination of work, leisure, and learning activities.

The Personality Style Hexagon

In conducting his research with interest patterns, Holland found that the six types geometrically arranged themselves in the shape of a hexagon (See Figure 4.3). The shape of this figure is significant because it shows some very important relationships among the six different styles. As you study this diagram, keep the following relationships in mind.

- Personality types that are adjacent to each other on the hexagon share some similar characteristics. For example, the "R," "A," "I" types prefer working alone to being with people. The "S," "E," and "C" types are far more socially oriented. The "A" and "I" types prefer unstructured activities that involve working with the mind and ideas. The "S" and "E" types are verbally oriented, gregarious, and enjoy being around people. The "C" and "R" types prefer structured work settings where they pretty much know what is expected of them and work roles are clearly defined.

- Personality types that are opposite each other on the hexagon share virtually no characteristics. For example, the "S" and "R" types are opposite: "S" likes to work with people, while "R" prefers to work alone; "S" doesn't like to work with machinery, but "R" likes to work with machines and tools; "S" likes social situations with groups of people, while "R" would prefer to watch T.V. or engage in a solitary outdoor activity.

- The distance separating types on the hexagon represents the degree of similarity or difference between types. The closer the types are, the more alike they are. The farther apart the types are, the more different they are. For example, since "R" and "I" are next to each other, they are somewhat alike. They share some common characteristics. While there are differences between the two types, they are not as great as the differences between "I" and "E," represented by their opposite positions on the hexagon.

FIGURE 4.3 The Six Personality Types

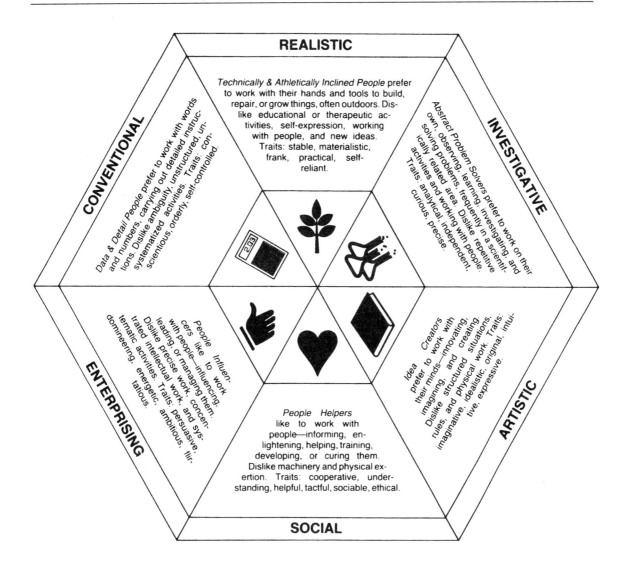

FIGURE 4.3 The Six Personality Types

REALISTIC

Technically & Athletically Inclined People prefer to work with their hands and tools to build, repair, or grow things, often outdoors. Dislike educational or therapeutic activities, self-expression, working with people, and new ideas. Traits: stable, materialistic, frank, practical, self-reliant.

INVESTIGATIVE

Abstract Problem Solvers prefer to work on their own, observing, learning, investigating, and solving problems, frequently in a scientifically related area. Dislike repetitive activities and working with people. Traits: analytical, independent, curious, precise.

CONVENTIONAL

Data & Detail People prefer to work with words and numbers, carrying out detailed instructions. Dislike ambiguity, unstructured, unsystematized activities. Traits: conscientious, orderly, self-controlled.

ARTISTIC

Idea Creators prefer to work with their minds—innovating, imagining, and creating. Dislike structured situations, rules, and physical work. Traits: imaginative, idealistic, original, intuitive, expressive.

ENTERPRISING

People Influencers like to work with people—influencing, leading, or managing them. Dislike precise work, concentrated intellectual work, and systematic activities. Traits: persuasive, domineering, energetic, ambitious, flirtatious.

SOCIAL

People Helpers like to work with people—informing, enlightening, helping, training, developing, or curing them. Dislike machinery and physical exertion. Traits: cooperative, understanding, helpful, tactful, sociable, ethical.

Exercise 4-F. LEARNING FROM YOUR PROFILE

After considering these illustrative examples, see what new insights you have gained from studying your own profile. Answering the following questions regarding your profile may be helpful:

1. Do I have a narrow range of interest areas, or do they spread across several areas?

2. Who are some people who have profiles similar to mine? What kinds of activities and/or interests did/do they seem to have? Does this provide clues for new activities and interests to investigate?

3. How do I feel about my profile? In what ways does it seem to be an accurate reflection of me? In what ways does it not seem to fit?

4. What insights have I acquired from this process? How can I use those insights?

Case Study Example

The following case study is presented to demonstrate the usefulness of the Holland model as a career/life planning tool.

One of this book's authors spent several years serving as a U. S. Naval officer. At one point, he was assigned to a two-year stretch as the Hangar Deck Officer aboard an aircraft carrier. His responsibilities included managing a division of seventy men in moving aircraft in and out of the hangar to support flight operations. He was also responsible for the security of a vast array of vehicles, machines, supplies, equipment, and people on the hangar deck.

This two-year job proved to be an extremely unhappy time in the life of the author. While he enjoyed the great liberty in ports visited by the ship, he found his required work activities highly disagreeable. He vividly remembers a particular incident that highlighted his general discontent with this job. One morning on one of his countless inspection tours of the hangar deck, he met another officer coming from the opposite direction and whistling his way down the deck.

The other officer instantly greeted the author by saying, "Isn't this a great life!" and "Aren't we lucky to have such a great job!" The author was shocked by this encounter because he had been feeling depressed, wishing that he were somewhere else, and counting the days until this tour was over. He wondered how there could be so much difference in the feelings of two people about this same lifestyle. Could there be something wrong with him? Or maybe the other guy was just crazy.

A few years later, the author was making the transition from military to civilian life. He used a career assessment and counseling service to help him decide where to go with his career. From these assessments, he became familiar with the Holland model and learned that his code was "AIS." Suddenly he realized why he had been so terribly unhappy in his shipboard assignment as Hangar Deck Officer.

The work activities he had been performing in that military assignment could be classified as "ECR" by the Holland system. Clearly the Hangar Deck job was simply a terrible mismatch for his particular personality style. It was reassuring to realize that there had been nothing wrong with him in being so discontent and depressed. That particular job was just totally unsuited to his unique interests. Someone else with interests more clearly matched to the job would have thrived in the same position. Suddenly, he understood the enthusiasm of his fellow officer. No doubt he and the job description shared matching Holland codes.

Through these career assessments, the author realized that he must get into a career that would enable him to express his creativity, investigative, and social interests. This story has a happy ending. The author now loves his job as a college career/life planning specialist who gets to create programs, assist people with their career goals, and write.

Summary

Personalities and interest patterns can be grouped according to six Holland personality types. While most of us have characteristics from all six types in our personalities, everyone has more characteristics from one specific group than from others. Everyone has a primary preference followed by a secondary and tertiary preference.

Identifying your own personality style will help you understand what kinds of people you prefer to spend time with, what kinds of activities you enjoy doing, and what interests you have. Once you have clarified this information about yourself, you can look for both people and occupations that will be compatible with your personality style.

Assignments

1. List your top hobbies and identify their Holland Codes.

2. From the list of personality characteristics below, check those that you would prefer in your co-workers:

intellectual	creative	popular
idea oriented	emotional	controlled
analytical	impulsive	orderly
self-reliant	imaginative	data oriented
independent	impractical	practical
curious	non-conforming	conforming
reserved	sociable	serious
adventurous	understanding	a loner
energetic	helpful	frank
aggressive	idealistic	involved with things
argumentative	cheerful	

   other _____

   _____   _____   _____

   _____   _____

3. Summarize in Appendix A^2 the most important insights you obtained from this chapter. What did you learn about yourself? What ideas did you get for career possibilities?

Additional Resources for Interest Areas

Introduction to Type and Careers, by Allen L. Hammer (Palo Alto, CA: Consulting Psychologists Press, 1993), helps you use your Myers-Briggs Type Indicator profile to choose or change your job/career. Order from Consulting Psychologists Press, Inc., 3803 E. Bayshore Road, Palo Alto, CA 94303 or call 1-800-624-1765.

It's in the Cards, by Joyce Cohen and Caela Farren, links 52 occupations to eight industries and color codes occupations to things, data, ideas, and people.

Occupational Interests Card Sort Kit, by Richard L. Knowdell, helps you identify and rank occupational interests from 110 occupational interest cards. Both this card sort and the one above can be ordered from Career Research & Testing by calling 1-800-888-4945 or in California 1-408-559-4945.

Notes

1. Adapted from Richard N. Bolles. "The Party Exercise" (Berkeley, California: National Career Development Project, n.d.).
2. John L. Holland, *Making Vocational Choices: A Theory of Careers* (Englewood Cliffs, New Jersey: Prentice-Hall, 1973).

5 Looking at the World of Work

. . . your career—is going to determine how you live.

DAVID P. CAMPBELL
If You Don't Know Where You're Going,
You'll Probably End Up Somewhere Else

DO YOU KNOW PEOPLE:

➡ Who dislike their jobs yet continue to go to work each day in hope that somehow they will find something better?

➡ Whose main source of satisfaction comes from their leisure activities and not from their work?

➡ Who are very dissatisfied with their jobs and frequently call in sick to avoid going to work?

➡ Who keep changing their academic program in search for one that really suits them?

➡ Who ignore their lack of enthusiasm for an academic subject and plow on, determined to get a degree in that field anyway?

If so, then you know people whose choice of job and/or academic program is incompatible with their personality style.

Bridging the Gap between People and Occupations

Now that you have derived your Holland Code and have some understanding of your personality style profile, you are ready to begin the next phase in the Career/Life Decision Making Sequence (see Figure 1.1, page 6). The next phase involves identifying occupational alternatives that would be appropriate for you. But how do you determine which alternatives would be appropriate for you? You need some way of matching people with occupations. John Holland's model is particularly useful in this regard in that it enables us to match our unique characteristics with occupational requirements. Holland's model provides us a way of bridging the gap between people and the world of work.

Structure of the World of Work

Fortunately, John Holland's research shows that occupations and academic programs have characteristic traits that parallel personality styles.[1] Accordingly, one useful classification of the world of work is based upon Holland's six personality styles model discussed in Chapter 4. The same hexagonal diagram, illustrating the relationship of each characteristic type to all the others, can be used to illustrate occupational types. See Figure 5.1 on the following page.

FIGURE 5.1 Occupational Groups

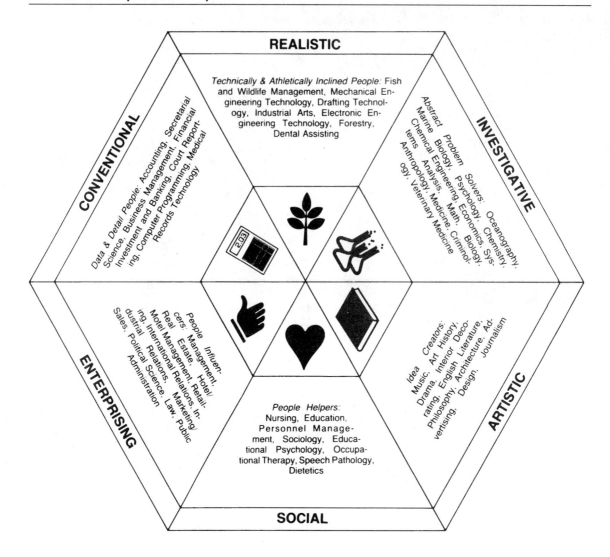

You are already familiar with the six Holland categories described in the following pages, but this time the explanations describe occupational types rather than types of people. Representative careers are listed in each category.

Occupations primarily *realistic* in nature usually involve working with tools and machines to build, repair, grow, or make things. Some typical realistic job tasks are operating a large crane, building a wooden cabinet, operating an X-ray machine, taking apart and repairing a clock, and wiring an addition on a house. Examples of primarily realistic occupations include: farmer, mechanic, electrician, civil engineer, carpenter, dental technician, forester, and industrial arts teacher.

Occupations primarily *investigative* in nature usually involve using intellectual effort to solve problems through observing, investigating, and analyzing, frequently in a scientific setting. Some typical investigative tasks are reading medical journals, developing a new computer program, analyzing tissue cultures for laboratory research, designing dental equipment and instruments, and analyzing statistical data for results. Examples of primarily investigative occupations include: economist, computer analyst, chemist, mathematician, astronomer, and doctor.

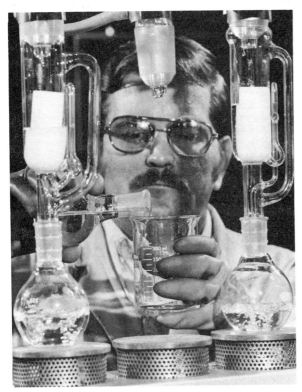

People who are analytical and precise and who prefer to work on their own frequently gravitate toward scientific and technical careers wuch as chemistry, biology, medicine, and mathematics, says author Borchard. Here, a technician measures chemicals during research at Goodyear lab. (Photo and caption courtesy of the World Future Society)

Artists and musicians, along with art historians, writers, journalists, and philosophers, are idea creators, individuals whose skills and interests place them in the Artistic category of vocational psychologist John L. Holland's models of personality styles. (Photo courtesy of Prince George's Community College; caption courtesy of the World Future Society)

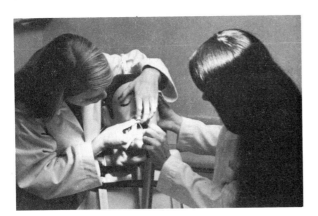

Dental-assistant students prepare for a career suited to Realistic type individuals—those who are technically or athletically skilled and like to work with their hands. Other Realistic careers of today include mechanical and electronic engineering, drafting, and forestry. (Photo and caption courtesy of the World Future Society)

People who like to work with other people—teaching, healing, developing, informing, or training them—are attracted to occupations in such fields as education, sociology, and therapy. This teacher has the rapt attention of his young pupils. (Photo courtesy of Prince George's Community College; caption courtesy of the World Future Society)

People who enjoy positions of responsibility and influence find personal satisfaction in Enterprising careers like sales, management, politics and public stations. Here a naval officer performs in a shipboard leadership capacity.

The average secretary's skills and interests place her in Holland's Conventional category—people who are orderly and efficient and prefer to work with words and numbers. Other Conventional types include accountants, medical records technicians, and computer programmers. (Photo courtesy of Prince George's Community College; caption courtesy of the World Future Society)

Occupations primarily *artistic* in nature usually involve creating artistic products or innovative programs, using music, various art media, words, or ideas. Some typical artistic tasks are doing a dramatic reading, writing poetry or stories, taking voice lessons, drawing caricature portraits, and designing clothes. Examples of some primarily artistic occupations include: literature teacher, writer, interior decorator, creativity consultant, program developer, public relations specialist, artist, and musician.

Occupations primarily *social* in nature usually involve working with other people to inform, help, train, develop, or cure them. Some typical social tasks are working with the Red Cross, helping a friend with a personal problem, taking care of small children, organizing a church bazaar, and teaching someone how to set up a budget. Examples of some primarily social occupations include: day-care director, massage therapist, counselor, nurse, social worker, teacher, and counseling psychologist.

Occupations primarily *enterprising* in nature usually involve persuading, leading, or managing other people for organizational goals or economic gain. Some typical enterprising tasks are chairing an important civic committee, starting your own business, running for political office, acting as spokesperson for a group, and persuading others. Examples of some primarily enterprising occupations include: TV announcer, personnel recruiter, bank manager, travel agency manager, lawyer, and salesperson.

Occupations primarily *conventional* in nature usually involve working with data, carrying out detailed instructions, or following a prescribed plan. Some typical conventional tasks are recording minutes for a meeting, keeping accurate financial records, typing letters and reports, operating office machines, and carrying out detailed instructions. Examples of some primarily conventional occupations include: financial expert, computer operator, secretary, accountant, and credit manager.

Personality Profiles and Occupational Profiles

The personality styles or traits of people and occupations are directly correlated. For example, people who are primarily *investigative* in nature like to observe, learn, investigate, analyze, and evaluate. Occupations that are primarily *investigative* in nature involve observing, learning, investigating, analyzing, and evaluating activities. Likewise, people who are primarily *enterprising* in nature like to work with people—influencing, persuading, leading, or managing for economic gain or organizational goals. Occupations that are primarily *enterprising* in nature involve activities that influence, persuade, lead, or manage people for economic gain or organizational goals.

From your work in Chapter 4, recall that while individuals are unique, everyone shares common primary personality styles with many other people. People also share personality profiles, the three dominating personality style codes, with a smaller group of individuals. In completing that chapter, you realized that you were especially compatible with individuals whose whole personality profile matched your own. There are similar compatibilities between individuals and occupations.

Occupations, like people, can be classified by the Holland Code system on the basis of activities or interests. Each occupation involves a pattern or profile of characteristic, task-related functions or activities. Figure 5.2 shows those characteristic profiles for a few occupations. The functions or activities performed by electronics technicians, for example, include working with their hands and using tools ("R" activities), diagnosing the cause of a malfunction ("I" activities), fixing the problem through knowledge of structural design, circuitry, and standardized electronic procedures ("C" activities). Electronics technicians, therefore, have "RIC" Holland Code classifications because the primary functions of their work involve "R" activities, the secondary functions involve "I" activities, and the tertiary functions are characteristically "C" activities.

Relevant codes can be assigned to all occupations. An "SEC" code is assigned to rabbis, since their chief functions are teaching and counseling ("S" activities). Perhaps the next most important kinds of tasks rabbis perform are to lead and influence their congregations and to decide questions of law and ritual ("E" activities). The next important priority of Rabbis may be the preservation of the substance of Jewish religious rituals ("C" activities).

Cranston had a feeling he needed a career change

FIGURE 5.2 Typical Profiles of Sample Occupations

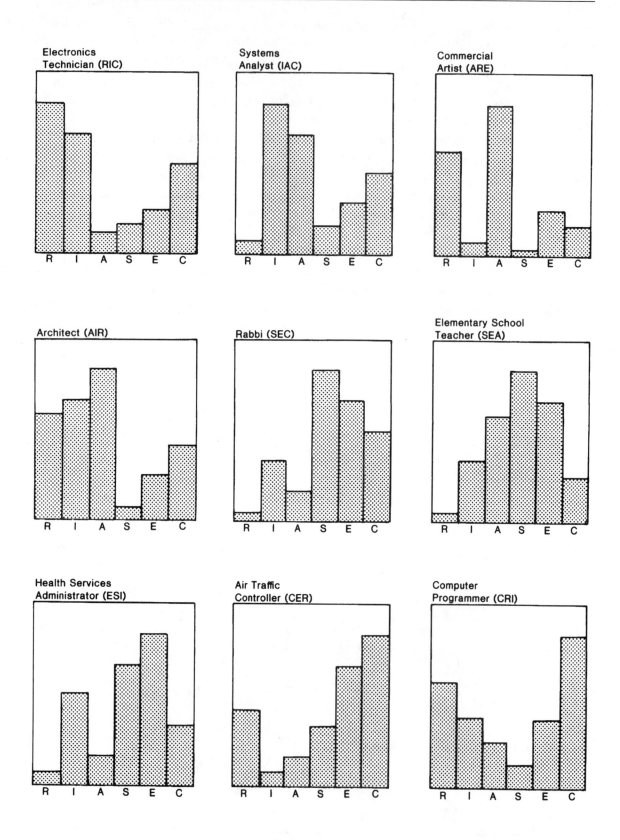

A "CRI" Code is assigned to computer programmers because they typically write detailed instructions for processing data in one of the computer languages ("C" activities). Programmers spend a considerable portion of their time working with their hands ("R" activities) and performing activities at computer terminals. The third code letter for a computer programmer might be either "E" or "I" depending upon whether the third order of activities is more management oriented ("E") or more analytical in nature ("I").

Finding Compatible Occupational Profiles

Find your most potentially compatible careers by looking for those occupations with Holland Code profiles that match your personality style. You will probably be bored and depressed by occupational activities with contrasting Holland codes. Don't let anyone talk you into pursuing a career with a completely different profile just because that occupation offers good job opportunities or good pay. You have a far better chance of succeeding (getting promoted, getting salary increases, getting more interesting challenges) in an occupation compatible with your Holland Code. Look in these compatible areas for careers with good long-range career opportunities.

Your task at this point of the career planning process is to discover occupations with Holland Codes similar to yours. As you compile your alternatives, keep in mind that there is a great deal of Holland Code variety among the different occupations associated with a particular field. Figures 5.3 and 5.4 illustrate the variety within two fields: library science and psychology. If you have an "ARS" personality profile and want to be a librarian, your tendency might be to reject such a career since most librarians have "CSI" profiles (see Figure 5.3). But that might be too hasty a conclusion. Notice that the Library Media Specialist occupation has an "ARS" profile. As a media specialist, you could use your artistic interest in developing audio visual programs ("A") while engaging in hands-on activities ("R") with equipment and materials and helping teachers to develop instructional materials ("S").

Also consider the long-term promotional opportunities within this field. With your "ARS" profile suppose you stay in the library field. The promotional path could lead to the position of Chief Librarian, a position whose Holland Code ("ECS") is very different from yours. Of course, other promotional paths lead to jobs with Holland Code patterns more compatible with "ARS."

The full range of possibilities within a particular occupational field is illustrated by the options available within the psychology area (see Figure 5.4). If you are highly motivated to help people live more effective and satisfying lives, you would probably want to consider the occupations of counseling psychologist or school psychologist. If, on the other hand, you are interested in assisting people afflicted with severe emotional or thinking disorders, you might choose to become a clinical psychologist. Should you have strong research and investigative interests, you might choose to become an experimental psychologist, an educational psychologist, or a psychometrist. Further, if you are interested in using the study of psychology to assist industry in managing its human resources more effectively, you might decide to become an industrial psychologist.

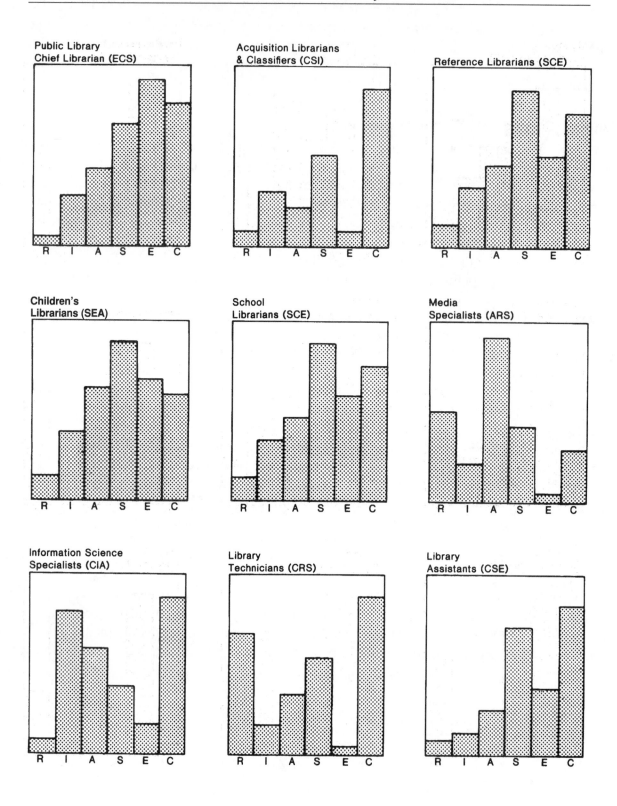

Public Library Chief Librarian (ECS)

Acquisition Librarians & Classifiers (CSI)

Reference Librarians (SCE)

Children's Librarians (SEA)

School Librarians (SCE)

Media Specialists (ARS)

Information Science Specialists (CIA)

Library Technicians (CRS)

Library Assistants (CSE)

FIGURE 5.4 Occupational Profile Variations within the Psychology Field

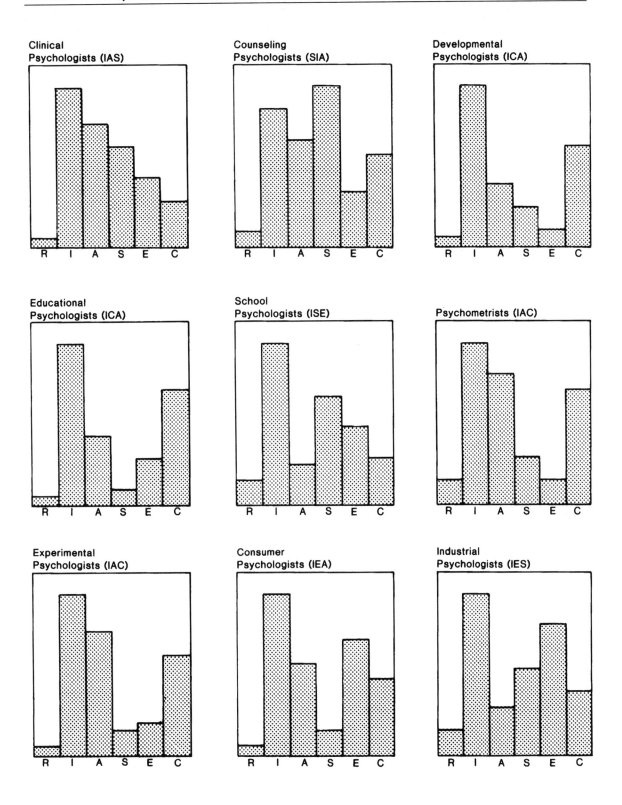

Clinical
Psychologists (IAS)

Counseling
Psychologists (SIA)

Developmental
Psychologists (ICA)

Educational
Psychologists (ICA)

School
Psychologists (ISE)

Psychometrists (IAC)

Experimental
Psychologists (IAC)

Consumer
Psychologists (IEA)

Industrial
Psychologists (IES)

Review your personality style from Chapter 4, and fill in your Holland profile below. Then fill in the profiles of four occupations that have Holland Codes similar to yours and four occupations that have profiles very different from yours. See Table 5.1, Personality Types and Occupational Characteristics, on pages 106–108 of this chapter for a list of Holland Codes for different occupations.

Your Profile

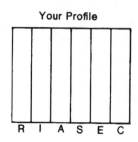

R I A S E C

**Profiles of Occupations
with Holland Codes Similar to Yours**

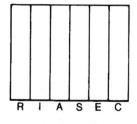

R I A S E C

Occupation

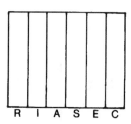

R I A S E C

Occupation

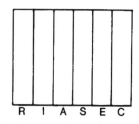

R I A S E C

Occupation

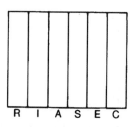

R I A S E C

Occupation

**Profiles of Occupations
with Holland Codes Unlike Yours**

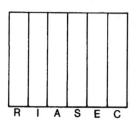

R I A S E C

Occupation

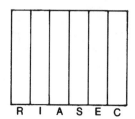

R I A S E C

Occupation

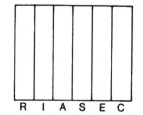

R I A S E C

Occupation

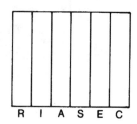

R I A S E C

Occupation

Predicting Outcomes of Occupational and Academic Choices

After studying the table and figures in this chapter, you should see clearly the similarities and differences among the six occupational categories. With this kind of insight, you can predict what is likely to happen if a particular personality type enters a specific occupation or academic program.

For example, essentially artistic personality types are likely to experience satisfaction if they enter occupations that are primarily "A" in nature. Holland's research shows that people who enter occupations compatible with their personality type tend to be satisfied in their work and stable on the job. Of course, career success also depends heavily upon possessing the functional and self-management skills and thinking style essential for that occupation or academic program.

In contrast, essentially artistic people will be extremely dissatisfied if they enter occupations that are primarily "C" in nature. Again, Holland's research shows that people who enter occupations that are incompatible with their personality type report a great deal of job dissatisfaction and are very unstable in their jobs.

Essentially artistic people will be moderately satisfied, or at least they are unlikely to be significantly dissatisfied, if they enter occupations whose primary characteristics are adjacent on the hexagon—either "S" or "I." Keep in mind, however, that the greatest potential job satisfaction is attainable only in occupations that are compatible with your primary personality type.

What alternatives are available for people with Holland codes that are not adjacent on the hexagonal model? For example, what happens if the essentially artistic person with a primary "A" has a "C" or conventional code as the second or third letter in the personality profile? It is possible to find occupations with unusual Holland code combinations. Another alternative is to select an appropriate creative occupation, but choose a more conventional, orderly working environment for the specific job.

FIGURE 5.5 Good and Poor Matches

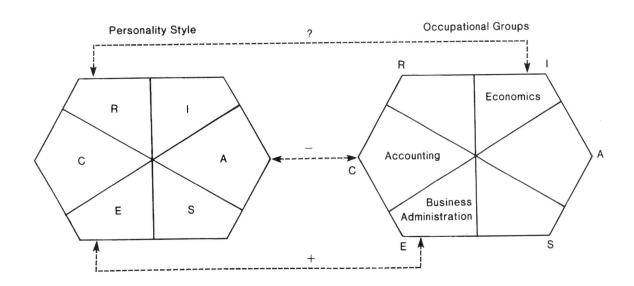

Make some predictions as to the most likely outcomes in each of the following examples. How satisfied and motivated do you think people are likely to be in each example? Why? Write down your thoughts, and then compare them with the authors' answers in Appendix B.

1. How successful and motivated is the "E" oriented person likely to be who enrolls in a biology curriculum?

2. How successful and motivated is the "I" oriented person likely to be who becomes a sales representative or a warehouse manager?

3. How motivated is an "A" personality type likely to be who enrolls in an interior design curriculum?

4. How well is a "C" type likely to get along in an occupation such as theater set design?

5. How enthusiastic are "S" oriented people likely to be if employed as electricians, surveyors, carpenters, or mechanical engineers?

Case Study of Billy

Through his school years, Billy had always been interested in music. He played the piano, guitar, and electronic keyboard. He organized a musical group with some of his friends, and they played until late into the night in his basement—usually until the neighbors complained or Billy's father put a stop to things.

Billy aspired to a music career, visualizing himself as a concert pianist, playing before appreciative audiences all over the world. He allowed his dream to be squelched, however, by his well-meaning father. His father advised him to be more realistic about his career, and he said that pursuing a career in music was impractical because of the limited employment opportunities. His dad warned him that if he pursued a musical career, he probably would not be able to support himself or a family.

Billy gave in and did what his father prescribed for him. He pursued an accounting career because his father had pointed out that he had always been good at math and that the employment outlook for accountants was good. After getting an accounting degree, Billy obtained a job with a large firm. He worked hard, and was rewarded with promotions and salary increases.

Eventually, Billy married his childhood sweetheart, and they had a child. Billy seemed to have all the ingredients for the good life—good job, steady income, wife, family, home. But there was one big problem. Billy felt terrible. He was anemic, sickly, and low on energy. He finally went to a doctor, assuming he had diabetes or some other major problem. His doctor was unable to find anything physically wrong with him. Finally, his doctor advised Billy that the cause of his problem was probably mental rather than physical. Suspecting job-related stress and dissatisfaction, his doctor referred him to the nearby community college career counseling center.

Billy came into the center looking emaciated and tired. He was so thin that his suit hung on him like a scarecrow. After discussing his situation with a career counselor, Billy decided to enroll in a career planning class. There he learned his Holland based interests were classified as "ASR." He realized then why he had been so unhappy in his accounting job, which had a "CIE" Holland code.

This Holland code incompatibility showed Billy why his personal energy and motivation were completely gone. His accounting job didn't allow Billy to express any of his strongest interests. Billy literally had to force himself to go to work each day—even though he had a good job and appropriate skills for that kind of work. He realized that he had made his career choice to please his father, but the cost had been especially heavy.

Unlike many people, Billy had limited options for change within his current environment. Also, his job was causing such serious conflicts that pursuing music as an occasional sideline job or leisure time activity was not enough. Besides, Billy's leisure time was already too limited. On the basis of this awareness, Billy and his wife decided to make major lifestyle and career changes. Billy's wife went to work and Billy went back to college to pursue his first love—music. For now, they are now getting by on a fraction of the income they previously had, but they feel energized and optimistic about their career and life possibilities. Billy has started putting on weight, and his health is improved.

Case Study of Gene

Gene, a 56-year-old engineer ("IRC" code), came to a career planning center to investigate a career change. In completing assessment activities with his counselor, he learned that he had an "ASE" Holland code. This was a major revelation to Gene. He had concluded that, in comparison with his engineering colleagues, he was lazy and not very bright.

Actually, Gene was unusually bright. But neither his interests or thinking style were compatible with the engineering "IRC" Holland code orientation. With Gene's interest pattern, he simply wasn't motivated to do the engineering activities associated with engineering. Gene's job used some of his skills, but they were not his best skills. He realized that his self-esteem and dignity had suffered needlessly as a result of an ill-suited career.

Since Gene has only a few more years to go to retirement, he has decided to stick with his current job. He is seeking constructive change in his leisure activities to express his strongest interests more fully. He has started acting in amateur theater productions, taking creative writing courses, and participating in social/learning activities with his church. Gene has also started to sing for the sheer fun of it, since he has a wonderful tenor voice.

Through his new leisure activities, Gene has been able to restore his energy, confidence, and sense of self-worth. By engaging in activities that match his interest patterns, Gene has literally transformed his life and creates enough satisfaction in his leisure activities to carry over and energize him in his work.

Miguel got off to a shaky start with his career counselor

Summary

The characteristics and activities that typify each of the six personality styles also apply to occupations and academic programs. Once you have identified your personality style, you can focus on occupations and academic programs that are compatible with your style. Trying to work in an occupation or study an academic program that is opposite, or at least not adjacent to your primary personality type on the Holland hexagon, is likely to lead to career dissatisfaction. Various creative combinations are possible, but compatibility of personality style and occupation is crucial for job satisfaction. It is crucial for life satisfaction as well, since your occupation has a major influence on your lifestyle.

Assignments

1. Follow the directions in Appendix C to conduct information interviews with two or three people in occupations which match your personality style or with instructors in educational programs that match your personality style.

2. In Chapter 4, you identified your 3-letter Holland code. Table 5.1, starting on p. 106, lists a number of occupations in each of Holland's six occupational groups. Look at the list of occupations corresponding to the primary letter in your 3-letter Holland code and circle those occupations that might be of interest to you. Then go on to the occupation groups corresponding to the second and third letters of your Holland code and circle any of these occupations that interest you. Write the names of occupations you have circled on Appendix A[2], under the "Career Possibilities."

Note

1. John L. Holland, *Making Vocational Choices: A Theory of Careers* (Englewood Cliffs, New Jersey: Prentice-Hall, Inc., 1973).

TABLE 5.1 Personality Types and Occupational Characteristics

Occupational Groups (Realistic)

Occupational Group	Occupation	Holland Code
REALISTIC "Hands On" Technically- Oriented	Architectural Drafter	RCI
	Agronomist	RIS
	Airline Pilot	RIE
	Animal Scientist	RIS
	Bridge Inspector	RCI
	Cable TV Technician	RIC
	Cook or Chef	RAC
	Electronic Technician	RIC
	Engineer	RIE
	Farmer	RIC
	Fire Fighter	RIS
	Fish and Game Warden	RES
	Forester	RIS
	Floral Designer	RAE
	Geologist	RIE
	Horticulturist	RIS
	Industrial Arts Teacher	RIE
	Landscape Gardener	RAS
	Land Surveyor	RIC
	Laser Technician	RIC
	Mechanic	RIC
	Medical Technician	RCS
	Optician	RES
	Piano Tuner	RAI
	Prosthetist	RSI
	Radiology (X-Ray Technician)	RCS
	State Highway Police Officer	RCE
	Tool Designer	RIC
	Robotic Technician	RIC
	Vocational Agricultural Teacher	RSI

21st Century Careers

Bionic limb technician

Robotic technician

Mechanics for new engines (solar, hydrogen, ion)

Space vehicle pilots

Health foods agronomists

Communication satellite television

Occupational Groups (Investigative)

Occupational Group	Occupation	Holland Code
INVESTIGATIVE Abstract Problem Solving Science Oriented	Aeronautical Engineer	IRE
	Anthropologist	IRE
	Anesthesiologist	IRS
	Astronomer	IRA
	Biochemist	IRS
	Biomedical Engineer	IRE
	Biologist	ISR
	Cardiologist	IRS
	Chemist	IRA
	Chiropractor	ISR
	Coroner	IRS
	Dentist	ISR
	Dietician	ISE
	Economist	IAE
	Geneticist	IRS
	Geographer	IRC
	Mathematician	IAE
	Meteorologist	IRC
	Natural Science Teacher	ISR
	Optometrist	ISR
	Pathologist	IRE
	Pediatrician	ISR
	Pharmacist	IES
	Physician	ISR
	Physician Assistant	IRS
	Psychiatrist	ISA
	Physicist	IAE
	Psychologist, Research	IAS
	Systems Analyst	IEA
	Veterinarian	ISR

21st Century Careers

Global economists

Genetic engineers

Artificial intelligence engineers

Ecological scientists

Astro physicists

Celestial geologists

TABLE 5.1 Personality Types and Occupational Characteristics *(continued)*

Occupational Groups (Artistic)

Occupational Group	Occupation	Holland Code
ARTISTIC Idea Creators Artistic and Self-Expressive	Actor/Actress	AES
	Advertising Art/ Writing	AEI
	Architect	AIR
	Archivist	AES
	Artist	AIS
	Art Teacher	ASE
	Cartoonist	AES
	Clothes/Fashion Designer	ASR
	Commercial Artist	AEI
	Dancer/Dance Instructor	AES
	Drama and Speech Teacher	ASE
	Editor	AES
	Entertainer	AES
	Graphic Designer	ARE
	Illustrator	AIE
	Landscape Architect	AIR
	Literature Teacher	ASE
	Make-Up Artist	AER
	Musician	AIS
	Music Instructor	ASE
	Paintings Restorer	ARI
	Pastry Chef	ARE
	Philosopher	AIS
	Photojournalist	AER
	Reporter/Journalist	AES
	Screen/TV/Radio Writer	AES
	Sculptor	ARE
	Set Designer	ARE
	Singer	AES
	Writer	AES

21st Century Careers

Computer assisted designers
Creativity facilitators
Restoration architects
Computer musicians
Global public relation consultants
New realities writers

Occupational Groups (Social)

Occupational Group	Occupation	Holland Code
SOCIAL People/Plant/ Animal Helpers Nurturing	Administrator, Non-profit/Public Service Group	SEA
	Career/Life Planning Counselor	SAC
	Coach	SEC
	Corrections Officer/ Counselor	SEC
	Cosmetologist	SAE
	Counselor, Educational	SEA
	Elementary Education Teacher	SAE
	Emergency Medical Technician	SRI
	Financial Planner	SEI
	Homemaker	SEA
	High School Teacher	SEA
	Interpreter, Deaf	SCE
	Instructor, Physical Education	SER
	Librarian	SCI
	Minister/Priest/Rabbi	SEA
	Nurse	SCE
	Occupational Therapist	SRE
	Organizational Develop-ment/Human Resource Developer	SEA
	Passenger Service Assistant	SCE
	Park Naturalist	SRI
	Physical Therapist	SRE
	Pre-School Teacher	SAE
	Psychologist, Clinical/ Counseling/School	SIA
	Psychologist, Industrial	SEI
	Recreational Therapist	SEA
	Recruiter, Educational/ Company	SEC
	Social Worker, Agency/ Hospital/School	SEC
	Special Education Teacher	SAI
	Speech Pathologist	SIE
	Vocational-Rehabilita-tion Counselor	SEA

21st Century Careers

Whole-brain accelerated learning instructors
Actualization psychologists
Cultural diversity consultants
Wellness counselors
Age 60+ career/relationship counselors
Global tourism counselors

TABLE 5.1 Personality Types and Occupational Characteristics *(continued)*

Occupational Groups (Enterprising)

Occupational Group	Occupation	Holland Code
ENTERPRISING People Influencers Power/Status/ Prestige-Oriented	Advertising/Public Relations Executive	EAS
	Airport Manager	ESI
	Budget Officer	EIC
	Business Manager	ESC
	Educational Administrator	ESA
	Funeral Director	ESR
	Foreign Service Officer	ESA
	Flight Attendant	ESC
	Fund Raiser/Grants Writer	EAS
	Golf Club Manager	ESR
	Head Chef	EAR
	Head Waiter/ Waitress	ESR
	Hospital Administrator	ESI
	Hotel or Motel Manager	ESR
	Judge	ECS
	Lawyer	ESI
	Lobbyist	ESA
	Marketing Research Manager	EIC
	Museum Manager/ Director	EAS
	Politician	ESA
	Postmaster	ESC
	Real Estate Agent	ESC
	Sales Manager	EAS
	Salesperson	ESC
	Stockbroker	ESI
	Supervisor	ESA
	Tax Attorney	ESI
	Travel Agent	ESC
	Umpire/Referee	ECR
	Urban Planner	ESI

21 Century Careers

Entrepreneur instructors
Hi-technology sales
Global attorneys
Ecological projects managers
Health food center managers
HMO managers

Occupational Groups (Conventional)

Occupational Group	Occupation	Holland Code
CONVENTIONAL Orderly and Efficient Data and Detail-Oriented	Abstractor	CIS
	Accountant	CEI
	Air Traffic Controller	CIE
	Bibliographer	CSA
	Bookkeeper	CIR
	Building Inspector	CIE
	Business Teacher	CES
	Certified Public Accountant	CIS
	Computer Programmer	CIR
	Court Reporter	CRS
	Customs Inspector	CEI
	Financial Analyst	CSI
	Insurance Under- writer	CSE
	IRS Agent	CEI
	Library Assistant	CSE
	Medical Records Technician	CRS
	Mortgage Clerk	CES
	Personnel Clerk	CSE
	Procurement Specialist	CSE
	Proofreader	CIS
	Quality Control Inspector	CER
	Receptionist	CSE
	Reservation Agent	CES
	Secretary/Adminis- trative Aide	CES
	Statistician/Actuarist	CIE
	Teller	CES
	Title Examiner	CSE
	Tourist Information Assistant	CSE
	Typist/Word Processor	CSR

21st Century Careers

Information system security managers
Robotic programmers
Office information system managers
Electronic library assistants
Wellness center records managers

6 Discovering What Motivates You

Man is a wanting animal and rarely reaches a state of complete satisfaction except for a short time.

ABRAHAM H. MASLOW
Motivation and Personality

DO YOU KNOW PEOPLE WHO:

- ➡ Struggle through life barely maintaining a roof over their heads and enough to eat?

- ➡ Never feel part of a group because they have difficulty relating to others?

- ➡ Drive themselves to be equally successful at everything they attempt?

- ➡ Consider their work devoid of meaning and purpose?

- ➡ Are unsure about what is important in their lives?

If so, you know people who have not clarified their needs and values and turned them into constructive influences.

Needs and Values

Of all the individual preferences explored so far, needs and values are the most deeply personal. When people are asked to talk about their own needs and values, they often give "socially acceptable" answers, rather than speaking frankly. Other people are confused about what needs and values actually are, since these forces have been totally unconscious influences in their lives. This is unfortunate because real needs and values are especially powerful motivators in most people's lives. Ignoring or distorting them in career/life planning can cause painfully wrong decisions and wasted effort. This chapter will help you clarify your own true needs and values and put them in proper perspective. Once this is accomplished, needs and values become invaluable "filters" for eliminating general career/life alternatives or specific environments that don't fit you.

Needs and Motivation

Have you ever seen anyone try to motivate somebody else by offering inducements or threats? The research of Abraham Maslow clearly demonstrates that this approach is useless in the long run. All people can be motivated, but motivation cannot be imposed from the outside. Instead, Maslow's work shows us that all people are motivated by inner drives or impulses called needs.[1] A need is an urgent requirement for something that is essential. Because needs reflect some vital deficiency, a strong sense of inner discomfort motivates people to get their needs met.

FIGURE 6.1 Relationship of Needs, Goals, and Satisfaction

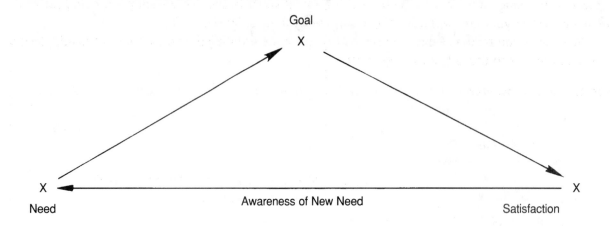

Although some basic needs are shared by all, higher-level needs vary from person to person. You might, for example, be strongly motivated by a need to compete with others, while a friend might be highly motivated by the need to help others. Some people have needs for security and others for risk taking. Some require independence, and others need dependency. Some needs may be readily fulfilled, but others remain unsatisfied for the greater part of our lives. Each of us, however, has a few dominant needs in our life at any one time.

Needs, Behavior, and Satisfaction

Your unsatisfied needs drive you; they provide the energy that directs your actions. Once you satisfy a dominant need, you reduce inner tension and experience fulfillment. You also cease to be motivated by any goals that were connected to this particular need. This dynamic is the reason it is a mistake to set up a career goal based solely on a temporary need. On the other hand, needs cannot be ignored because satisfaction itself is only a temporary experience. You undoubtedly know that it is human nature, once one pressing need has been satisfied, to quickly become aware of a new unsatisfied need. In this manner, the needs satisfaction process is cyclic, and everyone is destined to be motivated throughout life by needs. Perhaps that is fortunate. Wouldn't life be boring if all your needs were fully met, and you possessed no motivation at all?

Unacknowledged Needs and False Motivations

Your dominant needs motivate you regardless of whether you are consciously aware of them. And most people are not consciously aware of their real needs, even though they are revealed to others through actions. You may be ineffective at getting your needs met just because you need to clarify them.

Typically, when people lose touch with their real needs, they substitute a false need for a real one. For example, people who hunger for love and affection in their lives may substitute a false hunger for food. While these people appear to be motivated by the need for food, the underlying need is really for intimacy. Another example of "false" motivation is illustrated by people who mask a real need for security with a desire to dominate or to become subservient to others. None of the people represented by these examples are getting closer to getting their real needs met. Instead of fulfilling their deficiency, they are often creating other problems. The following exercise is designed to help you avoid making the same mistake.

1. Consider the things that are real needs at this stage of your life and are currently not being satisfied in any aspect of your life (work, school, leisure, relationships, family, etc.).

   Whenever you read a description below of a currently unsatisfied, really important need, place a check in the box to the left of that description.

Needs Assessment Inventory[2]

What I Need

(S) Having regularly scheduled activities like work, school, exercise, etc.

(P) An environment* where I am physically comfortable

(A) An environment* that allows me the freedom to grow as much as I can

(B) Being a member of a group (family, work, school, social, etc.)

(S) Having the protection of good benefits (hospitalization, insurance, compensation, retirement)

(E) An environment* that provides rewards (money, recognition, praise, promotion, etc.) for my performance

(P) An environment* where I'm not always pressured to produce results

(A) An environment* that enables me to contribute to a worthwhile cause

(E) Getting recognition for my skill or expertise

(B) Supporting, comforting, nurturing, or assisting others

(A) An environment* in which I can continually learn and apply new knowledge and insights

*In this context "environment" may mean work, home, school, etc.

What I Need

(E) Having a real sense of personal pride in my performance

(P) A job or similar obligation that doesn't cut into my leisure or personal pleasure time too much

(B) An opportunity to be a member of a team**

(S) An environment* that enables me to avoid pain, physical injury, illness, or hazardous situations

(A) Using my best and most preferred skills

(B) Being supported, loved, and guided by others

(E) Being acknowledged for my achievements

(P) A schedule that's flexible enough to provide adequate time for meals, breaks, and periods of rest

(S) An environment* where it's safe for me to experiment and make mistakes without being too harshly penalized

(A) An opportunity to use my time, talent, creativity, and energy in useful endeavors

(E) Knowing that I am one of the most competent members of my group

(S) An environment* where I am clear on exactly what is expected of me

(P) A lifestyle that assures me a place to live, some clothes, and enough to eat

(B) Being in the company of people most of the time

*In this context "environment" may mean work, home, school, etc.

**In this context "team" may mean work, sports, church chorus, community group, etc.

2. After completing step #1 above, add up the number of times each letter was checked and place the sum in the appropriate box below. For example, if four of the boxes coded as (S) were checked, then place a "4" in the "S" box below.

Do that for each of the five letters. You will be using these totals again later.

P   S   B   E   A

□   □   □   □   □

3. Each of the letters atop the boxes above represents a basic need in life. These basic needs are listed in Table 6.1, "Steps of the Basic Needs System," and explained in Tables 6.2 and 6.3, pages 114–115 of this chapter. Study this information carefully to understand your current basic needs better.

Maslow's Needs Hierarchy

Research psychologist Abraham Maslow found that people have patterns of needs that make behavior predictable.[3] Abraham Maslow classified all needs into five basic categories. Maslow concluded that needs conform to a hierarchy; that is, they are structurally organized from a lower to a higher level. The five needs from lowest to highest are: Physiological, Safety, Belongingness and Love, Esteem, and Self-Actualization.

Maslow's work shows that there is a natural progression and growth associated with the way that people experience their needs. This progression involves a step-like structure as illustrated in Table 6.1, page 114. The general tendency is for a person to move progressively from the lower to higher steps in the needs hierarchy. The lower steps represent deficiency needs for physiological survival and physical safety and then progress through emotional support to the need for self-esteem and self-fulfillment. People living at the highest need-level experience little difference between work and pleasure.

Maslow does not see these high-level self-actualization needs as deficiency needs. People become motivated by the self-actualization needs only when all of their deficiency needs have been satisfied as a general condition in life. Only then are people free to discover, explore, develop, and unfold their true potential. This upward moving tendency is what Maslow calls the growth process. Of course, not everyone grows at the same rate.

It is also possible to move downward on the needs hierarchy because of certain life events. For instance, the sudden, unexpected death of a spouse or loved one could result in belongingness and love reappearing as a strong motive when previously it had been satisfied. Or the devastation resulting from the loss of one's job and the inability to find another could plunge an individual all the way down the hierarchy to a personal need for safety and security.

The Basic Needs on the Job

So far we have discussed the basic needs hierarchy in general terms. These needs also operate in the work setting to motivate characteristic types of behavior. The needs and behaviors are presented in Table 6.3 on page 115. Study the table to see if you can identify on-the-job behaviors typical of you and of other people you know.

TABLE 6.1 Steps of the Basic Needs System[4]

The Need System	1 (P) Physiological	2 (S) Safety	3 (B) Belongingness and Love	4 (E) Esteem 1) Self-respect 2) Esteem of Others	5 (A) Self-actualization
Type of Need					Transcendent Needs
Specific Needs Involved	physical comfort food and water shelter warmth sexual gratification other bodily needs	avoiding risk feeling of being safe emotional security physical security harm avoidance predictability protection stability dependency freedom from fear need for structure and order, law, limits	friendship affiliation feeling part of a group belonging with someone else giving and receiving love affection relationships with people a place in a group or family intimacy	self-respect desire for acknowledgment demonstrate competency and mastery advancement recognition self-confidence independence and freedom reputation attention status sense of self-worth adequacy being useful and necessary	self-fulfillment achieving one's full potential desire to know and understand realization of the self personal growth meaning in life and work satisfaction through doing making a contribution serving a worthy cause

TABLE 6.2 Some Key Points about Needs

- An unsatisfied need produces a state of inner tension or discomfort which motivates the individual to satisfy that need.
- Unsatisfied basic needs are the primary sources of motivation in life.
- Basic needs that have been essentially satisfied in life no longer create discomfort and cease to be prime motivators of behavior.
- There are five basic needs systems that operate to influence most of human behavior.
- The five basic needs are arranged in a hierarchy from lower to higher.
- There is a natural tendency to progress from the lower level need system to the higher level need system.
- A person becomes aware of a higher order need system only when a lower order need system has been essentially satisfied.
- Should the satisfaction of a basic lower order need be blocked, a person will not become aware of or motivated by a higher order need system.
- While no need is ever fully satisfied, there is some minimal level of satisfaction at which a particular basic need ceases to be a major discomfort in life. At that point, the lower level need ceases to motivate behavior and a new, higher level need begins to capture one's attention and motivate behavior.
- Living at the higher level of needs is healthier and more satisfying than living at the lower levels.

TABLE 6.3 The Basic Needs on the Job[5]

The Basic Need	Work Motivation/Behavior
Physiological	Concern for subsistence (making enough money to survive). Concern for adequate time for meals and rest breaks. Concern for the physical working conditions and avoiding bodily discomfort.
Safety	Concern for fringe benefits such as retirement/pension plan, hospitalization insurance, safe working conditions, seniority protection, clear and consistent working standards (knowing exactly what is expected of a person).
Belongingness and Love	Concern for good relationships, harmonious interactions with peers and superiors, being a member of a working team or group, giving and receiving nurturing.
Esteem	Concern for ways of demonstrating skills and proving self to others. Seeking out opportunities for advancement and promotion. Obtaining work assignments to demonstrate special knowledges and skills. Preoccupation with the best work in return for various types of rewards available (titles, salary, praise, promotions, recommendations, status, etc.).
Self-Actualization	A concern for testing one's self (challenge), proving something to one's self. Preoccupation with personal growth, along with a need to be involved in challenging and interesting work that allows learning, growth, creativity, productivity, and contribution to a worthwhile cause.

A Case Study of Brad

After ten years with his company, Brad moved up to a position of considerable respect and responsibility. Then suddenly his life was thrown into chaos. Brad received notification that he was being laid off. Upon learning this, he was shocked, hurt, and frightened. How could he support his family? How could he obtain another job that would pay a comparable salary? How could he find work he liked and was interested in? How could he replace his friendships at work? Where could he have a comparable amount of responsibility and respect?

At this point, Brad sought the help of a career counselor to assist him in deciding where to go with his life. Brad's primary concern was finding work that would interest him, use his best talents, and associate him with people he really liked. This latter concern, being with people he liked, was Brad's major preoccupation at this point. Primarily because of this need, Brad decided upon a new career as a career counselor. Once he had chosen his new career, Brad worked hard to implement it, first by getting the necessary education and then by obtaining a career-counseling position.

When Brad acquired his new job, he was excited about it and very much involved. By belonging to an organization of his choice and by associating with clients and co-workers he liked, Brad's needs were being met. Gradually, however, Brad began losing his enthusiasm for counseling. Instead, he noticed that he was skilled at designing counseling materials as well as planning and developing counseling programs. This new love eventually became a problem for Brad. People seeking his counseling services were filling up his time, which he thought could be better spent in program development.

Eventually, Brad applied for and obtained a position where he could spend most of his time and efforts designing, planning, and developing programs. At this point, Brad re-experienced the interest and enthusiasm for his work that he had felt when he first acquired his counseling position.

Brad's primary motivation now is creating and implementing effective counseling programs to serve large numbers of people. His achievements have begun earning him recognition, and he feels very good about that. Recently, however, Brad has experienced a new tension; he feels he is still not using his strongest talents for a cause that is deeply meaningful to him.

Discussion of the Case Study of Brad

Brad's physiological, safety, and belongingness needs had been essentially satisfied in ten years at his old career. Upon receiving his termination notice, however, Brad was set back both physically and emotionally. His needs for security and belongingness suddenly became unmet needs. On the job, his primary motivation had been satisfying his need for esteem. Now he was plummeted all the way down the needs hierarchy to physiological concerns about how he was going to provide the basic necessities for himself and his family.

In counseling, Brad quickly learned that he possessed many employable skills. Although losing his job was a serious setback, his future was actually still quite secure. He was still young and employable, and he had sufficient savings to survive until he could obtain a new position. In looking at these aspects, Brad felt reassured. In fact, he really wasn't at the physiological or security level of the needs hierarchy. His primary preoccupation was at the belongingness and love level. His personal pride and esteem had suffered a great deal in his setback, but the primary motivation for his present career was with the need for affiliation, the need to feel wanted by and associated with others. Brad had chosen this career far more on the basis of his "hunger" for affiliation than out of consideration for his primary interests, talents, and personality style. And that proved to be a mistake.

Although Brad was an effective counselor, he quickly started losing his interest and enthusiasm for counseling as soon as his belongingness needs were generally satisfied. He then re-experienced the need for esteem. This occurred in the form of motivation to develop his skills and to produce significant achievements through work. In this respect, however, Brad became aware that his skills and interests were more in creative program planning and development than in personal counseling.

At the time he made his selection, Brad was unaware of how one's motivation changes when a need is satisfied. Had he been aware of this important dynamic, he would have developed plans for a career track that led more quickly to his fundamental interests and talents. Fortunately for Brad, his career choice and his organization allowed for a transfer that used his talents and fulfilled his current primary needs for esteem.

The closing statements in the case study suggest that a new shift in Brad's motivation may be occurring. His concern appears to be less in achievement for esteem and more in personal development for a worthy cause. Perhaps Brad's needs for esteem are becoming satisfied, and he is responding to inner needs for self-actualization.

Conclusions from the Case Study

While most of the lessons to be learned from the case study and the above discussion are obvious, a few points warrant further elaboration. We can infer from this case study that while needs must be included in the career-choice process, they should be considered as just one part of the whole picture. People must also clarify what they have to contribute through preferred talents, interests, values, and life goals. They must also be aware that although talents and personality styles change very little after the age of eighteen, the same is not true of needs. Needs change continuously over a lifetime. In career planning, therefore, you must take into account both where you are now regarding personal needs and where you will be in the future.

Now that you are more familiar with the basic needs system, return to Exercise 6-A on page 111 to process further your Needs Assessment Inventory results. Based on the totals in each box, rank the five letters in order, starting with the highest score. When there are ties, decide from Maslow's hierarchy and your own experience which needs are more important at this time in your life. If still undecided, choose the lower level need as the top priority based on Maslow's assertion that lower level needs must be relatively satisfied before higher level needs can emerge. For example, if you were unable to break a tie between your Belongingness ("B") and Safety ("S") needs, then choose the Safety need as your top priority since this needs system must be relatively satisfied before your Belongingness need can take precedence.

Example
Assume that your scores were as follows:

Basic Needs Category	Total Checks	Priority Order
(P) Physiological	1	#5
(S) Safety	1	#4
(B) Belongingness	2	#3
(E) Esteem	4	#2
(A) Self-Actualization	4	#1

From this example you can see that:

- The lower order needs, "P" (Physiological) and "S" (Safety), having been checked only once each, are pretty well satisfied.

- The "B" (Belongingness) needs, having been checked twice, are less satisfied than the lower order needs but still sufficiently satisfied so that "E" (Esteem) needs have made themselves known.

- The higher order needs, "E" (Esteem) and "A" (Self-Actualization), having been checked four times, are the least satisfied. The "E" needs probably are the primary source of motivation at this time.

Estimating My Needs Satisfaction

Basic Needs Category	Total Checks	Priority Order
(P) Physiological	☐	
(S) Safety	☐	
(B) Belongingness	☐	
(E) Esteem	☐	
(A) Self-Actualization	☐	

The order in which you ranked your needs gives an indication of how much each need category drives or motivates you currently.

1. Which of the basic needs in your life appear to be the most fully satisfied? Explain why this is so.

2. Which basic need, because it is not fully satisfied, now appears to be your primary motivator? What would have to happen for this need to be generally satisfied in your life? (Look for clues in individual items you've checked on the Needs Assessment Inventory.)

3. If your current primary motivating need were generally satisfied, what need would then probably become your primary motivator? Include the possible ways your life could change.

4. How will you use the information gained from your needs assessment in your future career planning?

Needs versus Values

Clear, consciously held values are another important factor in effective career choices. The relationship between needs and values can be demonstrated by examining how each is acquired and how each influences current and future behavior.

Needs arise out of a perceived deficiency primarily physiological or social in nature. For example, the office manager whose work routine is disorderly and chaotic feels the need for a predictable sequence of work tasks. The perceived deficiency is one of structure, order, and organization. As soon as the office manager gets the safety and security of a structured and ordered work environment the need will disappear.

Unlike needs, values do not arise from perceived deficiency and do not disappear once satisfied. Values are learned and chosen from one's life experiences. For example, children whose strong interest in reading is supported and whose curiosity about natural phenomena is encouraged by understanding parents and teachers will most probably value education. As adults they may later seek out both formal and informal continuing education and encourage their children to do the same.

Both needs and values change over time although values change to a far lesser extent than needs. Needs change as they are temporarily satisfied, while values change due to life adjustments and/or personal growth resulting from changing circumstances. As crises occur and circumstances change over time, needs emerge and re-emerge up and down the hierarchy. If what seems to be a need remains consistently strong after being satisfied, it has become a value.

Needs are the key motivators for current behavior, while values serve as guides to current and future choices of action. Your immediate behavior is strongly influenced by potent, unmet needs. Clear, consciously held values aid you in making consistent decisions about appropriate courses of action.

The interplay of needs and values can be illustrated by the following example: Your neighborhood suddenly experiences a sudden increase in theft, harassment on the streets, and other similar occurrences. The sense of safety and security in your community is threatened. You and your neighbors are motivated to take specific action to return the area to its former state. The neighborhood improvement association calls a meeting of interested parties, and suggestions are elicited from the group.

Proposed actions include initiating a Neighborhood Watch Program, increasing illumination in the neighborhood after dark, maintaining a lookout and reporting system for unfamiliar people and vehicles in the neighborhood, investing in a security system, and purchasing handguns. While you may agree and actively support most of the suggestions, the purchase of handguns you deem unacceptable. Here your values regarding the sanctity of human life guide your decision not to purchase a handgun and to dissuade your neighbors from such a purchase.

The need to restore your community to its previous safe and secure condition motivates several types of behavior. But your clear, strongly held values determine the types of actions you would support and those you would oppose. Your needs motivate the necessity of taking immediate action, but your values guide the choice of actions that you would take or support.

The Importance of Values in Going for What You Want

There used to be a popular television beverage commercial that implored us to "Go for it with all the gusto you've got." "After all," it continued, "you only go around once in life." For those involved in career decision making, this is excellent advice, but going for what you want in life is not an easy task. In fact, few people really know what they want in life because they have never really taken the time and effort to determine what matters in their lives. To determine what you want, you must first know what is important in your life—the values that give your life meaning and relevance.

Values are not lofty ideals dreamed up by experts in ivory towers and held up as examples by which you ought to live. Instead, people choose, formulate, and reformulate their values as they direct their lives. Values can be seen most clearly in your everyday actions as you make decisions. You are not always consciously aware of your values, however, unless you dig deeply and search widely through your life experiences.

You will discover that values are the principles or standards upon which you make all decisions that shape the course of your life. Life in our culture is enormously complex, and each day we are bombarded by a wide array of lifestyle choices. Some are simple. For example, when you shop for groceries, do you choose nutritious foods such as grains, fresh fruits and vegetables, and low-fat dairy products? Or do you choose prepared foods that save you time? Do you look for money-saving bargains? Or do you prefer to pay more for brand-name items? Even these simple choices reflect your values.

More complex choices in your life require considerable and often difficult deliberation. Young people, for instance, face decisions such as whether to live at home where their basic needs are met or to risk moving out and fending for themselves. Young couples are often faced with the dilemma of how to balance the demands of family and career. Men and women of all ages ponder whether to terminate relationships that are not working. Men and women at midlife contemplate significant career and lifestyle changes. Older people often face the difficult choice of living alone in familiar surroundings or moving into living complexes with other senior citizens. People can best make these and other important decisions on the basis of clear, consciously held values.

Defining and Clarifying Values

Directing your life in a world full of confusion and conflict is like charting a course through unknown and often dangerous waters. Values clarification provides a means of charting a course through the unknown waters of your life. Through values clarification, you can carefully examine your own experiences to discover the content and strength of your own values system. This self-assessment method will help you discover what values you actually live by or act upon rather than what you think your values should be. Values clarification is a positive, forward-looking process that focuses on both your current values and your evolving values.

Before you can clarify your values, however, you must first be clear on what constitutes a value. According to values researchers, for something to be considered a value, it must conform to seven criteria. These criteria can be summarized best by the words *prizing, choosing,* and *acting. Prizing* emphasizes the emotions or feelings, *choosing* relies on thinking and reasoning, and *acting* implies behavior. Therefore, our values are formed by a combination of our feelings, thoughts, and behavior. The seven values criteria include the following:

Prizing

1. *Prized and Cherished.* To prize and cherish something is to have an emotional attachment to it. This attachment may be to an intangible concept or to a tangible object. For example, political activists who have been imprisoned in their own countries for opposing dictatorial regimes experience strong emotional ties to free political expression. To them the concept of freedom is prized and cherished. Other people may cherish a family ring or family heirloom not for the object itself but for what it represents: a deceased parent, a loving family, a proud cultural heritage.

2. *Publicly Affirmed.* Public affirmation is simply acknowledging a belief, feeling, or attitude to others. For example, local activists who make their views known to their neighbors through a community newsletter represent one method of public affirmation. Wearing a uniform (scout, military, religious order) is another more subtle way of publicly affirming certain values.

Choosing

3. *Chosen Freely.* Freely chosen values are those you have ultimately chosen yourself rather than follow the subtle or overt influence of others. For example, choosing a religious or political affiliation of your own volition (or choosing not to affiliate) rather than merely following what your parents or family believed illustrates the idea of free choice.

4. *Chosen from Alternatives.* Without two or more alternatives, there is no choice and no true value. A true choice involves awareness of the widest variety of possible options or alternatives. For example, young people graduating from high school have a bewildering array of educational, career, and lifestyle choices available to them. Milestones such as high school graduation are critical in the lives of young people, and they are well advised to seek help from parents, friends, teachers, and counselors both in identifying and exploring their alternatives.

5. *Chosen after Consideration of Consequences.* Making the choice that is right for you first requires a careful examination of the probable consequences of each of your identified alternatives. For example, when deliberating upon a career change, factors such as job security, salary and benefits, seniority, degree of dissatisfaction, the possibility of lateral movement, etc., should all be weighed and considered carefully before reaching a decision.

Acting

6. *Acted Upon.* You affirm your values by acting upon them. Unless you act upon something, it is not a value but a good idea or belief. For example, if you valued your role as citizen, then you would demonstrate it by voting, supporting candidates, lobbying, publicizing officials' actions, etc. Failure to act can prevent an idea or belief from becoming a value.

7. *Acted Upon Repeatedly and Consistently to Form a Definite Pattern.* A single act alone does not constitute a value. Examining your life for patterns of repeated and consistent action will help you identify your values. For example, if you consistently arrange regular physical and dental checkups, exercise three times per week, plan and eat nutritious meals, and sleep 6–8 hours per night, then you undoubtedly value healthful living. Your repeated pattern of consistent actions promotes health as one of your values.[6]

Directions

1. Place an X on the line next to each of the values that are truly important in your life right now. For a value to be truly important in your life it must be reflected in your behavior on a regular basis. For instance if variety is one of your current values then you may behave in ways that result in frequent changes in various aspects of your life, such as your job, location, friends, physical appearance, recreation, etc.

2. Circle the ten values that are currently most important in your life.

_____ Achievement (accomplishing something important)

_____ Adventure (seeking challenging new experiences)

_____ Aesthetics (appreciating beauty in all its forms)

_____ Affection (giving and receiving love)

_____ Authenticity (genuinely being yourself)

_____ Creativity (freedom to express new ideas/develop new things)

_____ Cultural Heritage (appreciating your ethnic background)

_____ Economic Reward (earning a high rate of compensation)

_____ Emotional Strength (managing your feelings in positive ways)

_____ Ethical Living (living morally and justly)

_____ Expertise (being good at something worthwhile)

_____ Family (having a strong bond through shared heredity and/or experience)

_____ Friendship (affiliating with others)

_____ Future Orientation (seeking to learn what the future holds)

_____ Health/Fitness (actively maintaining vitality)

_____ Inner Serenity (seeking peace within)

_____ Integrity (maintaining congruence of your words with deeds)

_____ Intellect (having a keen and lively mind)

_____ Leadership (having influence over others)

_____ Orderliness (living an organized life)

_____ Personal Development (continuing self-exploration and growth)

_____ Personal Freedom (making choices independently)

_____ Personal Safety (being safe from bodily harm)

_____ Pleasure (enjoying fun activities)

_____ Recognition (being known by others)

_____ Risk-taking (seeking excitement via living on the edge)

_____ Satisfying Career (having meaningful and challenging work)

_____ Security (having a stable future)

_____ Self-Confidence (feeling positive about oneself)

_____ Service (contributing to the welfare of others)

_____ Spirituality (seeking the ultimate meaning in life)

_____ Variety (seeking change in activities and surroundings)

_____ Wisdom (seeking mature understanding)

3. List the ten you have selected in the space below.

Acquiring and Changing Your Values

The predominant view about how values are acquired has been that they are transmitted from adults to children. Parents or parent substitutes articulate and model the values that they desire their children to acquire. According to this traditional view, children take the values they have been taught and make them their own.

Proponents of values clarification reject the traditional idea that values can be taught or transmitted.[8] Instead, they believe that values are learned directly from an individual's life experiences involving various influences.

As you grow and develop, you change, and so do your values. What is a value to you now may diminish in importance as you gain new information and acquire additional skills, or as your life circumstances change in significant ways. For example, in first grade, children often value their relationship with the teacher above all else, but in the upper elementary grades, children place a higher value on their relationships with peers. In adolescence, relationships with the opposite sex are usually most highly valued. Later, young adults often find that family and career values take precedence. On the other hand, some values remain relatively stable throughout your life.

Discovering Your Hidden Values

Often you are not consciously aware of your values. Being asked to express your values directly is like asking you to count all the muscles in your body. Some are obvious and visible to you, but most are hidden from your view.

The way you choose to live your life provides clues to these hidden values. For instance, when you have free time, what do you choose to do with it? Do you read, jog, play the piano, or call a friend long distance? Other than obtaining the necessities of life, how do you choose to spend your money? What kinds of things get you riled up enough to take a stand or to take action? What do you fantasize or daydream about? When do you feel most alive and vibrant in your life? In answering these and other similar questions, you are focusing on your true values.

Clues to the discovery of your values constantly surround you. Everything you do or say tells something about what you value. If you find yourself living for those quiet, reflective moments when you can be alone, then you probably value time for quiet contemplation. If, on the other hand, you live for the moments of raucous, roughhouse play with your children or your friends, then you probably value noisy, physical activities with others.

Two good ways of discovering your hidden values are through examining past events or accomplishments in your life and by looking at your future objectives. The events or accomplishments represent choices you have made in the past and reflect what motivated you at that particular time. They tell you much about what you may still consider important in your life. Your future objectives come from the dreams and fantasies you have about the future. They, too, tell you what is important in your life right now.

Exercise 6-D. UNCOVERING YOUR HIDDEN VALUES[9]

I. This exercise requires you to imagine that you have just been given a gift of one million dollars with only one stipulation. That stipulation is that you must use the million only on yourself.

A. List below under Column A some of the possible ways you would like to use your gift. What would you want to do, have, or see? Some examples are provided to help start you thinking about this exercise.

Column A	Column B
Uses	Possible Values
Examples:	
1. Invest in stocks and bonds	1. Financial Security, Challenge/Risk-taking
2. Reserve season's tickets to symphony, theater, and dance performances	2. Aesthetics, Pleasure
3. Set aside funds for my continuing education	3. Intellect, Personal Development, Job Security
4. Start my own small business	4. Independence, Risk-taking Achievement

Uses	Possible Values

Your Selections:

B. Now that you have determined how you would use your million dollars, analyze each use for values content. In our first example for instance, investing in stocks and bonds represents the value of financial security to those who invest in safe, low yield securities. But to those who prefer more chancy, high return investments, it represents the value of risk-taking. The same use can represent different values to different people. Analyze each of your million dollar uses for the value(s) they represent to you and list those values in Column B. Refer to the list of Life Values from Exercise 6-C for possible values words.

II. You are the recipient of yet another million dollar gift, this time with a different stipulation. This gift is to be used only for the good of others.

A. Ask yourself what needs doing in your family, neighborhood, country, and the world. How could you best contribute? List the ways you would make a contribution under Column A. Refer to the examples below in Column A to stimulate your thinking.

Column A	Column B
Uses	*Possible Values*
Examples:	
1. Establish an institute for peace studies	1. Ethical Living, Freedom, Spirituality
2. Reform the educational system	2. Intellect, Personal Development, and Freedom
3. Establish parenting classes for young parents	3. Affection, Family, and Emotional Strength
4. Establishing a neighborhood watch in my community	4. Service, Personal Safety

Uses	*Possible Values*

Your Selections:

B. Again analyze your list of uses in Column A for the value(s) that each represents and place them (the values) in Column B.

The Importance of Values in Work

For your work to be satisfying, it must be compatible with your values. For some people, money, power, prestige, and status are what it takes for a job to be rewarding. Others may have these external rewards in their work but still find it unsatisfying. Some people must experience meaning or purpose in the work itself for a job to be satisfying.

Years from now when you reflect on your work life, will it be with a sense of satisfaction or a sense of regret? Satisfaction comes from knowing that what you did with your life was important, that your life's work had some significance and benefit for yourself and perhaps for others.

The following exercise contains a listing of values that can be derived from work. These are arranged in three categories: work conditions, work purposes, and work relationships.

1. Read the definitions of the work values listed in three categories below. Rate each work value according to its degree of importance to you. Use the following scale in assigning your ratings:

1 = unimportant in my choice of career
2 = somewhat important in my choice of career
3 = very important in my choice of career

Place the number corresponding to your rating in the blank to the left of each work value.

A. *Work Conditions.* The conditions of work involve:

_____ *Independence/Autonomy*—doing what you want to do without much direction from others.

_____ *Time Flexibility*—arranging your own hours, working according to your own time schedule.

_____ *Change/Variety*—performing varying tasks in a number of different settings.

_____ *Change/Risk*—performing new tasks or leading new programs that challenge the established order and may be initially resisted.

_____ *Stability/Security*—performing regular, predictable tasks in a job you are assured of that pays you reasonably well.

_____ *Physical Challenge*—performing dangerous tasks that challenge your physical capabilities and involve risk.

_____ *Physical Demands*—performing physically strenuous, but relatively safe activities.

_____ *Mental Challenge*—performing demanding tasks that challenge your intelligence and creativity.

_____ *Pressure/Time Deadlines*—performing in a highly critical environment with constant time deadlines.

_____ *Precise Work*—performing prescribed tasks that leave little room for error.

_____ *Decision Making*—making choices about what to do and how to do it.

B. *Work Purposes.* The purpose of work is to:

_____ *Truth/Knowledge*—pursue knowledge and understanding.

_____ *Expertise/Authority*—seek recognition as an acknowledged expert or leader in a particular area.

_____ *Creativity/Innovativeness*—develop new and different ideas, programs, and/or structures.

_____ *Aesthetic Appreciation*—seek out the appreciation of beauty in all of its various forms.

_____ *Social Contributions*—seek to improve the human condition.

_____ *Material Gain*—acquire and accumulate money or other material objects.

_____ *Achievement/Recognition*—seek public recognition for your work contributions.

_____ *Ethical/Moral*—act in accordance with a set of moral and ethical standards.

_____ *Spiritual/Transpersonal*—seek beyond ordinary consciousness to a more spiritual plane.

C. *Work Relationships.* The relationships at work entail:

_____ *Work Alone*—doing assignments by yourself with minimal contact with other people.

_____ *Public Contact*—interacting in predictable ways with a continuous flow of people.

_____ *Close Friendships*—developing strong interpersonal relationships with the people at work.

_____ *Group Membership*—belonging to a group with a common purpose and/or interest.

_____ *Helping Others*—assisting other people directly to obtain information and/or resolve problems.

_____ *Influencing Others*—affecting others in ways designed to change attitudes or opinions.

_____ *Supervising Others*—being in a position to oversee the work of other employees.

_____ *Controlling Others*—maintaining some control or power over the destinies of other people.

2. List below your top 3 or 4 most important work values in each of the three categories. Add any others that are important but which were not covered above.

Work Conditions	Work Purposes	Work Relationships
_____	_____	_____
_____	_____	_____
_____	_____	_____
_____	_____	_____
_____	_____	_____

1. List below your top 5 to 10 values from each of the values exercises 6-C, 6-D, and 6-E.

6-C	6-D	6-E
Life Values Assessment	*Uncovering Your Hidden Values* *Million/Self* *Million/Others*	*Work Values*

2. Combine the values in the four columns above in order to come up with your top 5 values. Pay particular attention to those values that appear in more than one column.

3. Place your top 5 values in the box below.

My Top Five Prioritized Values

1.

2.

3.

4.

5.

Summary

Your needs are experienced as an inner feeling that something essential for you is missing. This awareness produces a sense of acute personal discomfort or inner tension which motivates you to satisfy this need. Abraham Maslow has identified a basic needs structure comprised of five separate levels of needs—physiological, safety, belongingness and love, esteem, and self-actualization. These needs are arranged in a hierarchy, proceeding in steps from the lower level needs, which are physical, to higher level needs, which are social and spiritual. A person is motivated to progress through these needs one at a time, from the lower order to the higher order. The satisfaction of a lower level need allows a higher level need to emerge as primary motivator. This progression represents a satisfying growth process in life. For career planning, consider your needs seriously, but do not let them overshadow the importance of other personal attributes and preferences. Choose a career that will meet your currently dominating need and provide upward progression through the other needs. It is important to understand not only your current needs, but also the ways these needs are likely to change in the future.

The process of values clarification is also crucial to career/life decision making. Career choices must be based on some assessment of what is important in your life. Values clarification strategies enable you to clear up much of the confusion and conflict in your life in order to determine what gives your life meaning and purpose.

Values are not always conscious, being frequently hidden from consciousness and appearing only through the use of indirect values clarification methods. Using a variety of values clarification methods and then synthesizing the results is an effective way to derive a comprehensive listing of your top values.

People derive certain values from their jobs and careers. For some, work provides external values, such as money or material success. Others require the fulfillment of more internal values, such as helping others or seeking knowledge. You need to identify the important values you derive from voluntary or paid work before deciding on a career.

While closely related, values and needs differ in significant ways. These differences can be demonstrated best by examining how each is acquired and changed and influences current and future behavior. Unmet needs strongly influence your immediate behavior. Values determine the choices of action that you deem acceptable to satisfy your unmet needs.

Assignments

1. Reflect on what you choose to do when you have free time. Think of the free time you had last week. What did you choose to do with it? What, if anything, does this tell you about your values?

2. By answering the following questions, what values do you discover?

    a. Other than purchasing necessities, how do you choose to spend your money?

    b. What kinds of things get you riled up enough to take a stand?

    c. What do you daydream about?

    d. What do you find yourself doing when you feel most alive and vibrant in your life?

3. See Appendix E for further resources to clarify your values.

Notes

1. Abraham Maslow, *Motivation and Personality,* 2nd. ed. (New York: Harper & Row, 1970).
2. Adapted from Jay Hall and Martha Williams, *Work Motivation Inventory* (Conroe, Texas: Teleometrics International, n.d.). For further information, write to Teleometrics International, P.O. Drawer 1850, Conroe, Texas 77301.
3. Maslow, p.44.
4. Maslow, p.45.
5. Hall and Williams, *Work Motivation Inventory.*
6. Louis E. Raths, Merrill Harmin, and Sidney F. Simon, *Values and Teaching* (Columbus, Ohio: Charles E. Merrill, 1966), pp. 28–30.
7. Sidney Simon, *Meeting Yourself Halfway* (Niles, Illinois: Argus Communications, 1974), p. xi.
8. Adapted from the Intensive Course in the Crystal Life/Work Planning Process, John C. Crystal Center, Inc., 894 Plandome Rd., Manhasset, N.Y. 11030.
9. Same as #8.
10. Howard E. Figler, *PATH: A Career Workbook for Liberal Arts Students* (Cranston, Rhode Island: Carroll Press, 1975), pp. 77–79.

Making the Right Choice

Far too often, people tend to lay out alternatives for you. As a result, you may focus on only those alternatives. But you should always keep in mind that there may be other alternatives that haven't been mentioned by anyone. Also, you are bringing what is uniquely you to the situation, so that an alternative that may be best for most people may not be best for you.

GORDON PORTER MILLER
Life Choices

DO YOU KNOW PEOPLE WHO:

➡ Make decisions without knowing what their alternatives are?

➡ Have no idea how to find information about occupational alternatives?

➡ Can only seem to identify unsatisfactory choices?

➡ Seem to ponder their alternatives endlessly without ever deciding?

➡ Do you know people who just let others tell them what to do?

If so, you know people who lack the skills required to assess their available alternatives and make the best career/life decisions.

Alternatives and Decision Making

The world of work is a huge universe consisting of thousands of occupations. Statistically, picking a suitable occupation by chance or luck is inconceivable. You will need effective decision making skills.

What is your current approach to decision making? Do you immediately want to know the "right answer"? Most people do. Good chess players, however, realize that there is seldom a single best course of action. Instead, they contemplate their full range of options, each leading to different consequences. They are likely to be asking, "What strategy do I choose to pursue? What are my alternatives right now, and how might they change depending upon the next move?" Only after surveying the whole range of alternatives and their consequences, do successful chess players decide what move to make.

Successful chess playing is similar to effective career decision making. Chess players who cannot see the full range of alternatives available to them are unlikely to be consistent winners. People faced with career/life decisions are also unlikely to make winning decisions unless they too can see their full range of alternatives and evaluate their consequences.

At this phase of your decision-making process, try to be thorough, patient, and alert to all of your best possibilities. We have seen many people in the Career Planning Center who, after assessing their talents and goals, became impatient with the task of identifying alternatives. They wanted to pick the first seemingly good choice they found. Some people are afraid that too many choices will just confuse them. It is true that having a lot of possibilities makes choosing more complicated. But why miss your best available option because of impatience? We urge you to take your time with this chapter's exercises as an investment in your future.

Envisioning the Task

To help understand career decision making, consider the following example. Janet, Roy, Shirley, and Phil all have a "CIR" Holland personality code. At this point in their career planning, each has identified the following career alternatives of interest to them:

Janet	Roy	Phil	Shirley
Accountant	Electronic Technician	Computer Systems Analyst	Computer Programmer
Data Entry Clerk	Word processor	Radiologic Technician	Computer Systems Analyst
	Nurse	Social Science Teacher	Electronic Technician
		High School Athletic Coach	Radiologic Technician
			Accountant

Which person do you think has identified the best alternatives for a "CIR" personality style? Why?

All together, these four people have identified a total of ten alternatives. These alternatives vary in suitability for a "CIR" personality style. Below, these alternatives have been separated into categories labeled "good" and "poor." These alternatives are ranked on both suitability to the "CIR" personality style and on the job-market outlook.

The Five Best Alternatives

B_1 Computer Programmer
B_2 Computer Systems Analyst
B_3 Electronic Technician
B_4 Radiologic Technician
B_5 Accountant

Note:
B_1 = The best alternative
B_2 = The second best, etc.

The Five Poorest Alternatives

P_1 Social Science Teacher
P_2 High School Athletic Coach
P_3 Nurse
P_4 Word Processor
P_5 Data Entry Clerk

P_1 = The poorest alternative
P_2 = The second poorest, etc.

TABLE 7.1 Sample Occupations for the "CIR" Personality Style

Rating	Occupation	Holland Code	Comments
B_1	Computer Programmer	CIR	This is the best alternative. It represents the best Holland code match, and the job-market demand for computer programmers is excellent.
B_2	Computer Systems Analyst	ICR	This is the second best Holland code match, and, again, job-market demand is excellent.
B_3	Electronics Technician	RIC	This is the third best Holland code match of the alternatives identified with an excellent employment outlook.
B_4	Radiologic Technician	IRC	This is a good Holland code match with a fair job-market prospect.
B_5	Accountant	CEI	While the Holland code does not exactly match the example, with two out of the three letters the same, this would be a fairly good match. The employment outlook for accountants is excellent.
P_5	Data Entry Clerk	CRI	While the Holland code of this alternative matches fairly well, the employment outlook for this obsolete occupation is extremely poor, and not many skills are transferable.
P_4	Word Processor	CRS	The Holland code here matches fairly well. This occupation is fast becoming obsolete, although some of the skills could be transferred.
P_3	Nurse	SEC	While the job market for nurses is excellent, this Holland code is significantly different from the example.
P_2	High School Athletic Coach	SER	While this Holland code does share one letter with the example, it is a significantly different code. The employment outlook for coaches is fair.
P_1	Social Science Teacher	SEA	This is rated as the poorest alternative because of the disparity in Holland codes and because of the limited employment outlook for social science teachers at this time.

Assessing the Sample Options

Janet has identified only two alternatives, one in the "good" column ("B_5—Accounting") and the other "poor" ("P_5—Data Entry Clerk"). As a consequence, Janet's "best" choice is only a moderately good ("B_5") alternative. Her list does not give her much to choose from.

Roy's three alternatives can be ranked as follows:

B_3 for Electronics Technician
P_3 for Nurse
P_4 for Stenographer

As a consequence of his alternative selection, the best pick that Roy could make would be only slightly better than Janet's choice.

Phil has selected alternatives which can be ranked this way:

B_2 for Computer Systems Analyst
B_4 for Radiologic Technician
P_1 for Social Science Teacher
P_2 for High School Athletic Coach

Phil has more and better options than either Janet or Roy. On the other hand, his list also contains the two poorest options identified on the overall list. If Phil makes a poor decision, he could end up more dissatisfied than either Janet or Roy.

Shirley, through careful alternative assessment, has identified the five best alternatives on the total list. Accordingly, with a good pick, she could choose the one alternative capable of producing the greatest amount of eventual career satisfaction. Even with a poor selection, she would still be choosing from the "good" list.

Becoming Aware of Your Alternatives

In real life, it is difficult or even impossible, to identify all of the best career alternatives for yourself. However, you will be able to find many alternatives leading to considerable career/life satisfaction by completing the following exercises. They are designed to use both your creative and logical abilities to find a large number of alternatives. The time for narrowing down your options will come later. For now, concentrate on finding your full range of winning career alternatives.

Seeking Career Alternatives from Functional Skills

In Chapter 2, you listed your specific functional skills and figured out your top five preferred skills groups based on personal preference and feedback from others. A good way to begin developing your career alternatives is to review your favorite functional skills, brainstorming with others to discover what kinds of careers would welcome these capabilities. Brad, our case study from Chapter 6, used this process to begin developing his list of occupational alternatives.

Brad's Top Five Skill Groups were identified as follows:

1. Inventing/Developing New Ideas
2. Communicating/Teaching
3. Planning/Organizing Data
4. Analyzing/Evaluating/Researching
5. Investigating/Observing/Experimenting

Brad gave this list of preferred skill families, along with a copy of his specific skills list, to a small group of people. He asked them to come up with a list of possible occupations where these skills would be used extensively. In just six minutes of brainstorming, the group came up with the following list of occupations:

scientist
lecturer
developer of training aids
learning lab director
investigative reporter
teacher
researcher

developer of textbooks,
    educational materials,
    and programs patent
    investigator
inventor
trainer

technical writer
campaign manager
pollster
editor
speech writer
lobbyist

Brad was interested in most of these career ideas. Imagine the list this group might have completed if they had spent thirty minutes or more on the task instead of just six.

Exercise 7-A. ENVISIONING PROCESS

1. Review your specific skills from Table 2.1 on page 20 in Chapter 2. Rank the top five of these skills, based on the skills you enjoy using the most. Do not list any functional skills that you lack, but would like to possess. List the top five below:

   Note: *Be sure to prioritize your list on the basis of those functional skills you now possess and prefer using. Do not list functional skills you lack but would like to possess.*

   My Top Five Individual Functional Skills

   1.

   2.

   3.

   4.

   5.

2. Use the envisioning process described in Appendix D to begin developing your list of career alternatives. To do this, set aside about one hour of time in which you will be alone and undisturbed. Then do the following:

   a. Review the envisioning process described in Appendix D.

   b. Review your top five skills (Chapter 2), your thinking style profile (Chapter 3), your personality style profile (Chapter 4), and your needs and values (Chapter 6).

   c. With these skills, needs, and preferences fresh in your mind, prepare to do the envisioning process by asking yourself: "What kinds of careers might enable me to use my preferred skills and have the kind of life I want?"

d. Ask yourself this question several times. Can you picture yourself in the career(s) you are thinking about? Don't worry about whether you come up with anything or not. If the process doesn't work for you, go on to the other exercises.

e. After you complete the envisioning process, immediately list below any thoughts or images that you had and record any occupations you come up with in Appendix A.

NOTES ON THE ENVISIONING PROCESS

Exercise 7-B. BRAINSTORMING WITH INDIVIDUALS

Getting input from other people is helpful for developing your career alternatives. A good technique is to record your ranked individual skills on a piece of paper. Then give your list to someone like a career counselor, a personnel officer, a job-placement specialist, employers of people in several different occupations, etc. Ask them to look these skills over at their convenience and to advise you of any occupations requiring these particular skills. It is not usually a good idea to use close family or friends in this process, since they often have preconceived ideas about what is best for you. If you do use family or friends, give them your list anonymously, at least until they have provided some ideas. Record other people's career suggestions in Appendix A.

Brainstorming in a group is also a very good way to generate a list of career alternatives. Your best bet here is to get a group of four to eight people together, preferably people familiar with occupations and transferable skills. Then display your top five specific skills and top five skills groups on a large piece of paper or on a chalkboard. Next, have the group brainstorm ideas and record their suggestions on a separate piece of paper. This process will work best if you are not present in the group at the time they are brainstorming with your list. In fact, this exercise works best if the group is unaware of whose skills they are working with. Record the group's suggestions below. Then select those that interest you, and list them in Appendix A[2].

This exercise calls for using a Department of Labor publication called *The Guide for Occupational Exploration* (GOE) to identify occupational alternatives. The GOE can be found in most college career centers and in most public libraries. The GOE can also be purchased from the Department of Labor.

To complete this exercise, first read the directions in the beginning of the GOE on how to use it, and then follow these steps:

1. Identify interest areas to explore by reading the descriptions for all twelve interest areas at the beginning of the GOE. Record the name and number of each interest area that appeals to you.

	Interest Areas That Appeal to Me	Interest Area Number
Example:	Artistic	1

2. Explore the work groups within each interest area that appeal to you by completing the following steps:

   a. Open the GOE to the interest areas you have identified in #1 above, and read the general statement relating to that area.

   b. After reading that statement, if you are still interested, decide which of the work groups you want to explore. Record on the following page the work group and names you find interesting.

   c. Read each of the descriptions in the GOE for the work groups you have identified above. As you read the descriptions, answer the following questions:

   - Does this appear to be the type of work I would be interested in doing?
   - Is this kind of work compatible with my most preferred families of functional skills?
   - Do the activities I have done and enjoyed in the past suggest that I would enjoy or could do this type of work?
   - Does the preparation required for doing this kind of work appear to be something I am willing to do? For example, if it requires four years of education, am I now willing to go to college for that long?

Interest Area	The Work Groups and Work Group Numbers I Wish to Explore within this Interest Area
Example: Artistic 01	Literary Arts 01.01 Visual Arts 01.02

d. After answering the questions above, if that work group remains interesting to you, explore the subgroups for that work group:

- Record occupations of interest to you, along with the corresponding nine-digit DOT number in the space provided below.
- List all occupations that you think you would be interested in or are unfamiliar with.
- Omit only those familiar occupations that do not interest you.

Example: $\dfrac{\text{GOE Occupations of Interest}}{\text{Industrial Designers}}$ $\dfrac{\text{DOT\#}}{142.061.026}$

3. Select ten occupations of most interest to you from your GOE list and record these in Appendix A^2.

Exercise 7-E. COMPUTERIZED ASSISTANCE

A number of excellent computerized programs are available today to identify career possibilities. Computerized systems like DISCOVER, SIGI PLUS, CHOICES, CIS, etc., are available in most college career planning centers. If you have access to a computerized system, use it to identify additional career possibilities. Add these choices to your list on Appendix A^2.

Decision Making Time

Now that you have identified at least 30 to 40 alternatives, it's time to begin narrowing down the list to select your best choice. Your first step is to eliminate all but the best ten from your list. Then you will research your "top ten" to learn more about these fields to decide which one is your very best choice.

Figure 7.1 illustrates the steps in this process. Notice that the process shown here leads either to a tentative or a definite choice. Sometimes it is appropriate to make tentative choices when you have narrowed your list down to two or three choices but need more time to further explore these choices before making a final commitment.

A tentative choice, as we use it here, is different from the avoidance behavior of not deciding. A tentative choice involves allotting yourself time to explore specific options that you have identified. A tentative choice is particularly appropriate for a beginning college student who has the luxury of time to explore before needing to make a final choice.

Career changers rarely have that luxury, however, and will need to use this process to make a definite decision. The good news is that career changers usually have more experience and self knowledge to draw upon for a definite choice.

Following are two case studies to illustrate definite versus tentative decision making. The first example is that of Brad, a career changer described in Chapter 6. The second is Julie, a younger college student.

FIGURE 7.1 Making a Career Decision

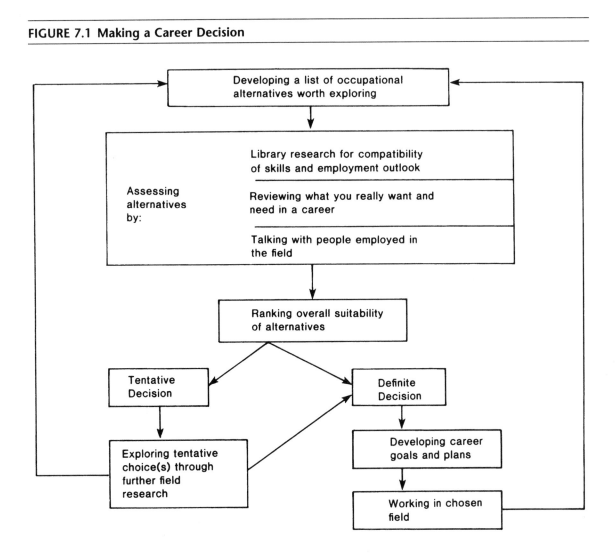

Brad and Definite Decision Making

Brad was confronted with a major crisis when he lost the job he had held for over ten years. With career-counseling assistance, Brad discovered that his personality style was incompatible with his previous job and career. He learned that his preferred families of skills were in the innovating, creative planning, writing, and teaching areas. Based on self-assessment, Brad developed a lengthy list of suitable alternatives and then narrowed the list down to the following:

Psychology
Counseling
Public relations/advertising
Cartooning
Journalism
College teaching

These were so appealing that Brad couldn't make any further instinctive decisions. He was advised to learn all he could about these occupations. Primarily, Brad accomplished this task through study of occupational literature and by identifying and talking with people working in fields he found interesting. He got their names from various directories and from friends and acquaintances. Initially, conducting these interviews was hard for Brad. He vividly recalls his tension and sweaty palms as he prepared to go talk with people.

Brad soon found, however, that if he called in advance, was considerate about people's time, and was straightforward about his purpose, most people really enjoyed talking with him about their work. Eventually, Brad started enjoying these information interviews. Best of all, he began learning what it would really be like to pursue a career in these kinds of occupations. At his counselor's suggestion, Brad carefully wrote down his observations and reactions from each of these information interviews immediately after conducting them. These notes were far more valuable than vague memories when he prepared to make his decision.

In conducting these interviews, Brad found that different people in the same occupation had completely different ideas and perspectives about the field. He realized how important it was to discuss the same occupation with several people. He learned, too, that there are wide ranges of differences within an occupation depending on the work setting. He also acquired a much better appreciation of what work settings were most likely to be hiring in the future, what settings offered the best advancement opportunities, what settings had the best salaries and benefits programs, etc.

After completing these interviews, Brad reviewed what he had learned from his field research about outcomes he could expect if he pursued various careers. He also reaffirmed that what he wanted most in a career was to be associated with people he liked, to continue learning and using his knowledge, and to develop creative methods for helping adults live more satisfying lives. Based on what he had learned, Brad chose counseling in a community college as his best career alternative.

Brad recalls both the relief and exhilaration that accompanied this selection. He knew that he still had to establish his specific career goals and develop his implementation plans, but he also realized what a giant step he had taken towards creating a new and satisfying career. Later, when Brad's needs changed again, be became aware of new suitable career alternatives available to him. This placed him in a new decision situation.

His experience in the decision-making process benefited Brad in many ways. First, he learned how to make career-choice decisions more effectively and easily than ever before. Secondly, he learned to view his career as a life-long process. As a result, he could recognize new alternatives and opportunities when they arose. He was also far more inclined to act on these opportunities.

Julie and Tentative Decisions

Julie, a gregarious young woman, graduated from high school with absolutely no idea of what she wanted to do, other than to go on to college. In high school she had acquired a large group of friends and concentrated on having fun. Julie was intelligent, attractive, and sociable but just had never discovered anything in school that really engaged her serious interests.

After graduating from high school, Julie decided to pursue a general studies curriculum at the local community college until she discovered a compelling career interest. After taking general elective requirements during her freshman year, she enrolled in a career planning course. In that course she discovered that she had skills, interests, and values that she had never really thought about before. She realized for instance that she had excellent communication skills which enabled her to establish rapport, make excellent presentations, sell her ideas, and entertain others. She was also an excellent organizer and planner when it involved some activity that really interested her. She realized that she enjoyed helping others and that she wanted to have a balance between family and career. A job that involved performing a useful service to others, perhaps to children, was appealing.

In the course, she identified about forty career possibilities, including many she had never considered or heard of before. Eventually she narrowed this list down to three: teaching, psychology, and communications. She felt unwilling to commit to any one of these at that time. She needed more information and some related experience to eliminate alternatives from this list she felt enthusiastic about. She found out that each of these choices was a broad field in itself. What age groups did she want to work with? What types of organizations were appealing? What particular work settings did she want? If she decided on teaching, for example, what age group did she want to work with? Did she want to go into special education, elementary education, or learn a specific subject matter to teach in high school, college, or business setting?

With the help of a career counselor, Julie worked out a plan of action that would enable her to explore all three areas and cover her bases until she was ready for a definite career commitment. She selected an arts and science major that enabled her to meet the general education requirements for each of the three fields. She also selected introductory courses in psychology, education, and communications to sample these subject areas and get a clearer idea of how her skills, interests, and energies would be useful.

In addition, Julie decided to participate in extracurricular activities that allowed her to express her interests and develop the skills she now knew she wanted to use in her career. These activities included being in a college play, working as a technical assistant in the college media department, participating in the readers theater, taking voice lessons, and trying out for and making the college forensics team. As a team member she won numerous awards and traveled across the country.

Upon obtaining her associate-in-arts degree from the community college, Julie decided to transfer to the University of Iowa. Based on her previous activities and course work, Julie decided to major in communications. At Iowa, Julie took advantage of work/learning experiences that included working with a local radio station, where she learned marketing activities and even got to develop and record a short advertisement. During the summer, she obtained an internship with PBS, where she became familiar with the research, marketing, and management areas of a large T.V. and radio operation. In her senior year in college, Julie is continuing to broaden her experience by working as a production assistant with the college cable T.V. station. She is also refining her resume and setting up job interviews through the college career planning and placement office.

Julie still wonders sometimes whether she has made the right choice. She occasionally catches herself thinking, "Maybe I should become a child psychologist or a speech teacher." She is now content to try out her career choice in communications and to gain some experience and wisdom in the "real world." She realizes also that she is young and that she can make a career change in the future. She is not afraid of that prospect because she now knows a useful decision making process and intends to use this process continually throughout her life. She knows that at some point in the future she will want to go on for a masters degree. For now, she wants to become financially independent and learn about about herself and her possibilities on the job.

Narrowing Down

Throughout the course of this book you have identified a number of occupations from the various exercises and recorded these in Appendix A². Now it is time to narrow that list down to the best ones for you. The goal is to select from this list the ten best choices for you and your unique interests, skills, and values.

Begin by crossing out those that are not particularly interesting or not practical for your situation. For example, you might aspire to be a jockey but are 6'2" and weigh 240 pounds. Or perhaps you want to become a psychiatrist but are not up to the ten years of education and training that would entail. Next, eliminate duplicate entries that have been entered with slightly different names.

Once you have cleaned up your list, reduce the number further by assigning Holland codes to the remainder and eliminating any obvious mismatches. This process will enable you to weed out not only the poor choices (the P's) on your list, but also some seemingly appropriate choices that wouldn't work out in the long run.

Holland Coding Your Career Alternatives

From your work in Chapters 4 and 5, you will recall that people have characteristic personality styles and that occupations can also be classified by 3-letter Holland codes. By comparing your own Holland code with the Holland codes of these occupations, you can determine how compatible an occupation is with your particular interests and personality style.

1. Refer now to that portion of Appendix A² entitled Career Possibilities. Under the column heading "Occupations of Interest" you have listed career alternatives based on insights obtained from the assessments you completed in Chapters 3, 4, and 5 and exercises included in this chapter. Identify the Holland Code, as best you can, for each of the occupations on your list and place it in the adjacent column under the heading Holland Code. If necessary review the information in Chapter 5 that relates to the Holland coding of occupations. Six examples are provided below to assist you in your identification.

Occupations	*Holland Code*		
Examples:			
Newspaper Reporter	A	E	I
Electronics Technician	R	I	C
X-Ray Technician	I	R	S
Office Manager	E	S	C
Accountant	C	I	S
Teacher (primary or secondary)	S	A	E

In the first example, newspaper reporter, "A" is listed as the primary letter, since a reporter's primary function involves the process of creative writing. The second letter is "E" because a reporter needs to elicit the cooperation of people in order to obtain essential information from them. Thirdly, a reporter needs to be a problem solver of the "I" kind.

Here are three additional sources of help in identifying Holland codes:

- John L. Holland, Table E-2 in *Making Vocational Choices*, 1973 shows how to translate DOT codes into Holland codes.

- *The Occupation Finder*, which comes with the Self Directed Search (SDS). Look for this resource in the career library.

- *Dictionary of Holland Occupational Codes*, Consulting Psychologists Press, Inc., 577 College Avenue, Palo Alto, California 94306.

2. After Holland coding each of your occupations, decide which are compatible with your personality style:

   My Holland code is   _____   _____   _____

3. If an occupation has none of the three letters that are contained in your Holland code, you may wish to delete that alternative from your list. For example, your Holland code is an ASI, and an occupation on your list has a CER code. That occupation is likely to be a very poor match for you.

   - If an occupation has one letter that is the same as a letter in your Holland code, you will need to decide whether to keep that occupation on your list or not. For example, your code is ASI, and an occupation on your list is CSE. If you have no interest in the occupation, you may want to delete it. On the other hand, if you are uncertain about it, retain the alternative for further consideration.

   - Be sure to retain for further exploration any occupations that share two or three letters in common with your Holland code. For example, if your code is an ASI, you would want to retain occupations with codes such as SAI, SIA, IAS, ISA, SEA, ASE, SIR, IAR, etc.

4. After completing your assessment, record the ten best occupational alternatives that are compatible with your Holland code on Table 7.2, pages 151–160 and following, in this chapter. List your alternatives under the column headed "Career Alternative," and leave all of the remaining columns blank for now. You will learn how to fill in that information later.

Exploring Your Top Ten

Now that you have identified your ten best career matches, you will need to apply the information you have already discovered about yourself and to acquire additional information about your ten selections. Table 7.2 has been designed to facilitate this process and contains a numbering system to support your assessments. The following exercises will guide your assessments and information searches to find your best and most compatible alternative. The information search will help you find crucial information about the employment outlooks of your top ten. The process begins with assessing how each of your "top ten" will enable you to use your "most preferred" transferable skills.

Review your transferable skill assessments from Exercise 7-A and from Chapter 2, deciding which skills are essential for you to use in your work. Rank these skills below, starting with the most important.

The Individual Transferable Skills My Work Must Have

My most preferred skill is

1. _____

2. _____

3. _____

4. _____

5. _____

---

1. Study the descriptions in the Dictionary of Occupational Titles (DOT) for each of the alternatives you listed on Table 7.2. Notice that the DOT provides concise descriptions of several thousand occupations. As you read the DOT descriptions pertaining to your alternatives, identify what functional skills are involved in these occupations, and record them in the appropriate subsection under the DOT column of Table 7.2. Also from the DOT, note the Data, People, Things (DPT) orientation of your occupations in the same DOT column.

2. After identifying the skills involved in each of your occupational alternatives, compare these with the skills you identified above as being essential in your work. Using the following scale, rate how well the skills involved in each occupation match your preferred functional skills. In the "Skills Rating" Column A of Table 7.2, list from the scale below the rating that most accurately evaluates the compatibility.

Transferable Skill Evaluation Scale

Rating

5 Would enable me to use all my preferred skills fully.

4 Would enable me to use most of my preferred skills to a considerable degree.

3 Would enable me to use some, but not all, of my preferred skills to some extent.

2 Would not enable me to use my most preferred skills, but would enable me to use my secondary skills to a considerable extent.

1 Would not enable me to use any of my preferred skills to any extent.

? Unsure how well this occupation would enable me to use my preferred skills. I need more information than the DOT provides.

---

3. In the "Comments about Skills Compatibility" column of Table 7.2, record any other information you may wish to remember about these occupations. Record any insights you discover about specific responsibilities and/or duties that are particularly appealing or unappealing to you.

Note: If you cannot locate a particular occupation in the DOT, get assistance from someone familiar with the publication. The occupation is likely to be listed under a different subject heading. If, however, your alternative is not listed in the DOT, you may need to seek other sources of occupational information.

Exercise 7-G. IDENTIFYING YOUR CAREER-RELATED NEEDS, WANTS, AND VALUES

Your next step in narrowing the options is to review what you really need and value in your career and life. Review your "what motivates me exercises" in Chapter 6 to refresh your memory about your primary values. Then consider the following:

1. Do these priorities still seem accurate? If not, what has changed, or what new insights have you acquired?

2. From your review, decide what is the single most important value in your career, and list that below. Then decide what are the second, third, fourth, and fifth important characteristics you value in your career, and list them below as well.

    The most important thing I need, value, or want in my career is

    The second important thing . . .

    The third . . .

    The fourth . . .

    The fifth . . .

After completing your employment outlook research along with your information interviews, you'll be ready to evaluate how well your occupational alternatives will satisfy these values.

Assessing Compatibility and Employment Outlook

In an age of choice, it would certainly be a mistake to select an occupation simply because it offers excellent employment prospects, especially since these can change. It would be equally a mistake, however, to select a suitable occupation without determining whether you have a reasonable chance of finding employment in that field.

To find the employment outlook of any career alternative, you can check occupational literature or obtain first-hand information from people in the field. These methods have some shortcomings, however. The job market changes so rapidly that printed occupational information quickly becomes outdated. People in the field often have more current information, but they may also have a biased view of the employment outlook. For these reasons, we strongly advocate that you use both recent occupational literature and information interviews.

A major printed source of occupational information is the *Occupational Outlook Handbook* (OOH). Be sure to use only the most recent issue of the OOH, which is updated every two years. Then keep its limitations in mind. OOH information is national in scope, so the situation in your local area or the area in which you wish to work may be different. Also, the OOH provides information about expected openings in an occupational field, but it does not tell you how many people may currently be preparing for a career in that field. The OOH, however, does provide an excellent general description of an occupational field and the best national employment-outlook information.

Exercise 7-H. STUDYING OCCUPATIONAL LITERATURE

For this exercise, you will obtain information about employment outlook and your personal/ occupational compatibility for each of your alternatives. The OOH will be your primary source.

1. Study each of the alternatives on your list that you can find in the OOH. You may not always be able to find information about a particular occupation you are exploring in the OOH. In such cases, you may want to go to other sources of occupational information found in most college career centers.

2. Review the "self-insights" you have listed on Appendix A[1]. With this information in mind, read the OOH. Evaluate how well each of the occupational alternatives you are exploring coincides with your own personal attributes. To what extent will each alternative fulfill what you need, want, and value?

3. In the OOH section of Table 7.2, record what you learned about each occupation, along with your impressions of how appropriate you think it would be for you. Again, be sure to make your comments clear and complete enough to refer to later and know what you meant.

4. Note and record in the OOH section of Table 7.2 the OOH employment outlook information for the next five years for each of the occupations you are exploring.

Exercise 7-I. CONDUCTING INFORMATION INTERVIEWS

The best sources of information you are likely to find are people working in the fields that interest you. These people can offer comments on employment outlook in their locality. They can also give you more detailed information about working conditions in their field to help you decide how well that kind of work suits you. A good way of locating these people is to ask your acquaintances if they know anyone involved in these fields. If they do not, perhaps they might know someone who might know and could give you a referral. Another good way of finding information is to call relevant companies and associations listed in the Yellow Pages of a city telephone directory. Ask for the Public Information Office and explain what information you're seeking.

1. Use the guidelines in Appendix C to conduct your interviews. Be sure to record your impressions and thoughts immediately after conducting the interview, while it is still fresh in your mind. If you wait, you are likely to forget.

2. As you conduct your information-gathering interviews, be sure to talk to more than a single person in a field. You are likely to find that one person's views are too biased to give you an accurate reflection of that occupation. Also, as you seek out information sources, find people who have been in that field long enough to have fully experienced it. That usually takes three years or more. You will also want to ensure that you are not talking only with people who are very unhappy in their work. Remember that an unhappy person may be misplaced in the field or "burned out," having done the same job too long. Even though that person is dissatisfied, the field involved might be perfect for you.

3. After conducting your interviews, record your overall assessment of the occupational alternatives in the "Information Interviews" section of Table 7.2.

Exercise 7-J. COMPLETING THE CAREER ASSESSMENT TABLE

After having obtained the data you need about occupational compatibility and employment outlook for Table 7.2, you will want to use your accumulated information to determine your best occupational alternative. To help you make this choice, we have provided an Evaluation Scale to assign numerical ratings to your alternatives.

1. Review the comments you have recorded in the "OOH" and "Information Interviews" sections of Table 7.2. Then use the Evaluation Scale to find suitable numerical ratings for Data, People, Things Preferences, occupational compatibility with what you want/need in a career, and employment outlook. Fill in Columns B, C, and D of Table 7.2.

2. After assigning your numerical ratings, add the scores on Table 7.2 from Columns A, B, C, and D for each of your occupations. Put the resulting score in the "Cumulative Score" column. Having computed this total for each occupational alternative, you will have a handy numerical guide for determining which of your alternatives is best.

3. Look down your "Cumulative Score" column to determine which alternative received the highest rating. Place a #1 in the "Overall Suitability" column for that alternative to indicate that this is probably your best overall choice. Place a #2 in the "Overall Suitability" column for the alternative that received the next highest score. Continue ranking all of your alternatives in this manner.

Evaluation Scale for Personal/Occupational Compatibility and Employment Outlook

Rating Score	*The likelihood that the occupation would be compatible with your Data, People, Things Preference*	*The likelihood of fulfilling your most important wants and needs in that occupation*	*The likelihood that you will be able to obtain employment in that occupation*
	Column B on Table 7.2	*Column C on Table 7.2*	*Column D on Table 7.2*
5	Totally compatible with my Data, People, Things Preference	Better than a 75% probability	Considerably more job openings than qualified applicants in the location you've chosen
4	Fairly compatible with my Data, People, Things Preference	Less than a 75% chance, but almost certainly better than a 50% chance	More job openings than qualified applicants in the location you've chosen
3	Slightly compatible with my Data, People, Things Preference	About a 50% probability	Number of job openings about the same as number of qualified applicants in the location you've chosen
2	Fairly incompatible with my Data, People, Things Preference	Less than a 50% chance	Fewer job openings than qualified applicants/stiff competition for available jobs in the location you've chosen
1	Totally incompatible with my Data, People, Things Preference	Highly unlikely to no chance at all	Far fewer job openings than qualified applicants in the location you've chosen and/or occupation becoming obsolete

TABLE 7.2 Developing and Assessing Your Career Alternatives

Career Alternative & DOT Number	DOT Information The Primary Transferable/ Functional Skills Involved in This Occupation	A Skills Rating	Comments about Skills Compatibility

Occupational Outlook Handbook (OOH) and Other Sources Comments about Personal/ Occupational Compatibility and Employment Outlook	*Information Interviews* Conclusions and Comments	B Data, People, Things Rating	C Wants/Needs Rating	D Employment Rating	Cumulative Score	Overall Suitability Ranking

Career Alternative & DOT Number	*DOT Information* The Primary Transferable/ Functional Skills Involved in This Occupation	*A* Skills Rating	Comments about Skills Compatibility

Occupational Outlook Handbook (OOH) and Other Sources Comments about Personal/ Occupational Compatibility and Employment Outlook	Information Interviews Conclusions and Comments	B Data, People, Things Rating	C Wants/Needs Rating	D Employment Rating	Cumulative Score	Overall Suitability Ranking

Career Alternative & DOT Number	DOT Information The Primary Transferable/ Functional Skills Involved in This Occupation	A Skills Rating	Comments about Skills Compatibility

Occupational Outlook Handbook (OOH) and Other Sources Comments about Personal/ Occupational Compatibility and Employment Outlook	Information Interviews Conclusions and Comments	B Data, People, Things Rating	C Wants/Needs Rating	D Employment Rating	Cumulative Score	Overall Suitability Ranking

Career Alternative & DOT Number	DOT Information The Primary Transferable/ Functional Skills Involved in This Occupation	A Skills Rating	Comments about Skills Compatibility

Occupational Outlook Handbook (OOH) and Other Sources Comments about Personal/ Occupational Compatibility and Employment Outlook	Information Interviews Conclusions and Comments	Data, People, Things Rating	Wants/Needs Rating	Employment Rating	Cumulative Score	Overall Suitability Ranking
		B	C	D		

Career Alternative & DOT Number	DOT Information The Primary Transferable/ Functional Skills Involved in This Occupation	A Skills Rating	Comments about Skills Compatibility

Occupational Outlook Handbook (OOH) and Other Sources Comments about Personal/ Occupational Compatibility and Employment Outlook	*Information Interviews* Conclusions and Comments	B Data, People, Things Rating	C Wants/Needs Rating	D Employment Rating	Cumulative Score	Overall Suitability Ranking

The following check list will assist you in making your decision.

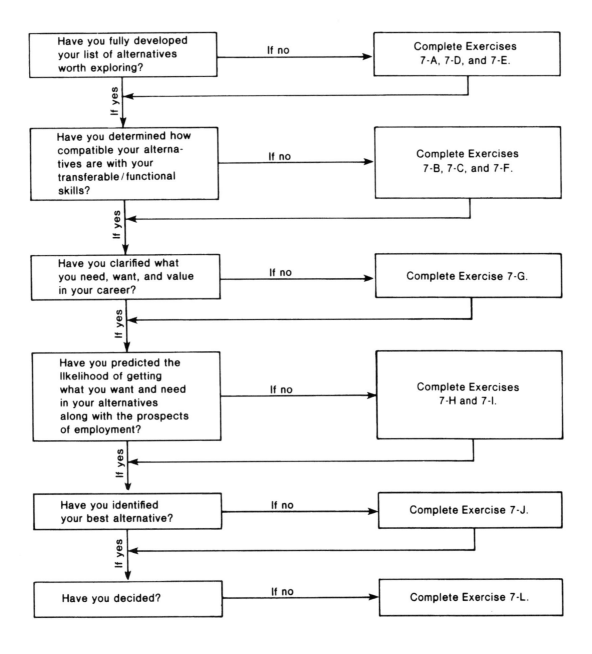

Making a Definite Decision

Having completed Exercise 7-K, you are probably in one of the following circumstances:

1. By clearly identifying your best choice through your assessments, you have chosen a career to pursue. Go on to the section of this chapter entitled "Deciding and Taking Responsibility."

2. Numerically you've identified your best choice, but you don't feel quite ready to decide.

3. You may have one choice with the highest numerical rating, but you're not sure that rating is accurate. Or you may have two or more choices that are so close numerically that you have a difficult time deciding which is the best option.

Note: An alternative is a good choice even if it only provided scores of 3 or better in all four columns A, B, C, and D of Table 7.2.

4. All your assessments have such low cumulative scores that you doubt that any of them are wise choices.

5. You feel frustrated because the alternative you prefer most has poor employment prospects (a low score in Column D).

If you find yourself in situation #2 above, you are probably close to selecting that alternative as your definite choice. However, it might be helpful to clarify what you would need to do in order to feel comfortable about deciding. What should you do if you find yourself in situation #3, 4, or 5 above? These are tentative decision situations. For situation #3, you need to consider the time you have available to choose. Depending upon your time, you might want to do limited or considerable field research in the occupation(s) involved to obtain sufficient first-hand information before making a definite decision.

Humpty decided to go back for another session with his career counselor

Should you find yourself in situation #4 or #5 above, ask yourself whether you've missed an alternative or alternatives that would provide a more promising outlook. If so, it would be well worth your while to spend some more time developing additional alternatives. If you are fairly certain, however, that you have already identified the alternatives that interest you most, your task becomes somewhat more difficult. Your best bet is to look for any alternatives that provide a cumulative score of 12 or better on Table 7.2. If you have one or more alternatives in this category, decide which consideration—skills compatibility (Column A), compatibility with your Data, People, Things Preference (Column B), Wants/Needs Preference (Column C), or employment outlook (Column D)—is most important to you. Then pick the best alternative with this in mind.

If you decide on an alternative with a poor employment outlook, we strongly encourage you to develop your job-hunting skills by studying Chapter 11. Even in a tough job market, there are almost always jobs available somewhere. However, job openings in crowded fields are unlikely to be listed anywhere. Therefore, usually the person with the best job-hunting skills rather than the best talents gets hired for these jobs.

Dealing with a Tentative Decision

In some situations it is very difficult to come to a definite decision. Perhaps you lack the information, experience, and/or time needed to make a realistic decision. In such cases, it might be best, if you are working, to remain temporarily in your present employment situation or, if you are in college, to pursue a general studies curriculum. Meanwhile, acquire further insight and experience with one of your better alternatives. You may want to explore several appealing alternatives, one at a time. Some good ways of exploring a tentative decision are discussed below under the heading "Need for Field Research."

Carol and Tentative Decision Making

Carol serves as an example of a tentative decision maker. She completed the decision-making process defined in this text, but felt that she could not make a definite career choice because of financial circumstances. She was interested in several art-related careers, but was unsure of her talent in these areas.

She was reluctant, therefore, to quit her job and go back to school full time to study. Accordingly, she decided to remain in her current secretarial job, maintaining her financial security, while exploring the art-related careers. She decided to accomplish this by enrolling in studio art courses at a nearby college. At the same time, she will be interviewing many people in art fields to obtain information about the art careers and about the job market. If Carol discovers that she does have marketable talent and finds the job market promising, she will then definitely choose an art career. In the meantime, she has the security of her present job. She also knows that if her pursuit of an art career does not work out, she still has other interesting alternatives to explore.

What can you learn from the previous example of Carol that you can apply to your own decision-making situation?

List those career alternatives that appear about equally suitable right now. Divide these into the following categories, according to which alternatives you find most appealing.

The Alternatives Which I Am　　　　　　　　*The Options I Am Less Certain*
Most Interested in Right Now　　　　　　　　*about Right Now*

Once you have identified the alternatives you want to explore now, decide your best method by answering the following questions:

1. Which alternative am I inclined to investigate first?

2. How much time can I realistically give myself to explore that option?

3. Given the above time consideration, what are the best ways I can explore this alternative?

4. What will I need most to learn about myself in this exploration?

5. What will I need most to find out about the job market and the career field in this exploration?

6. Are there any other things I need to do or keep in mind while undertaking this exploration?

7. If my exploration suggests that this alternative would not be a good choice, which alternative should I explore next? Have I meanwhile discovered other interesting alternatives missing from my original list?

Further Field Research for Tentative Decision Makers

The best way to explore your options further is through first-hand experience. If you must complete your exploration in a brief time, your best bet is simply to talk to as many people as you can who are working in your fields of interest. Follow the guidelines of Appendix C for these information interviews. If, on the other hand, you have enough time to conduct a thorough exploration, consider some or all of the following methods:

1. Interning involves spending time with people working in a field you find appealing to observe directly the nature of their work, their duties, and their responsibilities. This method lets you experience a typical day of a person working in a particular career. As you can imagine, this kind of investigation can be more revealing than just asking people what their work is like. Formal internships include collegiate work/learning experiences.

2. Volunteer work is also an excellent way of both gaining realistic insight and acquiring general work experience. You can obtain valuable job references and sometimes salaried job offers in the process. Many organizations are happy to use the services of a volunteer worker, particularly when the individual has enthusiasm along with some knowledge of the area.

3. Part-time or temporary work is another excellent way to acquire first-hand experience in an occupational field. You probably won't get a paid, part-time or temporary job in the position you really are interested in. However, you can often acquire a lower-level job in the general field. In addition to getting a job reference, you'll be in a position to find out whether you would enjoy working in that particular field.

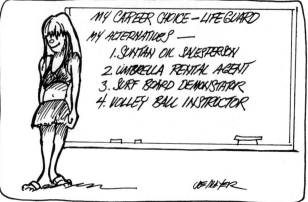

Your main goal in any kind of field research is to find out how appropriate an occupation would be for you. It is helpful to answer relevant questions as you explore the alternatives. Among the questions to consider are:

1. What specific kinds of information will I need to learn for this field?
2. Would pursuing a career in this field get me closer to what I really want in my career?
3. What are the least appealing aspects of a career in this field?
4. What are the most appealing aspects of a career in this field?

Deciding and Taking Responsibility

If you have followed the career/life decision-making model to this point, you have made a decision. Consider for a moment what a decision is and is not.

Your decision is not:

- someone else's responsibility
- the option you fell into or had to choose because there was nothing else to choose from
- a perfect choice that will make your life wonderful forever
- likely to be the last decision you will ever have to make about your career

Your decision is:

- fully your responsibility and no one else's
- made from among alternatives that you clearly identified and investigated
- your best alternative given your self-knowledge and your available options
- likely to create new decision situations that will enable you to continue freely making choices and taking charge of your career

Congratulations! Your decision is probably the very best one that you can make at this time. If your needs change later or the outcomes of your decision do not seem to be getting you closer to what you want, remember that you can make a new decision at that time. This is the freedom associated with "taking charge."

Summary

To come to a satisfactory decision about your career, you look for a match between self insights and your identified choices. This process starts with a systematic assessment of your skills and the skills required by your occupational alternatives. Next, you clarify your career needs, wants, and values to determine which of your alternatives are most likely to fulfill these. By studying the employment outlook, you can assess which of your alternatives will provide the best employment prospects. Once you have acquired and compiled this information, you are usually ready to make a realistic decision. A realistic decision offers a high probability of obtaining employment, achieving satisfaction, and being productive in your career.

Career/life decision making is a unique experience for everyone. Because no two people are the same, no two people are likely to come to the same decision after completing the same process. No two people are likely, either, to complete the process in the same amount of time. Some people complete the entire process and reach a definite decision in just a few weeks of concentrated work. Others may need many months to complete the process. It is far preferable to take the time you need to make a realistic decision than to hurry through the process and make a poor decision.

If you have completed the career/life decision-making model, you can have confidence that you have made a good decision, either tentative or definite. Having learned this process, you can use it whenever you are faced with major career/life decisions. While the model has been used in this book to make career decisions, it can be used to make other major life decisions.

Assignment

The following situations are provided for you to consider how willing you are to make and implement a career decision in the face of typical pressures people often experience. Answer the following questions candidly, telling how you really believe you would respond in each situation:

1. You decide on a career that really interests you, but others are discouraging your plans, saying that only men/women do that kind of work (Example: You are a woman deciding to pursue electrical engineering or a man deciding on a secretarial career.) What would you do or say?

2. After pursuing a career for many years, you decide at age forty-nine to return to college to prepare for a new career. People around you call your decision a mistake. They say you should stay with what you are doing because of your age, and besides, you're too old to go to college. How would you handle that?

3. In completing this workbook, you decide that a career in an enterprising field (E) is exactly what you want, but your parents, spouse, or friends try to pressure you into a career in an investigative (I) area. How would you respond to them?

4. You are a thirty-four-year-old housewife whose children no longer require constant personal care. You decide to return to college to begin preparing for a new career. Your spouse, friends, and/or family strongly discourage you from that, arguing that a mother and wife's role is in the home. How would you answer? What would you do?

5. Although you like your job, you decide to retire early to begin doing some of those things you have always planned but have never accomplished. Friends and associates tell you that you are foolish to quit a job you like and that people generally are not very happy in retirement. What would you do and why?

6. You have gotten into a career you dislike, but it offers good benefits and a high salary. Based on what you learned from career planning, you know you want to make a career change. But the career you want requires further education or training. Your family, friends, and/or acquaintances say you are foolish to give up your job benefits just to pursue something you are interested in. How would you respond? What would you do?

8 Designing Your Future

Control starts with planning. Planning is bringing the future into the present so that we can do something about it now.

ALAN LAKEIN
How to Get Control of Your Time and Your Life

DO YOU KNOW PEOPLE:

➠ Whose careers suffer today because they failed to plan adequately yesterday?

➠ Who are so focused on future goals that they neglect the present?

➠ Who set objectives and then just expect them to happen?

➠ Whose lives have been made inflexible by overly detailed plans?

➠ Who plan without realistically taking future conditions into consideration?

If so, you know people who do not effectively use goal setting and planning to take charge of their careers and lives.

The Future in Perspective

Futurists maintain that through collective actions, everyone participates in creating the future. Thus, the decisions made in the present will determine the shape of the future world.[1] The validity of this statement is most dramatically proved through historical examples. For instance, President Kennedy and others decided in the early 1960s to place a man on the moon by the end of that decade. This decision ushered in the space age along with such major technological advances as spacecraft design, rocket fuels, space medicine, computerized information, communication satellites, etc.

Today, people take for granted the resulting changes in society, including instantaneous, low-cost communication with countries all over the world, immediate access to information that used to take months to compile, and simultaneous television viewing of live events, such as the Olympic Games, via space satellite.

Unfortunately, historical examples also prove society's capacity to warp the future. When the decision was made to develop and use the atomic bomb, many people considered the world indestructible. Yet this decision to develop atomic weapons has resulted in the current frightening potential to destroy the human race. Previous atomic testing caused long-term damage to human health through radioactive fallout, and no adequate plans existed to cover this possibility. Nuclear accidents such as the Chernobyl disaster have also had wide ranging world consequences. The immediate death and destruction as well as the potential long-term damage to human health and agriculture from Chernobyl signal the need for worldwide cooperation and planning in the use of nuclear energy.

FIGURE 8.1 Designing and Building Your Future Career and Life[2]

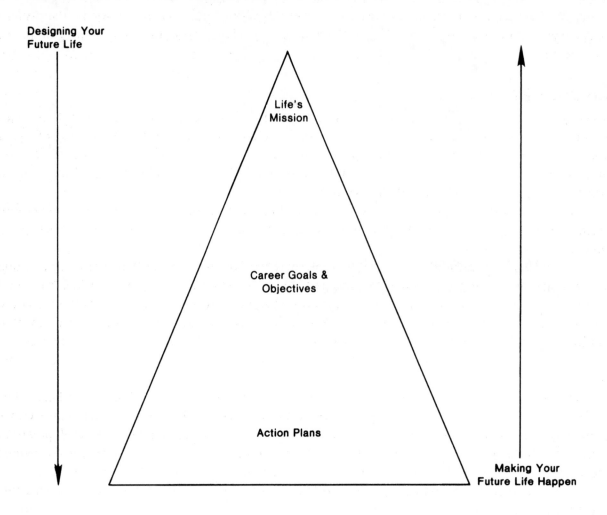

Designing Your
Future Life

Life's
Mission

Career Goals &
Objectives

Action Plans

Making Your
Future Life Happen

Influencing Your Career Future

Just as collective actions shape the world's future, your individual actions shape your personal destiny. As you will see in Chapter 9, your own mindset can strongly influence your future through the power of suggestion. The term "self-fulfilling prophecy" describes this phenomenon of individual expectations influencing future results. For example, if you approach a job interview fully prepared and expecting to perform well, you are likely to succeed. In contrast, if you expect to perform poorly ("I never do well in face-to-face contacts" or "I always choke under pressure") you are likely to fail.

Having chosen a career, you may be tempted to make minimal plans, sit back, and "let it happen." Unfortunately, what usually happens with this approach is failure. Like everyone else, you will probably experience some setbacks as you pursue a career. Lacking shorter-range goals and specific career plans, you may find these setbacks overwhelming and doubt that you can succeed. Feeling out of control, you might then reinforce your pessimism by expecting further setbacks instead of looking for other options and opportunities. Not surprisingly, a cycle of victimization develops, and few career choices are attained.

On the other hand, with comprehensive, short-range goals and plans, it is easy to view setbacks in a large perspective. You can recognize other, often better, alternatives that were not obvious before. Of course, no one can absolutely predict the future. Yet developing and following objectives and plans does give you far more control, direction, and motivation. In this way, your own self-fulfilling prophecy will be success.

Career Goals/Objectives

Career goals provide you with purpose and direction for your career and life. People without goals experience more conflict and uncertainty because they just react to whatever happens instead of trying to infuse their lives with meaning. These people are likely to have far more days when they have no compelling reason for even getting out of bed. In contrast, people with carefully chosen, clearly defined goals know what they want out of their lives and careers.

Another function of clearly defined goals is that they enable people to channel their energy into meaningful activity and may even create more energy in the pursuit of life goals. The following example illustrates this point.

Denise was a conscientious and efficient secretary whose true passion was hiking and backpacking in wilderness areas. Feeling unchallenged and tied down in her office setting, she decided to attend college as a way to initiate a career change. Unmotivated and discouraged by her lack of clear direction, she dropped out her first semester. She was unable to see how her love of the outdoors had any relationship to a possible new career direction. Through the assistance of a career counselor, however, she saw that conserving natural resources for the enjoyment of everyone was the motivating force in her life.

With renewed purpose, Denise re-entered college, majored in geology, and made the Dean's List her first semester back. She joined the Appalachian Trail Conference in its mission to maintain sections of the Appalachian Trail. Currently she is collaborating with an architect friend on the development of a design for an energy efficient home utilizing solar and geothermal power. Having a clearly defined career objective has enabled Denise to channel her energies towards results that amaze even her.

In effect, having clearly defined goals brings the future into the present. Instead of procrastinating, you can take appropriate present action because you are clear about what direction you want to go. Accordingly, you can also see what actions will move you in your chosen direction and what will not.

In this way, goals enable you to take charge of your life. Rather than just sitting back and letting things happen to you, you can use goals as catalysts for action. People who just let things happen to them are actually at the mercy of circumstances. They use up their energy fighting, denying, or rationalizing unpleasant realities.

As you create goals and act upon them, you influence your future. In other words, your mental images and attitudes about the future largely determine the shape of your future. No one can totally control the future because of unknown circumstances over which there is little control. Goal-oriented people, however, tend to be far more successful at getting what they want rather than simply taking what they can get.

Defining Your Goals/Objectives

Goals and objectives are specific, future-oriented statements of purpose and direction accomplishable within a definite time frame. The time frame can be long, medium, or short range. Although the terms *goal* and *objectives* are often used interchangeably, sometimes the term *goal* is used for long-range aims while the word *objectives* is used for related short-range intentions. Being well within our grasp, short-range objectives enable us to establish and reach tangible outcomes on the path towards our long-range goals. As we complete our objectives, we are then in a position to set and accomplish new ones.

The word is out, Farmer Brown has crummy long range goals for us

Goals may be stated in a variety of ways corresponding to the strength of your commitment to complete them. The way you state your goals clearly indicates how determined you are to achieve your desired outcome. According to David Ellis, there is a hierarchy of goal statement categories, each successively more powerful than the preceding one.

FIGURE 8.2 David Ellis' Hierarchy of Goal Statement Categories[3]

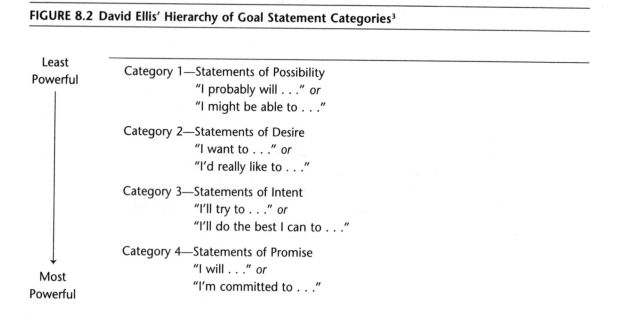

Least Powerful

Category 1—Statements of Possibility
"I probably will . . ." or
"I might be able to . . ."

Category 2—Statements of Desire
"I want to . . ." or
"I'd really like to . . ."

Category 3—Statements of Intent
"I'll try to . . ." or
"I'll do the best I can to . . ."

Category 4—Statements of Promise
"I will . . ." or
"I'm committed to . . ."

Most Powerful

Notice that with each higher category, the language gets increasingly stronger and the likelihood that the goal will be completed gets more believable. In people's daily interactions, the strongest language (category 4) is reserved for activities requiring the highest level of commitment, such as marriage vows or promissory notes. In a court of law where the truthfulness of witnesses can mean the difference between life and death of an accused, the most powerful language is used when swearing in witnesses: "I promise to tell the truth, the whole truth, and nothing but the truth."

Pay attention to the language you use when you state your own objectives. If you state a goal in the language of category 2 (desire), "I want to get a better job," examine your willingness to make a stronger commitment to reaching that objective. Then restate your goal in the language of category 3 (intent) or category 4 (promise). "I'll do my best to get a better job," or "I will get a better job."

Clarifying What You Want in a Career

Knowing what you really want in a career is necessary before you can develop believable career goals. Clarifying your wants, however, may not be so easy. Wants are often confused with "shoulds" that are beliefs about what you ought to do, be, or have. "Shoulds" usually are influenced strongly by the thinking of others. Your parents, social institutions, the media, public opinion, current popular values, etc., try to convince you of what you should do, have, or be. At your place of worship, you may be reminded of your duty to contribute your time and money to the support of the congregation. Television commercials bombard you with overt and subtle secular "should" messages: "remove unsightly hair," "take the fear out of being close," "blonds have more fun," "double your flavor, double your fun." "Should" messages from a variety of sources serve as nagging reminders of what we are "supposed" to do.

"Wants," on the other hand, are expressions of what you really desire to have, do, or be. They reflect those things that attract your interest or enthusiasm, those things that grow from your wishes, dreams, aspirations, and fantasies. They reflect the inner you—the real you.

"Shoulds" can prevent you from being in touch with your true "wants." For this reason, it is important to clearly separate your "shoulds" from your "wants." Career goals created out of "shoulds" do not work because they are too much like New Year's resolutions, full of good intentions, but in the end, usually resisted. Career goals developed out of true "wants," however, enlist our full energy and provide a winning combination. Here is an example of how to transform a "should" into a "want":

- I *should* lose 15 pounds.
- I *want* to maintain my weight at a neat and trim 130 pounds.

The following exercises are designed to assist you in identifying your "wants" and separating out your "shoulds."

1. Before identifying what you do want in your career, it is important to know what you don't want or want to avoid. List below those things you have currently in your life, career and/or job that you do not want.

2. Some elements of your current life, career and/or job give you energy and pleasure. List below these current elements in your life, career and/or job that you do want to retain.

3. Now that you have more clarity about your skills, interests, and values and have made a tentative or definite career choice, what else is important for you to have in your career? List below things you truly want in your future career and/or job that you don't have now.

4. From parts 2 and 3 above, develop a list of your top 10 career wants. Eliminate those that are really "shoulds" from your list or restate them as "wants." Now prioritize your list of 10, assigning "1" to the most important and "10" to the least important.

My Top Ten Wants
1.
2.
3.
4.
5.
6.
7.
8.
9.
10.

5. Take the top five career wants from your prioritized list of 10 above, and restate each one as a specific career goal.

Examples:

a. I want to work with people who are highly committed to the customers/clients they serve.

b. I want to obtain recognition from others for the work that I do.

c. I want to make enough money to maintain the lifestyle I currently enjoy.

d. I want a job that is within walking distance from my residence.

e. I want a career that will enable me to use and develop my foreign language skills.

Guidelines for Expressing Statements of Career Goals and Objectives

Career Goal and Objective statements follow certain guidelines to define effectively the direction you want your future to take. The most important guidelines are listed below.[4] True career goals and objectives are:

1. *Achievable:* Achievable outcomes can be completed given the physical and mental limitations of the people setting the objectives. For someone five feet tall, the goal of becoming the center of a professional basketball team is neither realistic nor achievable. Similarly, most people would not be able to achieve the objective of reading a 1,500 page book in an afternoon.

2. *Believable:* To meet this standard, people need to feel confident that they can complete the goal or objective that it is within the realm of possibility for them. Some people are so fervent in their belief that they will accomplish something that they actually do it despite considerable obstacles. Grandma Moses is an example of a person who defied the odds and became a recognized artist in her 80s.

3. *Specifically Stated:* In so far as possible, true objectives are stated in concrete terms. Short-range objectives can be stated more specifically than long-range goals because of the uncertainty of the distant future.

4. *Presented without Alternative:* True objectives are clearly stated without any either-or's. "I'm either going to buy a house or rent one" presents two opposing alternatives. The person setting up this objective may be undecided about the primary objective. In either case, objectives stated in this way simply need clarification: "I intend to buy a house, if I can find one I can afford. My second choice is to rent a house."

5. *Compatible with Your Values:* True statements of goals reflect the values that you profess. If someone values doing things together as a family unit, then that person's vacation objective would be to set a time when every family member could participate.

Exercise 8-B. REVISING YOUR STATEMENTS OF CAREER OBJECTIVES

Check over your top five career objectives to see if they correspond to the guidelines listed above. Then, make any revisions that you feel are necessary.

1. Career Objective:

   Your Revision:

2. Career Objective:

   Your Revision:

3. Career Objective:

   Your Revision:

4. Career Objective:

   Your Revision:

5. Career Objective:

   Your Revision:

Comprehensive Career Goals and Objectives

Establishing reachable long-range career goals is crucial for providing future direction and perspective. But a long-range goal is less useful in clarifying what step you should take next. Long-range goals extend at least ten years into the future. It would be nearly impossible to sit down today and produce a detailed plan for the next ten years that would help you attain these goals. Even if you had the patience and perspective to do this, your plan would be foolishly rigid. Your own life will change, and the working world will present new opportunities. Accordingly, your plans and long-range goals will change.

For this reason, the easiest and most productive approach is to devise medium-range and short-range career objectives based on your long-range goals. A medium-range objective generally covers one to five years. As these medium-range objectives are reached, you can devise new ones to direct your progress towards the related long-range goal. Sometimes, you will want to change these medium-range objectives when they no longer are suitable. Short-range objectives cover up to one year. You will frequently revise short-range objectives.

The advantages of medium and short-range objectives are numerous. First of all, they are totally flexible. As changes and opportunities occur, these short-range objectives can easily be revised. Also, you don't have to wait ten or more years to attain them. Successfully achieving short-range objectives keeps you motivated. If you feel discouraged because you have not yet found a suitable career choice, setting short-term objectives will provide direction for your continuing exploration. Finally, short-range objectives are specific enough to provide guidelines for making step-by-step plans. And without these plans, your future becomes a question mark—or worse.

Table 8.1 defines these three types of Career Objectives. Table 8.2 provides examples of all three types, illustrating the difference between vague objective statements and more effective precise statements. Look these over carefully before devising your own short-range objective statements for Exercise 8-C.

TABLE 8.1 Types of Career Goals and Objectives

Long-Range Goals: These goals establish the general career direction you want to achieve over the long run or at least ten years into the future. Occasionally, you will find better alternatives and change your long-range goals.

Medium-Range Objectives: These are the career objectives you want to achieve in the next one to five years, so they are more specific. As these objectives are reached, you will establish others to progress towards related long-range goals. Medium-range objectives are frequently revised and sometimes changed completely as new options appear.

Short-Range Objectives: These are career objectives you want to achieve in one year or less, so they are very specific. These objectives are frequently revised or changed completely as new options appear.

TABLE 8.2 Examples of Career Goals and Objectives

Long-Range Goals

Vague	More Effective
1. I want to make a good salary.	1. Within fifteen years, I will be making a salary equivalent to $50,000 in today's money.
2. I want to work with people I like.	2. I will work with people who are caring, creative, and intelligent.
3. I want to use my best talents in my work.	3. In my career, I will be using and developing my research skills, ability to organize ideas, and creative writing skills.

Medium-Range Objectives

Vague	More Precise
1. I want to get a good education.	1. Within five years, I will have obtained a B.A. degree in psychology.
2. I would like to get a job in the computer field.	2. Within two years, I will be working as a computer programmer with an aerospace firm or agency such as NASA.
3. I want to be an artist.	3. Within three years, I will be working as a commercial artist for a TV station.

Short-Range Objectives

Vague	Precise
1. I will finish my A.A. degree.	1. Within one year, I will have completed my A.A. degree in respiratory therapy.
2. I will get a good, first job soon.	2. In six months, I will obtain an entry-level position as a secretary with an international banking and finance firm.
3. I will attempt to learn about owning my own business.	3. Within three months, I will have researched the local opportunities for opening my own health food store.

Exercise 8-C. DEVELOPING COMPREHENSIVE STATEMENTS OF CAREER GOALS

For this exercise, you will further revise your long-range statements of career goals from Exercise 8-A. Using these long-range career goals as references, you will then establish related medium-range and short-range objectives. To illustrate, we will follow the example of Marlene. Initially, Marlene completed the following prioritized list of career-related life objectives:

1. I will be doing worthwhile, important work related to my math skills.

2. I will obtain professional recognition.

3. I will have opportunity for self-improvement.

4. I will have financial security.

5. I will be contributing to the solution of our inflation problems.

After Marlene's preliminary research with her work options, she decided to become an accountant. At that point, she was able to develop and refine her long-range career goals. Her revised goals are listed below:

1. I will work in a large public-service accounting firm, serving in a leadership position.

2. Within ten years, I will receive recognition for my excellent work as a C.P.A.

3. I will work for an organization that encourages personal and professional growth by sponsoring workshops and funding continued education.

4. Within twelve years, I will be earning a salary equivalent to $60,000 in today's money.

5. I will be helping to solve our economic problems by teaching sound financial management and fiscal responsibility to my clients.

Marlene then developed the following medium-range and short-range objectives related to her top long-range Career Goals:

Long-range Goal #1

I will work in a large public-service accounting firm, serving in a leadership postion.

Medium-range Objectives

1. In one and a half years, I will obtain an entry-level accounting position in a firm of my choice.

2. Within two years, I will have received my first salary raise.

3. Within three years, I will earn a major promotion.

4. Within five years, I will have earned through part-time study my M.B.A. in accounting.

Short-range Objectives

1. Within one year, I will obtain my A.A. degree in accounting.

2. I will graduate with a B+ average.

3. While in college, I will research fully the types of accounting business I consider potential employers.

Directions:

1. Revise your top five long-range career objectives from Exercise 8-A, so they are stated as precisely as possible at this point in your life. If you have made a tentative career choice in Chapter 7, your long-range career goals will be more vague. However, state them as precisely as you can, and concentrate on constructive short-range objectives to aid your career exploration. Fill in your top two long-range goals in the appropriate spaces on the diagrams that follow.

2. After writing your long-range goals, write your related medium-range and short-range career objectives. Use Marlene's example as a guide.

3. As you complete this exercise, study Tables 8.1 and 8.2 to assist you in writing effective statements of goals and objectives.

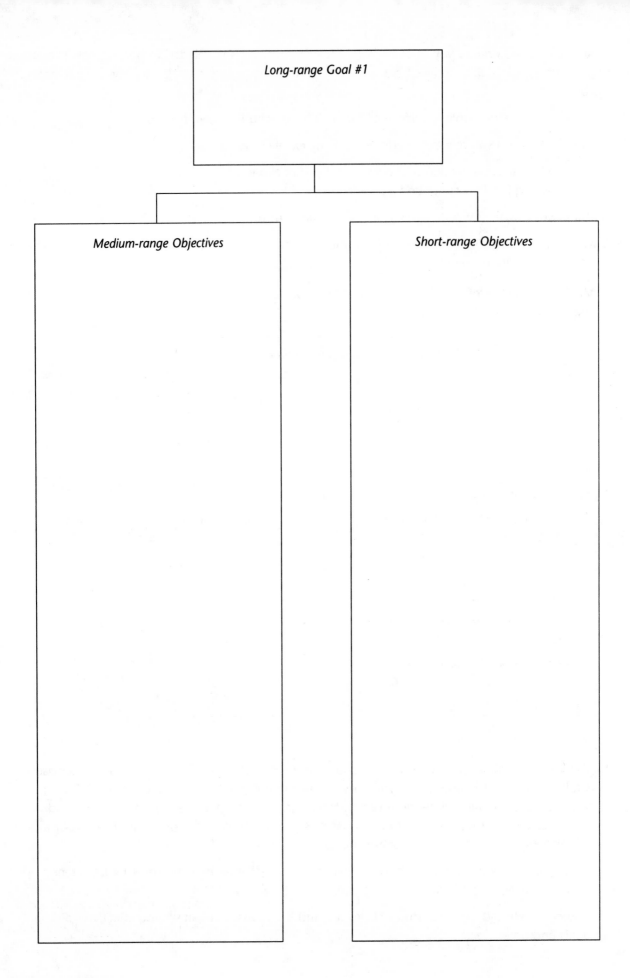

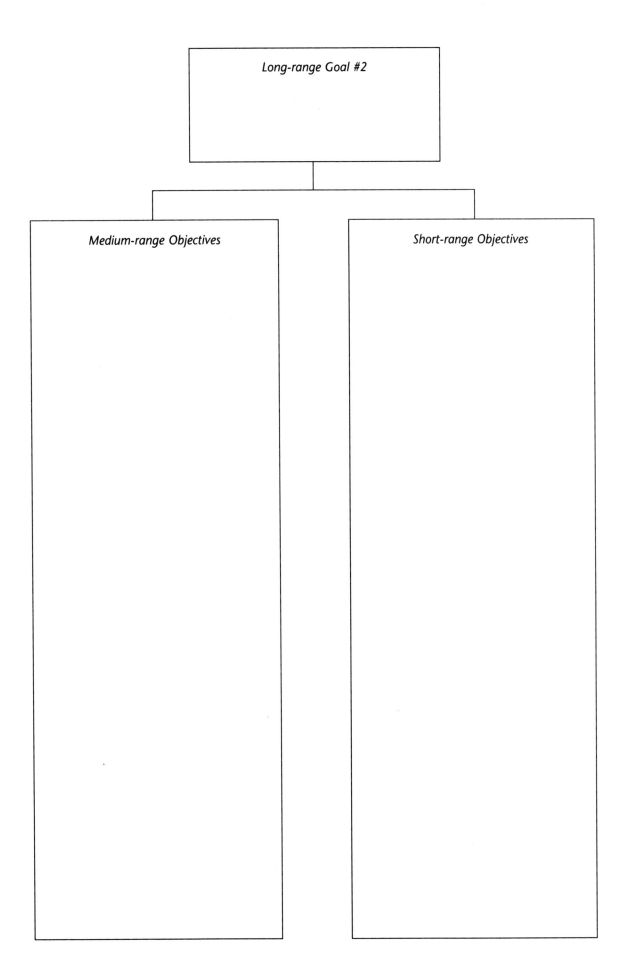

Long-range Goal #2

Medium-range Objectives

Short-range Objectives

FIGURE 8.3 From Life Goals to Action Plans

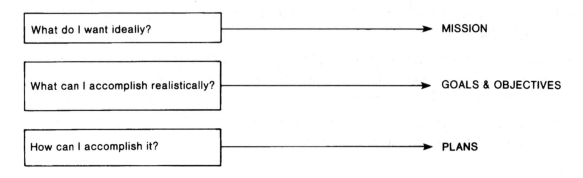

Mission statements are the ideal outcomes you seek in your life.

Career Goals and Objectives are the realistic outcomes you seek in your career.

Action Plans are the specific actions required to achieve your objectives.

Exercise 8-D. ACTION PLANNING

Figure 8.3 portrays the relationships among mission, goals, and plans. Notice that your mission is your ideal or ultimate outcome while your objectives and goals define what you can accomplish realistically within a specified time frame. Plans lay out the steps required to get what you want. In this exercise, your task is to identify the steps necessary to accomplish the short-range objectives you listed to support your longer-range goals. Start the exercise by identifying your first significant step towards achieving your short-range objective and determining when you can complete that step. Use the following example as a guide as you develop your own action plans.

Example:

For long-range goal #1, Marlene's short-range objectives were as follows:

1. Within one year, I will obtain an A.A. degree in accounting.

2. I will graduate with a B+ average.

3. While in college, I will research fully the types of accounting businesses I consider potential employers.

From these objectives, Marlene developed the following action plans:

Steps to Take	*Complete by*
1. I will change my major from general studies to accounting.	May 15, 1995
2. I will talk with my academic advisor to see what courses I need to take.	June 1, 1995
3. I will investigate financial aid possibilities at the Financial Aid Office, so I can afford to take four courses a semester.	June 1, 1995

	Steps to Take	Complete by
4.	I will enroll in two summer school courses.	June 15, 1995
5.	I will increase my study time to 30 hours a week to improve my current grades.	July 1, 1995 to May 20, 1998
6.	I will research public-service accounting firms in the area by calling the Chamber of Commerce, looking at government directories, and consulting Dun and Bradstreet directories.	Sept. 1, 1995 to May 20, 1998
7.	Through the college, I will arrange for an accounting internship with one of the firms I've identified in step #6.	Jan. 1, 1996

Directions:

1. Using the above example as a guide, develop a list of action steps for the short-range objectives associated with your top two long range goals.

2. As you review your cluster of short-range objectives for each long-range goal, think through all the related steps required to complete those objectives. List your steps on the following pages in logical sequence.

3. Indicate the approximate deadline for completing each of the steps you identify.

Action Steps for My First Short-Range Objective   *Desired Completion Date*

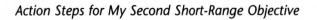

Case Study of William

William was a high school misfit. His parents took him out of public school and placed him in a private, parochial school where William did his best to prove that his parents had made a mistake. The culmination of his efforts came when he failed religion his senior year and was unable to graduate with his class.

After completing summer school to obtain his high school diploma, William jumped from one job to another, either leaving when he got bored or getting fired. He attempted to enlist in the Marine Corps but was unable to pass the physical. Angry and discouraged, William hit bottom when he was apprehended for reckless driving and placed in his parent's custody.

Given an ultimatum by his parents to "shape up" or suffer the consequences, William reluctantly agreed to try the local community college. He took just two classes his first semester, a career planning class and an art class (art was the only subject William had enjoyed in high school). Finding an environment where his creative interests and talents were recognized and encouraged, William began to believe in himself. Through the career planning process he discovered that what he really wanted to do was express himself creatively, especially through photography.

Prior to the start of his second semester, William changed from an undeclared to a visual arts major. Filled with enthusiasm and having educational and career direction for the first time in his life, William took a full academic load his second semester, narrowly missing the Dean's List. One of his photographic collages was chosen for the student art show, and he received a second place ribbon.

This summer, William is working as a photographer's assistant. In his free time he wanders the countryside taking pictures. He is learning how to develop his pictures to obtain the special effects he wants. The best prints will be placed in a portfolio for when he transfers to the Art Institute in one year.

Through realistic goal setting and effective action planning, William has found direction and focus for his career journey.

Muriel waited and waited, knowing that Ralph had unrealistic long-range planning skills

Final Notes on Goals, Objectives, and Plans

Setting goals and objectives and devising action plans are skills that can be developed. Both are also ongoing processes. Many people are reluctant to set goals and objectives or make the supporting plans because they fear they will then be committed to them no matter what. Others are afraid of even positive change or afraid of failing to meet the objectives they have set. All of these emotional reactions are perfectly understandable and normal. However, consider that the only purpose of goals, objectives, and plans is to provide productive direction and motivation, along with the time to accommodate change. Therefore, they should never be turned into nonproductive rigid commitments or burdens.

Since people and the working world change, goals, objectives, and plans should change whenever it is in your best interest. You will need to make these minor or major changes as you learn about new options or challenges in your career. In other words, career planning is a life-long process. Effectiveness in this process involves skill in the interrelated activities shown in Figure 8.3 on page 182. The more you practice these skills, the more effective you will become in taking charge of your career and your life.

Summary

By developing a view of the future, you can build the kind of future you really want to have. No one can predict your fate exactly. However, the taking-charge method of career/life planning does allow you far more control and influence over your prospects. The career/life planning process includes clarifying what you want in your future career and life, setting prioritized goals to get what you want, and translating these into realistic objectives and planned action steps.

As your personal needs as well as aspirations change and the working world changes, you will repeat parts of this process with increasing skill and confidence. Thus, career/life decision making becomes a life-long process, leading you to as much fulfillment as you seek.

Assignment

YOUR FUTURE STORY

For this assignment, imagine that you have been transported magically to a point ten years into the future. From this perspective, you will write an autobiography of what has happened to you over the past ten years you have projected. Thus, your autobiographic summary will cover the future as you envision it. Use your mission, career objectives, and plans along with the envisioning process described in Appendix D for help.

One purpose in completing this exercise is to become more comfortable with and enthusiastic about your future changes. Another purpose is to reaffirm what you ideally want to happen in your career and life. This way, you ensure that your self-fulfilling prophecy will be even more positive and suitable. Most students who complete this exercise find it enjoyable, revealing, and rewarding. After writing your future autobiography, why not put it away to be reviewed periodically over the next ten years? You may want to update this autobiography as you progress in your career and expand your expectations and plans.

DIRECTIONS

1. Assume you have been transported ten years into the future. From that future perspective, write your autobiography for those so-called past ten years. We recommend writing at least five to ten pages of summary.

2. Imagine that you are writing your future autobiography to send to some important person in your life whom you have not seen for ten years. Therefore, you want to tell this person all the significant aspects of your career and life over this period. To make the project seem more real, you may want to give your summary to this person, asking him/her for comments.

3. Base your future autobiography on the goals, objectives, and plans you have already created.

4. Use your imagination to envision your life having turned out the way you ideally want it.

5. Give special emphasis to:

   - Some of your top and most enjoyed achievements during this period.

   - Some of the high priority objectives that you accomplished.

   - Some of the most satisfying experiences in your work, your leisure, and your learning.

Notes

1. Edward S. Cornish, *Planting Seeds for the Future,* a booklet prepared for Champion International Corporation by the World Future Society. Copies can be obtained by writing to Champion International Corporation, Department 5360, 1 Landmark Square, Stamford, Connecticut 06921.

2. This figure is adapted from the Intensive Course in the Crystal Life/Work Planning Process, John C. Crystal Center, Inc., 894 Plandome Road, Manhassett, New York 11030.

3. David Ellis, *Here & Now Instructor's Newsletter,* November 1986, pp. 1 and 4. This newsletter can be obtained by contacting College Survival, Inc., 2650 Jackson Boulevard, Rapid City, South Dakota 57702.

4. James D. McHolland, *Human Potential Seminar Basic Guidebook* (Evanston, Illinois: National Center for Human Potential Seminars & Services, 1976). The publisher's address is 2527 Hastings Avenue, Evanston, Illinois 60201.

Hurdling Your Barriers

Argue for your limitations and sure enough, they're yours.

RICHARD BACH
Illusions

DO YOU KNOW PEOPLE WHO:

➡ Feel completely dependent upon others in making decisions?

➡ Are highly motivated to discover and investigate possible career alternatives?

➡ Blame others or circumstances for everything that happens in their lives?

➡ Believe that their career path will be determined entirely by circumstances beyond their control?

➡ Can make informed decisions and follow through?

➡ Are optimistic about their ability to create a satisfying career through their own efforts?

If you do, you can observe the differences between self-victimizing and self-empowering people.

Three Kinds of Barriers

At this point, you may know what you want in your career and have some plans for achieving your goals. Unfortunately, many people come this far in the career planning process and then get bogged down. Three types of barriers or obstacles keep people from getting what they want or from even attempting to go after their goals. The first barrier is a negative attitude pattern or mindset. The second barrier is poor decision making skills. The third barrier is any external circumstance or situation that at least temporarily blocks career progress. In this chapter, you will have an opportunity to identify your own particular barriers and learn how to overcome them.

Mindsets

Have you noticed how some people tend to be winners in life and others losers? Ask people who are consistent winners in life what their secret is, and the odds are you will receive an answer like, "I don't know why. I just expect things to go well." Losers are likely to tell you about the same thing in reverse. Patterns of winning, losing, and just getting by often correspond to the distinctive attitudes or expectations that different people have about the course of their lives.

These distinctive viewpoints that most people have about life are called mindsets. A mindset is a characteristic pattern of thinking, feeling, and believing. Some people, for example, believe that others have all the luck while they never get any breaks and remain powerless to change their lives. Other individuals expect things to turn out basically well and anticipate success. We refer to these two contrasting orientations as the self-victimizing and the self-empowering mindsets. These attitudes become ingrained, characteristically shaping a person's reactions to every situation.

The Real Victim versus the Self-Victim

A victim is defined as someone who is injured in some way or suffering from some negative act, condition, or circumstance. Unfortunately, there are many true victims in the world. Some people are impoverished, mentally retarded, and physically disabled. Other people are imprisoned for crimes they did not commit or are victims of accidents they didn't cause. People like these do live with limitations or restrictions, and they truly lack some of the options that you may take for granted. Yet many of these individuals remain optimistic, gaining strength from dealing constructively with their obstacles to create better lives and careers for themselves. They don't consider their disabilities real barriers and often refer to themselves as simply having "*different* abilities."

In fact, most people who feel like victims are not really victims of external circumstances or fate. These imagined victims are called self-victimizers.

The Self-Victimizing Mindset

Self-victimizing people are inclined to be uninvolved, dependent, and inflexible in the career-choice process. They rarely generate much energy or enthusiasm for the process of career choosing or career changing. They may underestimate their potential capability for making good choices. Typically, self-victimizers will rely on others to decide for them or wait for circumstances to determine what happens. Self-victimizers are unlikely to explore the full range of available career alternatives out of the rigid conviction that it doesn't make much difference anyway.

Self-victimizing people often feel harmed by circumstances, agencies, or people whom they perceive as hostile. They may say things like "I just can't get ahead because I am a member of a minority, a member of the majority suffering from reverse discrimination, short, tall, fat, thin, ugly, pretty, too smart, too dumb, too poor, too rich, too unskilled, too skilled, too old, or too young."

The legitimate victim is someone who qualifies for a job but doesn't get it because of race, sex, religion, etc. Self-victims are those who do not qualify for a job, but maintain that they were denied because of their age, ethnic background, social class or whatever. Self-victimizers use circumstances such as these to justify their belief that they are essentially helpless in the career-planning and job-hunting process.

Self-Victimizing Case Study

Jack obtained a job that he wanted very much. Yet he knew that the job didn't pay well and was a temporary position funded by a grant. Nevertheless, he hoped that the position would somehow continue, that his salary would somehow be increased, and that the job would somehow lead to a promotion within that organization.

Since the job had temporary funding, Jack's boss repeatedly advised him to begin searching and preparing for a more secure position. His boss also advised that their organization had no plans to create any new positions or hire additional staff for the foreseeable future. Jack chose not to act on this advice, however, feeling that things would somehow turn out all right.

Three years later, the funding ran out, and Jack's job was terminated. He expressed shock and anger. Jack accused the organization of callous unconcern considering his years of service. Just as he was about to leave, a vacancy did open up. Jack applied for that position but was not hired, losing out to a better qualified woman employed by the same organization.

Upon learning this, Jack threatened to bring an affirmative action suit against the organization, claiming reverse discrimination. Jack could not admit that this particular woman was better qualified for the position and that the selection had been carefully made by a committee of both men and women. Even if this hadn't been the case, Jack's negative behavior had ruined his reputation at the organization.

Jack clearly exhibits numerous self-victimizing traits. He was unwilling to even consider the future seriously, let alone explore career alternatives. He felt so strongly dependent upon the organization that he expected "them" to take care of him. He was uncompromising in his attitude about considering other options, stating that he was just not interested in working somewhere else and wanted to stay on.

Jack's surprise and anger after his inevitable layoff shows his dependency and lack of responsibility for his career and life progress. When problems arose, Jack blamed others for what happened. Several months after this incident occurred, Jack remained unemployed and was making no progress towards another employment goal. Instead, Jack's energy was tied up in feeling wronged by the organization and complaining about his "unjust" treatment.

The board was having second thoughts about appointing
Cecilia as public relations director

The Self-Empowering Mindset

"Empowering" means giving someone permission to exercise some type of strength, influence, or power. Self-empowering people give themselves internal permission for exercising power. People with " self-empowering mindsets" feel free to engage in activity geared to getting what they want, and they are optimistic about getting it.

Self-empowering people take responsibility for creating the conditions they want in their lives while self-victimizing people take whatever comes their way. Both groups may begin in exactly the same conditions and circumstances. Because self-victimizing people conclude that they are powerless to change or create, they passively take what they get in life, perhaps hoping for the best. In this sense, they make themselves total victims of chance and circumstance. Self-empowering people, in contrast, will be actively inclined to create and implement desired goals. What happens in the life of the self-empowering person is likely to occur more as a result of self-motivation than external circumstances and conditions.

Self-Empowerment and Career Choice

Self-empowering people go about choosing and implementing their careers far more actively and effectively than self-victimizers. They are also more involved, independent, and flexible in the career-choice and implementation process than are the self-victimizers. Although the self-empowerers are more likely to achieve satisfying careers, they, too, will end up in some unsuitable situations. However, unlike self-victimizers, they actively initiate career changes that will provide greater satisfaction.

Self-empowerers take the time and effort to learn what they need and want in a career and then go ahead and do whatever is required to achieve it. Once they have established career goals, they are inclined to pursue these optimistically and enthusiastically. But self-empowerers recognize that no career decision is likely to produce perfect results. For this reason, they remain flexible and strive to obtain the best results, given their unique situation.

Self-Empowering Case Study

At the age of 37, Anne gave up a successful and fulfilling career in teaching to become a full-time mother and housewife. She put her whole energy, enthusiasm, and creativity into this job, just as she had done with teaching. Years later after her kids had grown up, Anne decided it was time for her to return to an outside career. Since she had been out of the job market for a long time, Anne decided to enhance her credentials by obtaining a masters degree in education. While working on her M.A., Anne began establishing contacts. Through her networking, Anne obtained a part-time educational research job at a community college. She obtained the job even though other candidates had educational backgrounds far better suited to the position than her own.

Soon this job experience, her new M.A. degree, and her networking efforts paid off, and Anne landed an excellent full-time position as an educational researcher with the American Association of Junior Colleges. Through her energy and positive thinking, Anne had created a new career for herself when many were advising her that she was too old to start over again. However, Anne realized that this career was not her final step. While she got outstanding evaluations, Anne was just not energized by her work.

At this stage most people would probably have said something like, "Oh well, I'm just lucky to have such a good job. At my age, I'd better just keep what I have." But not Anne. Anne had far too much to contribute to simply hang in there and wait it out. She didn't know what kind of work would enable her to use her talents more fully. But Anne knew how to ask questions and then seek out answers. She found out that Dick Bolles, the author of *What Color Is Your Parachute,* conducted workshops to help people identify their top skills and interests and set goals aimed at self-realization. Anne went to Dick's two-week course and came away determined to use her talents as a career/life planning specialist.

Once again Anne was faced with a barrier. Her educational background was in high school education and college administration areas. What she wanted to do now involved counseling and teaching in a college setting. The difficulty of making that kind of transition would stop most people. Anne was determined, however. She would either make it on her own as a consultant in private practice or get a job at a college that was looking for talent above "the right" credentials. Anne did the latter through networking. She identified what colleges within commuting distance had strong career/life planning programs and targeted her first choice.

At the time, however, Anne's potential employer had no immediate or anticipated positions. But the people at that organization were impressed with Anne, and she was a patient and persistent problem solver. As a result, within six months she was teaching a career decision making course there and working in a part-time career/life planning specialist position. Within one year, she had been hired as a full-time professor of career/life planning. Over the past ten years, she has helped hundreds of individuals find themselves, clarify their career/life goals, and move into careers that utilize their skills and engage their interests. At this point she has established a reputation for herself within the career/life planning field and is a very popular instructor, guest speaker, and well-paid consultant. Her success has clearly not come through luck. Anne is where she is today because she knew what she wanted, went after it, and didn't let her barriers stop her.

TABLE 9.1 Traits of the Self-Victimizing and the Self-Empowering Mindsets

The Self-Victimizing Mindset	*The Self-Empowering Mindset*
• sees little or no choice available.	• sees life full of choices.
• sees problems as hopeless barriers.	• sees problems as challenges to be solved.
• believes people who get ahead are just lucky.	• feels that people get ahead primarily out of their own efforts and preparation.
• is resistant to change and unwilling to seriously consider other options.	• is open to change and willing to change for a good reason.
• feels career is determined by external circumstances beyond control.	• feels career is determined by personal efforts.
• feels unable to influence own career.	• feels empowered to influence own career.
• is uninvolved in own career development.	• is totally involved in own career development.
• gives little consideration to personal desires in career and life.	• gives serious consideration to personal desires in career and life.
• does not know or investigate the career options available.	• thoroughly investigates the career options available.
• allows others and events to make personal decisions.	• actively makes personal decisions.
• has either no career objectives or sets unrealistic goals.	• sets realistic and achievable career objectives.
• avoids future career planning.	• carefully plans career future.

1. After reviewing the material on the two mindsets, including Table 9.1, determine your self-victimizing and self-empowering traits.

I am like self-victimizers in that:

I am like self-empowerers in that:

2. Rate yourself on the scale below by placing an "X" at the place that best describes your assessment now. Make this assessment based on your current general attitudes rather than your particular mood at this moment.

The Self-Victimizing versus Self-Empowering Scale										
0	*1*	*2*	*3*	*4*	*5*	*6*	*7*	*8*	*9*	*10*
Totally Self- Victimizing		Somewhat Self- Victimizing			A Little of Both		Somewhat Self- Empowering		Highly Self- Empowering	

3. a. What are the main things you learned about yourself in doing this assessment?

b. How do you feel about your assessment?

4. After you have decided where you are currently on the self-victimizing versus the self-empowering scale, decide where you want to be. Go back to the scale now and place a large "G" (for Goal) at the point you really want to be.

5. a. What would you have to change in order to become as self-empowering as you really want to be?

b. Are you willing to make the effort to change?

How to Become Self-Empowering

Fortunately, your place on the self-victimizing versus self-empowering scale results far more from the way you perceive the world currently than the way the world actually is. Your attitudes were not acquired at birth. Instead, they were developed over the years through learning a certain style or bias that continues to influence your thinking and behavior today. Just as your attitudes were acquired through learning, they can also be productively changed through learning.

To become more self-empowering, start changing your self-victimizing attitudes now by working on the following steps:

1. Become aware of your actual attitudes and beliefs involving career choice.

2. Don't allow your behavior to be controlled by your ineffective attitudes. You can accomplish this through good decision making. Make carefully considered decisions. Then carry them out, even though your traditional biases may cause you some initial difficulty.

3. Set productive and accomplishable goals, and complete them. By accumulating minor accomplishments over a period of time, you make a habit of success. In this process, your old self-victimizing attitudes will fade.

4. Acknowledge your successes. Whenever you have a successful experience (big or small), reward yourself. Most people get a perverse kind of payoff in some way from their old self-defeating habits. Acknowledging your successes can help you trade in your negative payoffs for positive ones.

5. Create affirmation statements. Write them out, and place them where you will see them. Repeat them to yourself a number of times. An affirmation statement might be like this: "I am a powerful and effective person. I learn from and am successful in all I do."

Priscilla learned to be a risk taker after becoming self empowered

The Competencies Involved in Career/Life Decision Making

How effective you are as a career/life decision maker is determined both by your mindset and your competencies. A competency is a special skill, expertise, or facility that you have developed through practice over a period of time. For career planning, you will need to have the following five basic competencies:

Self-Assessment

Identification of Options

Goal Selecting

Planning

Problem Solving

The Five Competencies for Making Career/Life Decisions

1. *Self-Assessment*

   This competency is the ability to analyze your career-related attributes, such as your personality style, interest patterns, potentials, needs, and values. It also involves objectively assessing your strengths and weaknesses and being able to see how these influence your career. Knowing yourself is an ongoing life process. The better you come to know yourself, the better able you are to make realistic and satisfying career choices. With poor self-assessment skills, you are unlikely to be able to make realistic career choices.

2. *Identification of Options*

   This competency is the ability to identify available career options. It is one of the biggest problem areas in the career decision process because of the large number of available choices and the scattered sources of information. There are over 20,000 occupations to choose from and over 40,000 different job titles. First, you need to become proficient at acquiring information and data about occupations, including knowing what resources are available and what information-gathering methods work best. Then, you need to get information about the particular jobs available in your chosen field as well as information about the job market in your chosen work location.

3. *Goal Selecting*

   This competency is the ability to select goals or targets that are likely to produce a sense of satisfaction, achievement, and direction. People who have selected meaningful goals experience a sense of purpose, and their goals provide guidance for their careers. If you lack meaningful goals, you are likely to experience frustration and indecision in your life.

4. *Planning*

   Planning involves the ability to translate goals into action plans. Meaningful goals have little value unless you set up realistic action plans to accomplish these ideals. Poor planners avoid planning because it is easier to just dream about reaching certain goals. Good planners envision their desired career goals and devise specific steps to accomplish them.

5. *Problem Solving*

   Problem solving is the capability of handling obstacles that arise in any phase of your career. While you might hope to avoid career problems, this is unrealistic. Incompetent problem solvers will be stopped whenever problems arise. They may give up in such circumstances, look to others to solve the problems, or just wait for things to work out of their own accord. In contrast, competent problem solvers expect such obstacles and develop a facility for approaching problems as challenges and opportunities to use their skills and to learn.

Use the following graphs to assess your current effectiveness in these five career planning competencies. Base your assessment on where you actually see yourself at this point in life rather than where you would like to be or think you should be.

1. Rate your decision making effectiveness below by placing an "X" at the point on each of the five scales that most accurately describes your current level of effectiveness. Use the "Clues for Assessment" to help you decide.

   a. *Self-Assessment (Knowing Yourself)*

   Clues for Assessment:

   - How effectively can you describe your best and most enjoyed talents?
   - How effective are you in describing your career-related interests and values?
   - How effective are you in pinpointing what you really want in a job and in a career?
   - How effective are you in describing the working conditions that most appeal to you?

0	1	2	3	4	5	6	7	8	9	10
Very Ineffective		Somewhat Ineffective			A Little of Both		Somewhat Effective		Very Effective	

   b. *Identification of Options*

   Clues for Assessment:

   - How effectively can you identify kinds of occupations that best match your interest and ability patterns?
   - How effective are you in finding occupational information and using it in your career decision making?
   - How capable are you of developing possible options from your imagination?
   - How familiar are you with current job-market conditions in your field of interest?
   - How effectively can you analyze occupational outlooks for the future?

0	1	2	3	4	5	6	7	8	9	10
Very Ineffective		Somewhat Ineffective			A Little of Both		Somewhat Effective		Very Effective	

c. *Goal Selecting (Knowing What You Want for the Future)*

Clues for Assessment:

- How effectively can you define what you want in a career in the form of specific goal statements?
- How effectively can you define what you want to accomplish in your life?
- How effectively can you use self-knowledge and knowledge of the world of work to develop meaningful goals for yourself?

0	1	2	3	4	5	6	7	8	9	10
Very Ineffective		Somewhat Ineffective			A Little of Both		Somewhat Effective		Very Effective	

d. *Planning (Knowing How to Get to What You Want)*

Clues for Assessment:

- How effectively can you identify specific actions or steps that need to be accomplished to achieve your ideal goals?
- How effectively can you predict possible outcomes of specific actions over a long period of time?
- How effectively do you manage your resources (money, time, energy, etc.)?
- How effective are you at regularly getting the things done that you really need to accomplish?

0	1	2	3	4	5	6	7	8	9	10
Very Ineffective		Somewhat Ineffective			A Little of Both		Somewhat Effective		Very Effective	

e. *Problem Solving (Creating Alternatives as Possible Solutions)*

Clues for Assessment:

- How effectively can you identify the problems that could keep you from accomplishing your objectives or goals?
- How effective are you at foreseeing possible alternatives when obstacles keep you from achieving what you want?
- How effectively can you select those alternatives that make the best sense for you?
- How effective are you at seeing problems as challenges to be solved?

0	1	2	3	4	5	6	7	8	9	10
Very Ineffective		Somewhat Ineffective			A Little of Both		Somewhat Effective		Very Effective	

FIGURE 9.1 Becoming a Star through Career/Life Decision Making

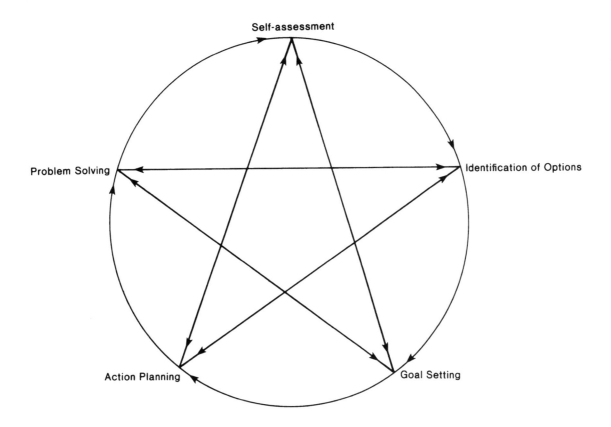

2. After you have decided where you are currently on the five competencies, decide where you want to be. Go back to each of the five scales and place a large "G" (for goal) at the point you want to be.

3. a. From completing the preceding scales, what did you learn about your current effectiveness level in making career/life decisions?

b. What do you see as your main strengths as a career/life decision maker?

c. What do you see as primary problem areas in your current ability to make effective career/life decisions?

Common Situational Barriers

A joke floating around the computer field, where huge projects are commonplace, goes like this. Question: "How do you eat an elephant?" Answer: "One byte (bite) at a time." For most people the process of selecting and reaching a career goal seems as overwhelming as the huge challenge of "eating an elephant." The computer programmer approaches this challenge by acknowledging the whole elephant (goal/design phase) and then programming one byte at a time. Having set your own general career goal, you should now approach the goal one step (or bite, using the elephant comparison) at a time. You can no more get a new career going in "one bite" than you can gulp down an elephant in a single mouthful.

By now, you have already taken several big bites out of your career development elephant. You have selected the kind of occupation you want and developed goals to give definition and direction to your career and your life. That is impressive progress. There are still a number of big bites remaining to make that choice a reality. You have problems to solve, barriers to get over, and actions to take.

By clearly identifying these barriers, you can devise a series of appropriate steps to navigate over, under or around them. Without this kind of awareness, however, your barriers may remain insurmountable roadblocks, leaving your career/life goals in the realm of dreams rather than reality. The previous sections of this chapter have discussed overcoming barriers involving negative mindsets and faulty decision making skills. This section will focus on overcoming career barriers common to situations faced by college students without significant job experience and by career changers.

TABLE 9.2 Common Barriers to Getting Started in a New Career

College Student Preparing for a Career	Career Changer
1. Fear of beginning a career	1. Fear of change
2. Procrastination	2. Procrastination
3. Undefined career identity	3. Lack of support
4. Lack of experience	4. Feeling boxed in by current job stereotypes
5. Establishing competencies for initial job in a chosen career field	5. Establishing credibility and competencies for a job change within a new career field
6. Not knowing what entry-level jobs are available	6. Not knowing what is available
7. Shyness about networking with contacts in the field	7. Shyness about networking with contacts in the field
8. Lack of trust in own ability to make and follow through on personal decisions	8. Relationship conflict about change
9. Inability to visualize job specifics within new field	9. Inability to visualize self working in a new career
10. Lack of job hunting "know how," experience, and tools	10. Lack of an ongoing plan and time frame for making change
11. Lack of self-confidence	11. Poor self-concept or lack of self-confidence
12. Unassertiveness	12. Unassertiveness

Barriers Facing College Students

The barriers facing college students are often related to a lack of working experience. As a member of this group, you may be feeling some fear and concern about getting that first, entry-level job within your career field. Welcome to the club. This is a common "anxiety" with most college students, particularly for liberal arts majors and increasingly for general business majors.

A common response to fear is procrastination, putting off those things you need to do to find out what jobs are available within your new field and then making yourself "marketable." Procrastination has left many students with a college diploma but without the foggiest notion of what to do about an entry-level job. Many students decide to go on to graduate school, not with any clear career goal, but mostly to avoid entering that big, strange world of work. But what do you do after getting a masters degree with no specific career goal? Get a doctorate?

Lack of job and career experience can be a real barrier. A crucial part of career implementation is being able to visualize or mentally picture yourself doing what you want in a work setting suited to your tastes. That can be hard to do if you lack work experience. Yet a clear career image of yourself gives you the kind of self-confidence needed to take the next step and to sell yourself effectively to prospective employers. Lack of a clearly defined career identity, however, can fill you with uncertainty and render you unassertive. The "taking charge process" advocated in this book is incompatible with unassertive behavior.

How do college students demonstrate that they have the capabilities needed to perform effectively in an entry-level career position? Employers have businesses and organizations to run, and they need to hire people whom they can trust to get the job done. That means you are going to have to demonstrate clearly your superior strengths and capabilities for doing the job. If you can't, you are not going to get hired. That may sound harsh—but competition and no-nonsense qualifications are a reality. How to establish your credibility is a problem you must solve if you really want to obtain gainful employment in your field.

If you are a young college student, you should start implementing your own life and career plans now, step by step, to gain more confidence and competence. Unless you are a very unusual student, you have probably been depending upon the help and support of parents or other adults in making your decisions. It's a new ball game now. On one hand, you can no longer rely on others to make and follow through on your most personal career/life decisions. On the other hand, as an inexperienced career and life decision maker, you are afraid to trust your own guidance.

You might be inclined either to avoid decision making or to be reluctant to move ahead with your decision until after graduation. The problem is that unless you start taking effective action on your decision now, it will remain a fantasy.

Another major hurdle to overcome is finding out what kind of entry-level jobs are available and how to prepare yourself for getting hired. This requires researching publications and getting out to talk with people in the field. Finding the necessary time can be difficult when you're struggling to find time to prepare your college assignments, do term papers, prepare for exams, and have a social life. In addition, talking with people in your potential or chosen career field can be scary. It's all too easy, therefore, to put off these activities until tomorrow and tomorrow and tomorrow. The problem with tomorrow is that one of those tomorrows will be graduation. At that point, suddenly getting a decent job and implementing a career will seem like eating that elephant in one gulp.

If this section seems depressing, we're sorry. We wouldn't be doing you a favor, however, by avoiding those "hard realities." The good news is that you can hurdle these barriers if you confront them head on with a realistic plan of action. That will leave you with far more confidence and competence than many other people in your same situation. Remember, everyone who has ever been employed had to start somewhere. The point is that you want to target your entry-level position, not be grateful for anything you can get.

Start clearly identifying your own barriers now by completing Exercise 9-C below. Then read further for ideas and suggestions on "hurdling your barriers" by developing an appropriate plan of action.

Exercise 9-C. COLLEGE STUDENT BARRIERS

Review Table 9.2 on page 203 for the list of common barriers faced by college students, circle any barriers that you believe are particularly pertinent to you, and add others, if necessary. Then list the five barriers below that you are the most concerned about:

1.

2.

3.

4.

5.

Strategies for College Students

Now that you have considered the bad news, the good news is that most barriers can be overcome. In fact, almost every barrier you will ever face is not so much a "bad condition" that exists in the world as it is a "mental state" that exists in your head. The way to overcome barriers is with positive thinking from which you develop a unique, workable plan of action. The following ideas and suggestions are offered to help you get started.

1. Visualize the kind of entry job you want to have and mentally rehearse being in that role. Use the visualization technique described in Appendix D of this book. Give yourself about 20 minutes of quiet relaxed time for this process once a week. The visualization technique is a way to bring the future into the present and reduce fear of the unknown. You can then create a clear picture of what you want so that you know what you are going after. This will decrease your fear and procrastination while increasing your confidence.

2. Gain more confidence about your decision making capabilities by reviewing the steps outlined in Chapter 7 or in additional books on decision making that your librarian can recommend. Your college counseling center may even offer workshops in decision making. Start practicing decision making by looking for all the opportunities available to make decisions and evaluate your performance. When you're in a decision situation, follow the steps in a conscious way, making sure that you both gather and analyze the available facts and draw upon your intuitive powers. Keep in mind that only you have the inner knowledge necessary for making effective decisions. Call on other people for information, ideas and reactions, but don't let anyone else make your decisions for you.

3. Complete your short-term plan from Chapter 8 to achieve your visualized entry-level job. Your plan will probably include information research at a local library, college career center, business or government library, or personnel offices. Your plan might include visits to the college career planning and placement center to discuss job-getting strategies with a career counselor. It might also include activities like networking (conducting information interviews) with people working in your field of interest to learn what those jobs are really like, to see what differences exist in jobs within different settings, to become familiar with businesses and organizations hiring people

in that field, and to get tips on getting hired. Your plan could also call for summer work associated with your field, internships, volunteer work, related club and organization activities, and class projects or assignments that help your learn more about your field.

Setting goals, developing a plan, and following that plan is a strategy for career success. Post your plan in a place where you will see it daily—try a piece of newsprint over your desk. Make notations on your plan, indicating what you did and when you did it as a record of your progress. Discuss your plan and your progress with counselors, faculty, friends, and network contacts. Ask them for ideas and suggestions on steps for achieving your goal, and revise your plan whenever necessary. Your plan will be both your tool for success and anti-fear and anti-procrastination assurance.

Here are some ideas for clarifying your career goals while in college and gaining job-related experience and skills:

1. Use class projects to focus on personal career issues. Term papers can be an excellent way to research subject areas related to your chosen career field and to establish your writing, thinking, and communicating competencies. Consult with your professors about ideas for such projects. A useful research project would involve visiting and communicating with companies and organizations that you want to learn more about and talking with people who are performing work of interest to you. Keep some of your best papers as examples of some work-related skills that can be applied on the job.

2. Visit the college career center to investigate summer jobs, volunteer work, internships, and co-operative education experiences. Summer jobs are excellent opportunities to gain work-related experience in your field and to establish your competencies. Don't take summer jobs just to earn money. Be creative and look for ways to gain experience, self-information, job possibilities, and job recommendations.

   Cooperative educational experience and internships are wonderful opportunities to acquire job-related experiences and to develop your own career identity further. Volunteer work with businesses and organizations related to your field can also be an excellent source of exposure. Perhaps you can include a volunteer work experience as part of a class project or a special study project. You might develop a volunteer project on a career-related activity with a favorite professor. Be sure to ask any employers you have worked for and professors in your field for letters of recommendation. Add these to your job credential file.

3. Take advantage of the numerous clubs, organizations, student government, and work activities available on almost every college campus. If you are thinking about a career in writing, look into opportunities with the college paper. Interested in communications? Check into possibilities with college radio and cable TV stations. Want to become a manager? Investigate possibilities with the college governance board or involvement in a leadership activity with a campus organization. Considering psychology, philosophy, or anthropology? Become active in the clubs associated with these disciplines.

4. Develop your job hunting skills and your awareness of what's available in the job market by reading Chapter 11 carefully. Don't wait until graduation to begin the job hunting process. If you are visionary and creative, you can move through entry-level job preparation in an organized way and even have fun with it. Since the job market is vast, there are always openings available. Start with the career planning and placement office to find out what is available.

Networking is often the most valuable source of job information. How does the shy or unaggressive personality handle networking? Remember that assertiveness can be learned. To become a more confident speaker, take speech classes, practice speaking out in class, and join activities that involve improving your skills. Drama classes and psychology workshops teach assertiveness skills and help you

Louise had difficulty establishing trust with her career counselor

improve your self-confidence. Remember also that you can "feel" unassertive but act in an assertive way.

College Student Case Study

Dick is a big amiable guy with a ready grin and a "laid back" appearance. You soon learn from talking with Dick that he loves to discuss ideas and is a diversified reader, particularly in science-related areas.

Dick comes from a family of professionals. His father is a Ph.D. biologist, and his mother is a chemist. Dick is the youngest child with a brother and sister who have also gone on to become practicing scientists. In comparing himself to his family, Dick always felt intellectually inferior. He was pretty much a "C" student in high school and a bit of a loner. He tried college for a while after high school, but dropped out before finishing his freshman year. He just hadn't discovered anything of interest, and he failed math to further confirm that he wasn't much of a student.

Dick bummed around for a couple of years trying odd jobs here and there, but generally was just drifting along with his life. Eventually, he learned about a career planning class being offered at the local community college and decided to give it a try. In the course, Dick decided that he wanted to be a science writer. He was still concerned, however, about his ability to do college-level work. Dick's counselor helped him see that his barrier wasn't lack of intelligence, but lack of self-confidence. Fortunately, finding a career goal had already given him a big boost over that barrier. This really was the first time Dick had ever felt energized about any kind of goal in his life.

Dick started back to college and was amazed at how well he was doing now that he was motivated by his career goal. He worked diligently, and his efforts paid off. He even found that he could "get" math. He obtained a tutor and worked hard. To his amazement, he now got straight "A's," even in math.

Dick still had some questions about his ability to be a successful student and a science writer. He knew that he had enjoyed creative writing in high school and that he loved science fiction reading. He had some doubts, however, about whether his family would accept him as a "writer," since he assumed they wanted him to follow the family tradition of becoming a scientist.

Dick began talking with his professor about his science writing goal and obtained names of local science writers to contact for information interviews. Dick set up some interesting research papers to do, including one that involved spending a weekend with a yogi who claimed that he could levitate. Dick's eyes really gleam when he talks about this project and what he learned from the yogi, though he didn't actually observe him levitate. Dick's instructor regarded his paper highly and suggested he share it with others. Dick did, and received validating feedback on his developing skills. Dick also arranged to take an anthropology course and write a paper on an archeological dig taking place at the site of an old home in the southern part of the county.

Dick has now completed his A.A. degree at the community college and enrolled in the journalism program at the state university. After his first semester there, he arranged to be a summer research assistant with a university biologist conducting research on bats in southern rural Ohio. Dick was optimistic that the results of this project might produce a significant breakthrough in improving intelligence in human beings. Dick maintained a journal for this project to use it either in a course project or a feature story in the college paper or alumni journal.

Dick is now serving as a writer on one of the university's numerous publications. He also plans to continue conducting information interviews with science writers and to develop his job hunting network during his last year in college. Through his networking so far, he has learned that his chances of getting an initial job with a major paper like the *Washington Post* right out of college are slim, but he has several ideas about getting an entry-level position with a smaller paper. Dick continues to check in with the folks in the career planning and placement office on a regular basis. He is in the process now of adding to his credentials file, refining his resume, and feeling good about himself as a learner, a writer, and a person.

Exercise 9-D. A COLLEGE STUDENT'S PLAN OF ACTION

Using the ideas and suggestions above, develop a plan for how you intend to overcome the specific hurdles you identified in Exercise 9-C, on page 205. Be as specific as you can. Identify real activities that you can and will do to move yourself through your barriers and onto the road to a satisfying entry-level job in your chosen career field.

I plan to take the following actions to hurdle the five barriers I have identified:

Barrier	Action
1.	
2.	
3.	
4.	
5.	

Barriers Facing Career Changers

Have you noticed how many people talk about career change but never do it? By career change, we mean a shift to a different kind of work, often in a totally different field. We know people who are desperately unhappy or bored with their jobs or even on the verge of losing their jobs and yet make no move to improve their situation. Why? Fear of change seems to be the biggest culprit. You may not like the situation you're in, but at least you know what you've got. This fear of change is often disguised with concerns like: "I'm too old to change" or "I've got my family, kids, parents, dog to support" or "I've been a widget technician, lion tamer, tank driver all my life. Who would want to hire one of those?" Procrastination usually goes hand in hand with fear. It's hard to get started on a task you fear. It's much easier to complain about the current situation or to engage in "if only I had done it differently" daydreams.

What is frightening about career change? If you have been at a job for a while, you are probably making a stable salary, with some benefits. Even a bad job provides some structure for your life. Changing careers certainly can involve a significant reduction in income and lost benefits. A career change situation also usually involves uncertainty about one's marketable skills and what they may be worth. People under stress tend to discount their worth and ability to make productive changes. It's unusual for people to be positive, realistic, and optimistic about themselves under such circumstances.

Career changers often find it difficult to obtain much support for making big changes in their life from mates, family, friends, and colleagues. That's particularly true the longer you have been in a career, the older you are, and the bigger your salary and/or benefits. It's often difficult to support yourself without the nurturing support of at least one other significant and trusted person. Career change talk has been known to produce serious conflict in relationships.

Another common barrier faced by the person in a career transition is feeling so boxed in by current work that it is difficult to visualize doing something very different. A person's current job title also makes it difficult for others, particularly prospective employers, to see an employee performing in a very different role. How do you develop a belief that you can do something very different from your current work? How do you establish your credibility and competence for doing a different kind of work?

Next, how do you find out what positions are available, where your prospects are best, and how to make the change? Most people have fallen into their careers as a result of circumstances. Few people really know how to make a career switch and job hunt effectively.

With all of these barriers to career change, it's no wonder that most people feel trapped in their current situation. But does it have to be that way? We think not. Are you feeling so unhappy with your current career that it is hurting your emotional and physical health or your personal development? Unless your distress is connected only with your current job, it's worth making either a career change or career redirection. A career redirection involves remaining in your line of work but negotiating some satisfying changes in your job, such as moving out of supervision and into technical applications, for example. To begin resolving your barriers, however, you first need to know what they are so you can take appropriate action. Take a few minutes now to clarify your specific barriers to career change by doing Exercise 9-E. Next, read further for suggestions and ideas to overcome these obstacles.

Review Table 9.2 on page 203 for the list of barriers to career change. Circle any barriers that might keep you from making a career change. Add any additional barriers to the list which affect your situation. Then list below the five barriers which you feel are most likely to keep you from getting what you want in your career.

1.

2.

3.

4.

5.

Strategies for Career Changers

Here are some ways to overcome negative mindsets and other psychological or emotional barriers:

1. Overcome the barriers of fear and procrastination by making your vision of what you want more vivid than your vision of what you fear. It is impossible to achieve what you really want without knowing clearly what that is. We are not advocating here that you develop some utopian vision, but a realistic picture of where you could use your actual talents more happily. At least twice a week use the visualization process described in Appendix D to imagine the kind of job you want to be doing and to mentally rehearse doing it. The clearer you can make that picture, the more likely you are to actually achieve it. You will be shifting your energy from fear and avoidance of an unknown future into enthusiasm for where you are going.

2. Conquer the lack of support barrier by establishing a support group to help motivate you. Look for people who can really support you, listen to you and provide suggestions, ideas, and feedback. You want the kind of support that will be both honest and constructive. Avoid both pure critics and well-intentioned, but inexperienced supporters who might lead you down a blind alley with naive ideas. Make a contract with your support structure to check in with them on a regular basis. We highly recommend that you seek out the assistance of a professional career counselor to include in your support structure.

3. Prepare in advance for the possibility of conflicts with your spouse, partner, or family over career change. Communication is the key here. Share your vision with your mate and include him/her in the planning as much as possible. Remember also that you have more to bring to a relationship when you are fulfilled in your work than you do when you're unhappy, bored, depressed or feeling blocked, trapped and helpless.

   What do you do if your mate simply is unable to support your change? Some individuals have found it necessary to leave their spouse in order to make the kind of career change needed for a better, fuller life. Their spouse simply could not support the change. Only you know what your situation really is, what your possibilities are, and what decision to make.

4. Make an action plan that becomes your "anti-procrastination" program of specific steps required to transform your vision into reality. See the previous section for college students to get more details on sources of information for this plan. As you clarify your visualized future, make any necessary changes. Post your plan in a spot you will look at often. A prominent spot over your desk is a good place.

To find out about specific job alternatives and market yourself effectively, read Chapter 11. Then consider the suggestions below:

1. Clarify what you really can do in a new career by giving up your current job labels and focusing on your transferable skills along with a vision of what you want. Your goal is to identify specific accomplishments you have achieved in your paid or voluntary jobs that are related to your new career goals. Using the guidance provided in Chapter 11, capture these in concrete terms on your resume.

   Developing your resume in this manner will help you build up your credibility and your competency for your career change both on paper and in your mind. You must do that for yourself before you can ever hope to convince prospective employers of your suitability for a job within a new career field. Also consider approaching prospective employers with a two-page marketing or resume letter instead of a standard resume with cover letter. These letters are often a better strategy for career changers because you can emphasize relevant achievements without calling so much attention to the job titles you have held that are outside the occupation you are targeting.

2. Networking and job hunting effectiveness are vital skills and activities in a career change. Networking is how you find out what's actually available, where you want to work, and how to get hired there. To overcome shyness or unassertiveness barriers that most people experience about networking, consult a career counselor for guidance. Perhaps all you need is a few names to begin your networking, along with a little encouragement. If your confidence is still lacking, practice information interviewing with your friends first. Remember that you can learn to be more assertive, even if you feel shy. Don't use shyness as a reason to avoid getting out and talking to people.

Career Changer Case Study

After a dozen years as a professional hockey player, age caught up with Nels. It was time to look for a different kind of work, but what does an ex-jock do? Nels hadn't been a superstar, so he considered that his days in the limelight were over for good. He had no career preparation, and, as far as he knew, no skills or personal contacts that would qualify him for anything more than a physical labor job. Based on that assumption, Nels felt fortunate to obtain a job as a forklift operator in a food chain warehouse.

After a couple of years of hoisting boxes, Nels decided there had to be more to life than this. The switch from the roar of the crowd to the endless boxes of the warehouse was too great a change for him. But the dilemma remained: what could he do? After an acquaintance told him about a career planning course available at a nearby college, Nels enrolled.

In the course, Nels discovered that he in fact had a number of valuable skills and that his strongest interests were in science and technology. He thought it would be wonderful to be a geologist or a petroleum engineer and search for oil wells. At first Nels rejected the idea flat out. He just couldn't picture an "ex-jock" who had never taken a college course doing that. How could he do all that math? Nels wasn't even sure he could spell thermal dynamics, let alone understand it.

Little by little, however, the idea began to shape into a clear vision in his mind. After numerous sessions with his career counselor and considerable self-assessment, Nels reluctantly did a couple of information interviews with a geologist and an engineer. After these interviews Nels was hooked. He knew he wanted to be an engineer. While he wasn't sure if he could do the college work, he decided "to give it a whack."

A year after taking the course, Nels stopped in to visit his career counselor to ask if there was a follow-up course he could take to verify his career decision. The counselor learned that Nels was getting "A's" in his college course work. His self-doubts came from the lack of support his wife and friends had for his new career decision. They were incredulous that the "ex-jock" was considering something so different like engineering. His counselor was able to reassure him on that score and assist him in finding a way to get the support he needed from his wife and friends.

Nels' career counselor saw him again a year later, when he stopped by the office to share a "breakthrough" success he had achieved. From the contacts established over the past two years, Nels had landed a job as an engineering technician with a petroleum exploration firm. He would be working with and assisting a team of geologists and engineers in the kind of work he had dreamed about. Nels confided that it was only because of his interests, his good grades, and most of all the contacts he had established that he had obtained the job. In fact, he really didn't have the A.A. degree yet that was listed as a job requirement.

Best of all, the company would pay Nels' way to a bachelors degree in engineering after he had been with the firm for one year. Nels was elated. He realized that if he hadn't been willing to visualize himself in this role and then check out the realistic possibilities, he would still be hoisting boxes in the warehouse. True, he would never be in the "limelight" again, but for him, this would be just as good. Nels would be doing interesting work and developing himself in a direction that appears right for his skills and interests.

Career Redirection Case Study

Cheryl came to the "Career Direction" workshop looking for promising alternatives to her career as a nurse. It was not so much that Cheryl disliked nursing, but rather that she was just "burned out" after ten years in the profession. She was tired of waiting on patients and taking orders from doctors. Cheryl just didn't want to do that any more.

In reviewing the data from her career surveys, the career counselor saw that the problem was more than just a career burnout situation. Cheryl's thinking style profile showed her to be a left-brain oriented, logical, and controlling thinker. While Cheryl could be empathetic and feeling, that was just not her strongest suit. She liked technical activities and was good at planning and organizing. Cheryl was introverted and liked to think things through on her own more than to interact with people. She particularly resented following the directives of doctors rather than deciding on her own.

Cheryl discussed alternatives with her career counselor. The problem was that Cheryl had some rigid requirements. She had to maintain her current income level, did not want to lose her benefits, and definitely did not want to go back to college for years as part of a career change program. Based on her situation and the information available, the counselor suggested that Cheryl consider redirecting her career within the health field rather than starting a totally new career.

The health field has enough variety and occupational possibilities to enable one to move away from the service delivery side of nursing and into a more technical specialty. As a technical specialist Cheryl would be able to utilize her top strengths much more fully and would not have to carry out doctors' directives. There were a number of possibilities in the area: computer diagnostics, medical technology, technical consultant, etc. By selecting a career track that would count much of her previous job experience and by taking selected courses, Cheryl could probably maintain her current income while making the switch.

Cheryl was not in a career change situation but rather a career redirection. The career center could only provide limited information on what kinds of jobs within the health area would best utilize her skills, where these jobs were, and how to get them. Cheryl needed to learn specifics and get more strategic advice by conducting information interviews and establishing a network of contacts. She was excited about the redirection possibilities but discouraged about the need for establishing personal contacts with other health professionals, since she tended to be a loner.

But Cheryl went ahead anyway by talking to some of the nursing instructors at the college and a nurse who had held a variety of interesting jobs in the field. Cheryl began to engage herself more fully in the networking task and developed her career redirection plan. She realized that she could not make an immediate change, but at least now she had a goal to follow and was identifying what steps to take to get there. As a side benefit, Cheryl's new goal gave her hope and energy. She was no longer "burned out" as she took charge of developing her career in a more self-fulfilling direction.

Exercise 9-F. A CAREER CHANGER'S PLAN OF ACTION

Using the foregoing ideas and suggestions, develop your plan to overcome the specific hurdles you identified in Exercise 9-E on page 210. Identify specific activities that you can take to move yourself through your barriers. Whenever you can, specify dates for when you intend to accomplish a specific activity.

I plan to take the following actions to hurdle my five major barriers to career change:

Barrier	Action	Date
1.		
2.		
3.		
4.		
5.		

Summary

Successful career/life decision making requires effective attitudes and decision making skills along with methods to overcome situational barriers. Your attitudes largely determine how effective you can and will be in implementing your career choices. People develop characteristic outlooks, some inclining to pessimism and others to optimism. Self-victimizing people are characteristically uninvolved, dependent, and inflexible in the career-choice process.

In contrast, a self-empowering mindset gives yourself permission to think, feel, and know that what you do makes a difference in the outcomes of your life. Self-empowerers tend to be involved in the career-choice process, independent in decision making, and open to compromise in order to achieve the best outcome possible in a particular situation. While it is no simple task to transform a self-victimizing mindset to a more self-empowering inclination, the time and energy involved in making this shift are well worth it.

Career competencies are skills that can be enhanced through learning and practice. Five specific competencies are involved in career/life decision making: self-assessment, identification of options, goal selection, planning, and problem solving.

To overcome situational barriers, such as being a college student with no professional work experience or being an older career changer, you will need current information sources, realistic self-assessments, support groups, action plans, and development of personal contacts.

Assignments

1. Interview three or four people such as your spouse, parents, friends, acquaintances, colleagues, banker, service people, etc., to find out such things as: what kind of work they do, what turns them on and off about their work, how they got into that type of work, whether they would advise anyone else to get into their line of work. As you interview these people, attempt to discover whether they tend to be more self-victimizing or self-empowering about their work. Note: If they are self-victimizing, don't volunteer this opinion. Remember that change has to be initiated by each individual.

2. Questions to ponder:
   a. In what ways might a person with a self-victimizing mindset go about the career-choice process differently from a person with a self-empowering mindset?
   b. In choosing a career, is it more effective to be uncompromising or willing to compromise? Why?
   c. Is it preferable to make your own career-related decisions or to have an expert or knowledgeable person decide for you?
   d. Why might some people prefer to be uninvolved in the selection and implementation of their careers?
   e. In what ways is a person with a self-empowering mindset more likely to have a more satisfactory career than a person with a self-victimizing mindset?

References for Hurdling Your Barriers

James, Muriel and Dorothy Jongeward. *Born to Win.* Boston: Addison-Wesley Publishing, Inc., 1971.
Waitley, Dennis E. *The Psychology of Winning,* a cassette tape series. Chicago, Illinois: Nightingale-Conant Corporation, (n.d.) Contact the publisher at 3730 West Devon Avenue, Chicago, Illinois 60659. Telephone: 1-800-323-5552.

Financing Your Plan

"Money is not an end but a means: a means to help make the most out of ourselves by being able to pay for education, travel, medical care and a worry-free retirement."

MARSHALL LOEB
Managing Editor of Fortune *Magazine*

DO YOU KNOW PEOPLE WHO:

➥ Regularly save a portion of their salary each time they get paid?

➥ Always seem to be scrambling to get their finances in order?

➥ Spend recklessly almost all of the time?

➥ Are living beyond their means?

➥ Have a plan for getting out of debt?

If so, then you know people who approach the issue of finances, or money, from different perspectives.

Now that you have read this book and completed many, if not most, of the exercises, you know that you do have the ability to plan for change. You are empowered with the knowledge of what planful steps to take in order to reach your objectives and goals. Part of that planning includes getting your finances in order to implement your plan.

Attitudes Toward Money

Before we talk specifics of how to finance your plan, let's examine how you view money. Is it a means to an end? For instance, do you hear yourself saying or thinking things like, "I could buy that bike if I had $100." Is money dirty? Perhaps you've heard yourself or someone say something like, "He is filthy rich." Do you have enough money, right now? Would you like to have more? Are you embarrassed by how much or how little you have? Do you recognize having feelings of shame about money?

According to Phil Laut in *Money Is My Friend*, "money is a topic that activates shame for everyone. People are ashamed they have so little or so much and are ashamed that others have so little or so much. When you are ashamed about money, no amount seems right." Your attitude toward money may be limiting your ability to change your financial condition.

PART I

On a separate sheet of paper, list all the fears you have about money.

> *Sample:*
> I'm afraid I'll spend more if I make more.
> I'm afraid I won't have any money at all.
> I'm afraid I'll be viewed as too self-sufficient.
> I'm afraid I'll be expected to take on additional family responsibilities if I have more money.

PART II

After you have listed as many as you can think of, in a symbolic gesture of destroying those fears, tearup, crumple or scratch through them, and throw the paper away.

Eliminate the Fear

Are you afraid of starting or finishing? Are you afraid of succeeding or failing? Are you afraid to take the necessary steps to put your finances in better shape, allowing you to finance your plan? Are you afraid of becoming financially responsible? Are you afraid because you don't know where to start, and you don't know what questions to ask, or whom to go to for advice? Are you afraid you might sound stupid? These fears are not unusual. Everyone has fears of some type. Now is the time to recognize and identify your fears. Acknowledge your feelings, move forward and take that first step to eliminate or manage your fears.

Rather than feeling ashamed about money, you will find it easier to have more money if you accept that what you have now is okay, thereby subconsciously giving yourself permission to take positive action to increase your money reserves.

You do not have to view money as an obstacle anymore. You can change your negative and embarrassed feelings about money into affirmative ones. You might even be surprised to find that you can view money as your friend. It can become a vehicle to help you achieve goals leading to your dream. Now you are ready for some visionary thinking and creative approaches to what you may currently view as financial problems.

To get started, spend some time using your *most creative* energies on the following exercise:[1]

Make a list entitled "Ten ways I can produce an extra $_____ before
_____."

The amount of money and date you use are up to you. As you let your creative energies flow even more, it will become easier to increase the amount of money and shorten the timeframe. Here is an example of a completed statement and a sampling of possible ways to produce the results:

"Ten ways I can produce an extra $50 before the end of the month (sixteen days remain)."

1. Take my lunch two days each week (saves $12 weekly; $24 total).
2. Tune up/adjust neighborhood bicycles ($15 per bike).
3. Provide tutoring for two music students ($12/hr).
4. Work overtime on special project ($30 total).
5. Provide childcare for neighbor one afternoon ($25).

From the five possibilities shown, you can see that more than the required amount of money would be reached within the timeframe.

Now that you have your creative energies flowing, let's move along, taking positive steps toward financing your plan. Are you ready to begin?

Principles of Financial Planning or Financing Your Plan

Some of the same principles used in financial planning also apply to the idea of financing your plan. There are certain sound steps to take to protect your money and make it grow.

FIGURE 10.1 Three Straightforward Steps to Follow
1. Get out of debt as soon as you can.
2. Save regularly by paying yourself first.
3. Make a plan to reach your goal.

What do these mean? Step 1 means just what it says: get out of debt. Start paying cash for your purchases; stop using your "plastic" money. In fact, cut up your credit cards. Sometimes it takes such drastic action to make certain that you adhere to your plan. Of course, you could also benefit by establishing a budget to follow so that you could easily see where you could cut back on your expenses.

Step 2 means pay yourself just as you would pay your utility bill. However, you should pay *yourself* first; that way you will be certain to adhere to your plan. This is a good way to see your savings grow. If it helps, use automatic deduction for savings at your bank or make out a bill statement with your name on it including the amount of money you intend to pay yourself (save). This will help you visualize the concept of paying yourself first.

Step 3, making a plan to reach your goal, actually is building on the goal setting technique you learned from Chapter 8. Now you are applying these skills to a new area of your life. By writing out your goals and objectives, you will be able to see when you have accomplished each one.

While we do not claim to be experts in the matter of financial planning, we do hope that we can plant some ideas for you to explore in further detail in other printed resources devoted to this topic. Although the resources listed in Table 10.1 don't include all the possibilities, these we found particularly interesting and helpful.

TABLE 10.1 Financial Planning Resources: Annotated List

Marshall Loeb's Money Guide, by Marshall Loeb (Boston: Little Brown and Company, 1994). This very factual, straight forward and easy-to-understand book covers such topics as personal finances, investments, home, taxes, IRAs, savings, borrowing, education and career, insurance, retirement, and security. Loeb discusses a multitude of details in concise sections that get right to the heart of the issue.

Money Dynamics for the New Economy, by Venita Van Caspel (New York: Simon & Schuster, 1986). Van Caspel, recognizing that we are faced with a new economy based on knowledge rather than mass-production of goods, highlights the opportunities that the new economy will provide for investing. Individual sections address such topics as inflation, real estate, tax savings, investing, insurance and retirement, all as they are impacted by the new economy.

Terry Savage's New Money Strategies for the 90's: Simple Steps to Creating Wealth and Building Financial Security, by Terry Savage (New York: Harper Collins Publishers, Inc., 1993). Savage shows you how to make your money grow through saving and investing. She offers advice on how to set goals, get motivated, and put your plan into action.

Money Is My Friend, by Phil Laut (New York: Ballantine Books, 1989.) Laut examines the opportunity to make money through the pleasure principle and recognizes the obstacles that impede people: guilt, fear, pressure and feelings of helplessness. This book helps you examine your attitudes toward and feelings about money, an appropriate precursor to taking steps to increasing your money reserves.

Head & Heart: A Woman's Guide to Financial Independence, by Susan Weidman Schneider and Arthur B.C. Drache with Helene Brezinsky (Pasadena: Trilogy Books, 1991). These authors discuss issues such as insurance, salary and benefits negotiation, investing, taxes and retirement within the context of predictable life-cycle events that shape or alter women's lives: moving out of a parent's home, getting a job, marrying, having and raising children, handling divorce, caring for your own aging parents, and widowhood. The factual information is presented without ignoring the emotional side of situations with which you may be coping.

Setting Your Goals

Are you ready to implement your plan now or within the next five years? Or is your goal five to ten years in the future? Or longer? You have to determine at what point in time you need your financial resources assembled and have a reasonable idea of how much money will be required.

Does achieving your goal require that you get new skills or additional education? Since this is often the case in a knowledge/service-based economy, let's look first at how to go about financing your new training and education. The following case study shows one path to success.

Case Study—Karen

Karen attended a small, liberal arts college and majored in psychology. Realizing that job opportunities in her field without an advanced degree were scarce, Karen went to the career center her junior year to seek volunteer opportunities for the summer. She found a volunteer position in the adolescent wing of a mental hospital well-known as a teaching facility. She commuted sixty minutes twice a week, without fail, in her ten-year-old car. At the end of the summer she received rave reviews from both clients and staff. The next spring when Karen graduated, a full-time clinician position on the staff became available. From the hundreds of applicants, most with higher GPA's than Karen's, she was selected. As justification for hiring her, the staff singled out Karen's dependability and high performance as a volunteer.

After one year in the clinical position Karen was encouraged to pursue a graduate degree in social work. Her plan was to become a licensed clinical social worker (LCSW) so that she could establish a private practice doing therapy with adolescents. She applied to and was accepted at the state university school of social work. She began her social work program as a part-time student while continuing to work full-time as a clinician. Karen curtailed her eating out almost completely, jogged or rode her bike to work when she could, and convinced her two roommates that there was room in their two bedroom apartment for three by converting the laundry room into a third bedroom. In this way she hoped to save enough money along with low interest loans to attend school full-time.

She resigned from the clinician's job that summer and attended school full-time in the fall. Despite her best efforts at economizing, Karen realized about halfway through the year that she would need another source of income. She saw a help wanted ad in the career center for a step aerobics instructor. Karen had always been physically active since high school, playing tennis, softball, racquetball and jogging on a regular basis. Although she had never done step aerobics, she purchased a video and learned the techniques on her own. She put together a routine and passed the test the fitness center required of all new instructors. They hired her, and she was able to finance the rest of her way through graduate school by leading step aerobics classes.

Financing Your Immediate Education and Training Objectives

Are you ready to get started *now* on your plan by taking some training or pursuing a college course of study? If you have not done any previous planning for your future training or education, then you will have to rely on immediate applications for scholarships, grants or loans. There may not be enough time to do any serious investing to generate growth of principal and interest. However, if you are in a position to cut back on your everyday expenses, and if you have some discretionary funds, then you can do some serious saving to help reduce the size of loan you will have to borrow in year one of your education.

The following is a list of sources that can be tapped for funds to help pay for training/education without the benefit of having done future financial planning.

- *Federal grants*
- *Scholarships*
- *Federal student loans*
- *Employer-paid tuition*
- *Co-operative education*
- *Personal bank loans*

Scholarships

An often overlooked, or underplayed, souce of aid that can be applied for in a fairly immediate time frame is scholarships. These are frequently available—the applications, that is—on a short turn-around basis, depending on what the "open season" is for any given scholarship. These may fit very nicely into your immediate education financing plans.

Many local organizations provide scholarships, and more than we realize, scholarships are left unclaimed due to lack of applicants. Just as the saying goes for the lottery, "you gotta play to win," so also must you apply for any scholarship to find out if you are the winner. Civic groups may offer scholarships based on academic potential, career goals, or some combination of the two. Athletic ability, artistic or musical talent, or service to community may be the basis for selection. Churches may offer scholarships for their members who plan to attend college.

Contact some of your local clubs and organizations to explore what scholarship opportunities they may have for you. Some organizations you might contact include the local Jaycees, Civitan, Rotary Club International, The Lions Club, Chamber of Commerce, Soroptomist, a local chapter of the National Organization for Women, and YMCA, to name a few. Colleges frequently offer scholarships as well. It is worthwhile to contact the Financial Aid Office at the college you plan to attend to get detailed information about the particular scholarships, the eligibility criteria, and the application deadlines.

Goal Setting with Finances

Another method of financing your education or training might include attending a community or local college first if your goal is to earn at least a bachelor's degree. You might choose to live at home, attend the local or community college, earn as many credits as possible, and then transfer to the four-year college or university of your choice.

Let's look at examples of an immediate, short-range goal, and the related plans for financing. Then let's look at a medium-range goal and the different plans for financing it that can come into play.

Immediate/short-range goal: This Fall '96, I will begin working toward my A.A. degree in business administration by registering for two courses.

Plan for Financing:
1. Determine how much tuition, fees, books, supplies, and transportation will cost per semester. (How much will I need to get started?)
2. Evaluate my current income against my current bills to determine how much undesignated income is left to save.
3. Develop a budget to follow, including a regular payment to myself.
4. Open a savings account and commit to depositing the amount established per my budget.
5. Read and become familiar with federal aid eligibility criteria so I will know how to apply when the time comes.

Medium-range goal: By Fall '99, I will transfer to the university to earn my Bachelor of Science in accounting.

Plan for Financing:
1. Evaluate my current income against my current bills to determine where I can cut back.
2. Develop a budget to follow, including a regular payment to myself.
3. Open a savings account and commit to depositing the agreed-upon amount each time I get paid.
4. Discuss alternative saving methods with my bank's personal financial planning consultant for higher interest earning potential.
5. Explore non-bank savings and/or investing opportunities that will be feasible within a timeframe of six years (approximately).

Planning for Ten Years Out and Beyond

Planning for ten years into the future may seem too long- range right now, kind of dream-like, as if you are looking through a vaseline-covered glass that causes everything to appear blurry. But, if you have a goal of becoming something in particular, such as "I've always dreamed of being an architect," or doing something specific, such as "I've always wanted to be in business for myself," then you *can* make a plan to help you achieve your dream. A plan with objectives for achieving your goal just breaks things into manageable chunks and allows you to see that you are making progress towards accomplishing your goal. This is particularly important when it comes to finances since the plan for your future invariably will require spending or investing money. You will have to know how to acquire the most that you can by the time you want to implement your goal.

What if your long-range goal does not specifically include education but does involve opening up your own business? There still are steps you can identify, intermediate objectives, to help you reach your goal.

Long-range goal: By 2006, I will open my own bicycle shop.

Plan for Financing:

1. Talk with a personal investment consultant to map out a plan for investing, starting immediately, with a sum that the consultant and I agree upon.
2. Research the requirements for opening a private-sector small business with the county and state economic development offices.
3. Write out my strategic plan: here is what I want to do, who is the target market, where will my business be located and why (supporting market research data), how much money I have available up front, and a cash flow analysis.
4. Talk with my bank to find out my options for a loan when the time comes.
5. Explore joining associations related to my field of interest; join those that I can early on rather than waiting until I am in the business.

If your goal involves starting your own business or pursuing a dream you've had, then you may be inspired by this case study of Mike and how he plans to fulfill his goal of becoming his own boss.

Case Study—Mike

"To me, risk equals success." What a powerful and insightful statement. This said by Mike, a single man in his late thirties, who has just given his notice of intent to leave his computer support position. He gave three months notice so that he would still have the opportunity to accumulate sufficient funds to live on over the next four months while he goes to commercial diving school.

Mike is one of those action-oriented, "school of hard knocks" learners. He was basically bored with school, with the standard approach to teaching and learning, so he never stayed with education long enough to get a college degree. He did get computer training in the U.S. Air Force and parlayed that into a career field that he could excel at for as long as he wanted to. He considered computers his "fall back position" while he pursued his other interests. And he has returned to the field of computers several times. In Mike's own words, he is "driven to dream chase" and turn dreams into goals.

Mike fears almost nothing so is willing to try almost anything. He tries out something by doing it the same way someone else would research it, test it in theory, talk with others about it, and then give it a try. He thrives on risk and adventure where someone else would recoil in fear. According to him, change keeps him young and active.

His dream that he is chasing now, and which he believes is an attainable goal, is to purchase land for a bed and breakfast or small resort on a lake. He calculated he could make three times his current salary as a commercial diver, enabling him to save more quickly the necessary amount of money to make his purchase. He has given himself six to seven years to work as a diver before he will leave that and then go to culinary school. He also likes to cook and has experience as an assistant chef. He wants to have all the necessary training and certifications to help him achieve his goal and be successful at it.

How did he reach his decision? He quickly made four statements: he liked diving; he wanted to be "comfortable" by the time he was 50; he wanted to be his own boss; and he wanted to follow his own goals, not the company's goals.

You see, he has a plan, a goal, and a dream to follow.

The case study of Mike is an example of someone who has a goal of owning his own business, of being entrepreneurial, without pursuing a formal education. Mike is, however, financing diving school, so further training for new skills is involved. Meanwhile, he is capitalizing on skills that he already has.

Ten Tips For Starting Your Own Business

Here are ten tips for starting your own business that were offered by one of our associates who does this type of consulting with individuals who are setting up their own businesses.

1. Do a cash flow analysis. Project a monthly cash flow for at least a half year. Project cost for capital purchase, utilities, rent, payroll, payments, interest, etc. Bottom line: you should be able to fund expenses for six months without any income to feel confident that you are not under-capitalized.

2. Be conservative in your calculations. Assume you will be in business for six months without any income coming in to the business. Will you be able to survive?

3. Two simultaneous activities that will be beneficial to your business are the following:

    a. establish a good relationship with a bank and/or banker

    b. line up a relatively inexpensive but competent attorney and accountant.

    (In the first instance, this will serve you when you need more money or someone to back you. In the second instance, your taxes and withholding will be handled by professionals and done correctly. These areas are usually too complex for an individual just starting out.)

4. Engage in a strong campaign to reach out to associations. They can become a wealth of contacts, support, resources, and other help. Associations are interested in recruiting you as a member and would not see you as competition, as perhaps would a comparable small business owner across town.

5. Reach out to the small business administration (SBA), county and state economic development corporations, and incubator programs. Tap into their business expertise; don't just go after the funding that might be available.

6. Take into account what technology may do to the field in which you are opening your business. How will continued advances in computers and the information superhighway affect what you are trying to do? Computerize from the very beginning.

7. If you are going to hire employees, the very first ones MUST be implicitly trustworthy. You can not be diverted with personnel problems right from the beginning.

8. Do you have the entrepreneurial mindset and spirit? Remember, you can count on at least an eighteen-hour day, seven days a week for the first year, in order to get your business on solid footing.

9. Start out small. Save ten to twelve percent of any profit and reinvest it into the business. Operate on a shoestring for two to three years.

10. Have a blast being your own boss! Remember you're in this so that you can march to your own drum!

Planning for the Unexpected

We know that no one likes to think that he or she will be out of work for any period of time, but the reality of the world of work these days is that there is a good chance you will be without a paycheck at some time. This may in fact be due to your choosing to leave one job and look for another, or it may be due to a downsizing, leaving you looking for just the right fit with another employer. Whatever the circumstance, it is a good idea to have a "transition fund" set up to cover the times when you are between jobs. A transition fund can simply be a savings account that is designated for those times when you need a cushion to fall back upon. You can establish this fund at your bank or credit union and have it handled as a payroll deduction perhaps, to make it as easy as possible to save on a regular basis every time you are paid. No, don't keep it in a big glass jar or under the mattress. Besides, your money won't earn any interest there.

Any idea how much is recommended to keep in this "transition fund"? In order to calculate the amount of money you should minimally aim for, add up your monthly expenses (mortgage or rent, utilities, food, consumer credit, etc.) and multiply by three. Three months worth of cash reserves! It sounds simple enough to do on paper, but in reality this can be a tough order to fill. Bank officers recommend establishing a cash reserve of six months because all too frequently people's expectations fall short of what is actually the case. When people expect that they will need only three months of reserves, too often they find that what they really need is six months of reserves to get them through the transition.

Are you prepared to establish a goal of how much cash you want in this special fund and commit to depositing the requisite amount of money each payday? You might refer to this as your "peace of mind account," as you will certainly feel a sense of relief when you have reached your goal.

Saving for Retirement

It's well documented that the earlier you can start saving for retirement, the better off you will be. Although it may be difficult to picture planning for your retirement when you are in your early twenties, that is the most beneficial time to get into the habit of saving. The more years you have to let your savings earn interest, or your investments grow, the larger the sum of money you will have at the time of retirement.

For instance, assume you want to retire at age 62. If you can sock away $5,000 a year in a tax-deferred account that produces ten percent, you'll have one million dollars, as long as you start by the age of 31. If you wait until you are 41 years old, then you will have only $300,000. (See the dramatic impact waiting ten years can have on the final dollar figure?) And, if you wait until you are 51 years old, you will have less than $100,000.[2]

An adequately financed retirement can give you the flexibility to pursue leisure interests that you may not have much time for otherwise. You can start a new career without being overly concerned about the compensation, or make contributions to others or society in the forms of time and money. Actually, "retirement" isn't an adequate term anymore, at least not in the sense of how older people (parents and/or grandparents) viewed it. It is possible that you may have fully one-third of your life to live and enjoy after you "retire." That's a significant amount of time to make your mark, other than who you were in your career, through self-expression and contributions. Some people have reported these "retirement" years to be the best years! This may be reason enough for you to include retirement savings in your goal setting for your finances. It will be worth the effort.

Summing it All Up

Planning for change and transition and setting goals are important components of financial planning and financing your plan. As one banker pointed out, goal setting is *most important*.

Define what your goal is and then develop a road map to help you get there. Begin as early as you can. Nothing beats "a good 'ole" savings account. In fact, as much as things change, that is one factor that hasn't changed much at all. Keep a positive attitude toward your finances and cash reserves. Think of money as your friend, a means to help you achieve your goal. Go for the gold!

Notes

1. Phil Laut, *Money Is My Friend* (New York: Ivy Books, 1989.)
2. Source: "Big Money: Saving For Retirement," The Washington Post Business Section, May 25, 1994.

11 Getting Yourself Hired

. . . there is always someone in the market place who wants to buy your special talents. All you have to do is to let enough people know about the merchandise that is available.

CARL R. BOLL
Executive Jobs Unlimited

DO YOU KNOW PEOPLE WHO:

➡ Need a job but are so anxious about job hunting that they just can't seem to get started?

➡ Can get a job any time they want because they know what they have to offer and are self-confident and assertive?

➡ Just don't know how to get a job or make a job change?

➡ For "security," stay with a job they hate or have outgrown?

➡ Find security by remaining open-minded and flexible enough to make successful job changes when necessary?

If so, you have seen the difference between self-victimizing, reluctant job seekers and self-empowered, effective job seekers.

Great Jobs and Barriers

This chapter assumes that you have developed a clear career goal, gotten whatever education or training you need, and are now ready to find and obtain a great job. Incidentally, we define a great job as one that lets you fully use your top interests and skills to perform a valuable service and rewards you with both personal satisfaction and a good income.

Most of us find getting the right job one of life's most difficult challenges. Perhaps the main reason is that we aren't sure how to conduct an effective job hunt. It's also true that after hearing so much about employment problems, we're afraid there isn't much available out there. We feel inclined just to keep what we have or take any available job. Fear about job hunting limits our effectiveness and may keep us from going after those really great jobs.

This chapter is designed to help you break through your own job barriers and those created by our country's incredibly rapid change. Thousands of traditional jobs in manufacturing are disappearing while thousands of new service and high-tech jobs are being created and added to the job market. You are likely to be changing jobs and careers many times in your lifetime. By reading this chapter carefully and doing the work involved, you will become an effective, confident job hunter. Even better, you'll discover that getting a good job becomes a problem-solving game. Playing the "getting hired" game can actually be fun—and can be far more rewarding than Monopoly!

Understanding the Getting a Job Game

To play the game effectively, you need to understand the game board—that is, the job world. Picture this world as a market and yourself as a product. William Cohen sums it up well in the statement, "Job hunting is a sales situation. You are the product. Your prospective employer is your customer."[1] You are in great shape, however, because you have mastered the most important task in the game of salesmanship—you understand the product. The work you have accomplished in self-understanding gives you a tremendous advantage over the competition. Most other job searchers out there don't know what they are selling to whom, or even that they are in a sales game.

It's helpful to think of the job world as being two markets—the visible and the hidden. Job openings in the visible job market are listed in places like classified ads and on college placement office job lists. In contrast, the hidden job market is a whole world of jobs and potential jobs that are never listed anywhere.

Outside of knowing the product (you), knowing the difference between these two markets is the second most important piece of information you need to become an expert in the "getting hired" game. Job hunting experts like Richard Bolles (*What Color is Your Parachute?*) and Tom Jackson (*Guerrilla Tactics in the Job Market*) tell us that only about ten to twenty-five percent of the available jobs at any one time are ever listed anywhere. In other words, fully seventy-five to ninety percent of the jobs are hidden!

While you shouldn't ignore advertised openings in the visible job market, we advise most job hunters to focus on this hidden job market. Why? First, the hidden job market is where the greatest number of opportunities lie. And second, you will encounter less competition and less rejection in the hidden job market. Since most of our nation's job seekers are going after ten to twenty-five percent of the jobs, there are usually huge numbers of applicants for every listed job. So to play the "getting hired" game effectively, you need to address all those opportunities awaiting you in the hidden job market.

In his book, *Guerrilla Tactics in the Job Market,* job hunting specialist Tom Jackson provides us with a good idea of just how big the hidden job market is. Jackson informs us that over 400,000 employers in the United States employ more than fifty workers.[2] Almost every employer this size has current or potential openings caused by people quitting, about to quit, being asked to resign, retiring, or expiring. Additionally, millions of new jobs are created every year in this country—even in times of recession, downsizing, and corporate re-engineering. What this means is that in almost any area of the country, there are thousands of job opportunities awaiting you right now. But you are going to have to be creative in finding them because the great majority of them are not readily apparent.

At first, tapping the visible or traditional job market may seem like the easiest way to get a good job. You would answer a few classified ads each week, check in with one or two employment agencies, and perhaps mail out your resume to a list of employers you find in the Yellow Pages. Unfortunately, if you are a recent college graduate, a returning worker, or a career changer, you're not likely to get many acceptable job offers from these traditional approaches.

The visible job market best accommodates job seekers with training and experience in "high demand" job slots and those with special skills for which there is an urgent need. For example, the traditional approach can be effective for an experienced nurse, a computer systems analyst, or fund raiser who wants to make a job change (but not a career change). Otherwise, the visible job market offers you few alternatives, heavy competition, and a distorted, negative view of available opportunities. In a large organization a classified job ad typically gets several hundred responses, including responses from highly experienced people. While this situation may change in the years ahead with fuller implementation of interactive world-wide job data bases and electronic resumes, this is not a viable strategy for the great major of normal job seekers at this time.

As a 58-year-old career changer, Ralph had learned how to network with a younger crowd

Employment agencies can be another dead end. Private employment agencies stay in business by charging a high fee, even though their service is often just handing packets of resumes to prospective employers. If the employer pays the fee, he or she expects a well-qualified candidate with significant experience. Many employers won't use state employment agencies because they don't want to be inundated by massive numbers of job seekers, nor fee-based agencies because they can find people easily enough in today's highly competitive job market. If, however, you do consider using a fee-based agency, see whether they will guarantee to find you a job that fits your qualifications and meets your salary requirements. We haven't found one yet that does this. But again, if you have high demand skills, you may wish to consult with a service that specializes in placing individuals with your specific competencies.

For most people, a job-hunting strategy that concentrates primarily on the hidden job market improves the odds of being successful at the "getting hired" game.

Choosing Your Strategy

Here is the situation as you prepare to engage in the "getting hired" game. There are dozens, perhaps hundreds, or even thousands of employment opportunities in the vast playing grounds of the hidden job market that are well matched to your skills and motivations. They need people who can and want to perform the work necessary for the success of their business or organization. Their profits, the quality of their goods or service, the attainment of their "bottom lines," their future viability are dependent upon hiring people with the right match of skills, knowledge, personal attributes, and motivation. But the employers with these great jobs don't know that you are out there or what you can do for them. They would often welcome potential employees coming forward and identifying themselves. This saves them the expense of agencies or advertising and time lost in the job listing, interviewing, and hiring process. The bad news, of course, is that unless you assertively play the game with the right players, you won't find these unadvertised positions.

So your task in the game is to decide which employers you might really want to work for and to show them directly that you are the right person for the job. The great thing about this game is that every player can win. All you have to do is follow the steps and play the game assertively and skillfully. Figure 11.1 outlines the steps involved in the game. Whenever you are ready, start the game—it's your move!

1st Move—Know Your Product

Effective salespeople realize that to be successful they have to know and really like their product or service. Imagine trying to sell a car to someone when you can't quickly and accurately tick off a list of its best features or answer the customer's questions. Can you see yourself attempting to sell a product you don't believe in or personally care about? How convincing will you be, and how likely are you to make a sale?

Like it or not, when you're in the job hunting game, you're in a sales situation. What's true in selling a product or a service is equally true in selling yourself. By completing the earlier exercises in this book, you have already learned about yourself, the product in the "getting hired" game. You know your unique features, your skills, interests, needs, and values. Now you need to verbalize, summarize, promote, and answer questions about them—with enthusiasm! Your customers (potential employers) need to understand what your product/service can do for them. In this regard imagine yourself as a highly desirable product/service that customers are anxious to buy and can benefit from. When you can do this you will be much more effective in selling your talents to the right customers, for a fair price (we're talking salary here!).

FIGURE 11.1 The Getting Hired Game

1st Move Know your product	**2nd Move** Assess the product and market	**3rd Move** Develop sales tools
10th Move Complete the game and enter the winner's circle	**Winner's Circle Rewards** • Great job • Work satisfaction • Useful contribution • Positive self-concept • Good salary	**4th Move** Identify employment targets
9th Move Assess your offers		**5th Move** Design and kick off sales campaign
8th Move Get attractive job offers	**7th Move** Prepare for job interviews	**6th Move** Create a support group

Exercise 11-A. SELLING YOUR PRODUCT

1. Review your preferred functional skills, your top self-management skills, and interests along with your needs, values, and goals.

2. Make a list of your best attributes as if you were a service you were preparing to sell for a profit. Decide what things are most unique about your service. Why would a customer (employer) want to purchase your service?

3. Gather a few friends or acquaintances together and assign them the role of potential customers (employers) for the product you're selling. Practice your selling skills with them by relating your career sales pitch to your top personal attributes. Wherever possible, point to selected personal accomplishments that demonstrate the kinds of skills and motivations you are selling. Have your friends and acquaintances ask searching questions about what you can do for their organization and why you would want to work at such an activity. Practice really liking your product/service and learn to sell what you can do for an organization with genuine enthusiasm. Ask for honest feedback from the group and use their evaluations to improve your product knowledge and salesmanship. Switch roles after one session to get a dual perspective. Ask questions, observe their responses, and adopt anything of value.

2nd Move—Assess the Product and Market

For your next step in the "getting hired" game, remember this critical point—*don't sell your product/ service to the wrong customer.* Think of the mistake it would be to sell an elegant car to someone who just wants any old car as long as it will perform. This valuable car would soon deteriorate into junk. You want to sell yourself to the employer who values what you have to offer, uses your services appropriately, and treats you with the respect you deserve. In doing this, we do not advise the kind of misplaced self-confidence that translates as cocky or obnoxious behavior. We do advise that you present yourself as someone special—because you are! However, it's up to you to clearly and specifically show how you are special and to do that in job-related terms.

As a self-empowered job seeker, the responsibility of getting your product/service to the right customer is up to you. In contrast, self-victimizers take any job they can get and then gripe about being neither appreciated nor satisfied. Your Second Move is to decide what kind of customers (employers) you want to sell your services to and what you are best equipped to do for them. You'll also want to begin assessing what your product/service is worth in the current job market. Begin by posing these questions:

1. What markets (employers) have the greatest need for your services? (See Exercise 11-A)

2. What are the most valuable benefits you can bring to each type of employer? What past accomplishments prove that those benefits are real?

3. What should your product sell for (reasonable market salary for the service you can deliver)?

When you've found answers to these questions, you will be able to decide which kind of employers to target in your job sales campaign. Think of this as exactly the same kind of task that successful business people perform when they have a product or service to sell.

To help with your product/market assessment, here are some more specific questions to consider:

1. What kinds of people would benefit the most from your service (young or old, uneducated or well educated, male or female, majority or minority, etc.)? Note: All employers, including the government, are in business to sell or provide a service to certain kinds of people. Identifying the people you are most interested in serving and best prepared to serve could help you target those employers who cater to these populations.

2. What kinds of employers (businesses and organizations) would find your services most useful? (If, for example, you are a gifted idea person, then companies who need bright, innovative people could best use your skills—advertising agencies, political campaign offices, sales and marketing departments, fund-raising organizations, etc.)

3. What causes might your product (your talents, energies, values, and interests) best serve? Do you have a strong desire to improve the efficiency of the transportation system, clean up the environment, conserve energy, improve people's health and longevity, create more beautiful cities, etc.? What kinds of organizations deal in some way with the cause you most want to serve? (If, for example, your cause is to improve people's health, you might consider the opportunities available with health food stores, hospitals, wellness centers, government and world health organizations, athletic coaching staffs, sports programs, etc.)

To help you define characteristics of target employers further, answer these questions.

1. In what geographic location (city, locality, etc.) do you most want to work? What area might have the greatest demand for your services?

2. What size of business or organization do you want to work for? What size of organization is most likely to need your services? Do you want to work with a business with interests and concerns that are local, national, or international? Do you have foreign language skills that might be of service in an international firm, or computer competencies to bring to an employer in need of enhancing their capabilities? Examples: A young college graduate sold his computing knowledge to a printing company in the process of transitioning from a manual to an auto-mated operation. A mid-life career changer sold his computing expertise to a travel agency in need of enhancing its data accessing and reporting capabilities.

3. What kinds of products or services do you want your employer to be associated with (potato chips, computers, plumbing repair, counseling, electronic equipment, bakery goods, daycare cen-ters, toys, family therapy, financial information, etc.)? *Suggestion:* Review the index or table of contents to the Yellow Pages of a city telephone directory for product and service ideas.

4. Do you have a preference for working with a profit or nonprofit business or organization? Would you get a greater sense of satisfaction working for an organization or business that was com-mitted to maximizing profits or one devoted to providing valuable service to people or the environment?

5. What kinds of activities do you want your work associates to be doing? What people would find your skills and interests most useful? What kinds of businesses or organizations would employ those people? (For example, a high Holland Code "C" person with wonderful organizing skills who enjoys being around creative people might be able to create order out of chaos for a grow-ing electronics firm, a group of architects, or artists.)

Exercise 11-B. DEFINING IDEAL EMPLOYERS

1. After considering the above questions, make two lists to help you assess where your job-related skills and attributes can best be marketed. Entitle the first list "Types of Organizations" and the second, "Characteristics of an Ideal Organization."

    Under the first heading, develop a list of at least ten (preferably 20 or more) types of organiza-tions that you would both enjoy working for and where your abilities could be in demand. Use the index of a city Yellow Pages directory for general ideas, but be sure to make the categories as specific as possible. Entries like electronic sales companies or educational institutions are too general to be useful.

    Under your second heading, "Characteristics of an Ideal Organization," list those things that are important to you in an ideal job setting. List ten or more items under this heading.

Sample entries might look like the following:

What I'm looking for in an ideal employment situation

- an accounting firm
- a computer software salkes company
- a conservation consulting firm
- a men's clothing factory
- public broadcasting company
- an arts dealership
- a dude ranch
- a children's toy sales company
- a sports outfitting firm
- a primary daycare center

- medium-sized city in NW, USA
- company size of 50–100 employees
- community involved business
- associates knowledgeable about science and high technology
- equal opportunity employer
- team oriented leadership
- company with Asian operations
- location under a ten mile commute
- profit-making organization

---

a. After completing your two lists, prioritize the first one to identify your "top three" employer types. That narrows down the employers you're targeting to a manageable few categories. You will use these categories later to compile a list of specific employment targets.

b. Rank your "Characteristics of Organization" list, identifying the top five preferred traits. These specific characteristics will also help you find appropriate employment targets.

c. Print your two prioritized lists and post them near your work or "thinking" space as an ongoing reminder of what you aiming for.

2. After developing your two prioritized lists, create a mental picture of your ideal employment site through the envisioning process described in Appendix D. The purpose of this part of the game is to create a mental picture of the kind of work setting that fits your career objectives. Repeat this envisioning process once or twice each day until you get a clear mental picture of yourself working in your ideal job site. This will give you an intuitive sense of what to look for and where to look for it.

3rd Move—Develop Your Sales Tools

Your sales tools are the means by which you make potential employers aware of and interested in your product. You will need to develop four different tools to play the "getting hired" game. They are your resume, your personal sales letter, your networking skills, and your job interviewing skills.

The personal sales letter, networking, and job interviewing skills will be discussed later in the chapter. For now we will concentrate on the first sales tool you should develop—your resume. Your resume serves two important functions. First, preparing your resume causes you to clarify your career goal and your best and most salable attributes. A good resume also identifies selected accomplishments and relates these to the type of work you are seeking. Here your transferable skills need to be clearly and concisely revealed.

Keep in mind that your resume serves first and foremost as a tool of *career self-definition* and secondly to help potential employers assess how closely your qualifications match their needs. But—a resume alone won't get you a job. Jobs are obtained through interviews! Usually it's your networking efforts, sales letters, and telephone calls that produce interviews. A well prepared resume can help get job interviews by assisting your "targeted" employers in summarizing pertinent information about you. And, conversely, a poorly done resume will sabotage a job-search campaign.

Because there is so much information, good and bad, readily available on resume writing, we will not go into detail here. A number of excellent resume writing resources are listed at the end of this chapter, and we also encourage you to consult with your local library or bookstore.

As you develop your resume, we recommend that you keep these five guidelines in mind:

1. Be clear and organized. Write your resume with the knowledge that an employer is likely to take just a few seconds to review it! Your resume therefore needs to be concise but "hard-hitting."

2. List those top skills and accomplishments that are relevant to your career objective. Don't be repetitious, and don't put any information on the resume that doesn't relate directly to the job you want. Don't sell yourself to the wrong job!

3. Be ready to revise and customize your resume for specific employers. Do not have just one resume printed and mass mailed.

4. Make your resume look great—it represents you! Print it out on a laser or letter-quality printer and use only top quality paper (heavy bond with rag content) and traditional colors (white, off-white, gray). Be creative in the way you play the job hunting game—but not in your resume presentation.

5. Use your resume as a tool in your getting-hired campaign rather than your sole tactic. Often it's best to send a specially prepared resume to networking sources and/or a potential employers *after* an initial meeting rather than handing them a mass-produced, general resume that is likely to hit the trash bucket before you're out the door.

1. Remember, first and foremost, that your resume must clearly state exactly what you're selling! Begin by developing a clear and concise Career Summary. This summary should include these three elements:

    • an opening line that defines you career-wise. For example: "An articulate leader-manager with six years experience creating, organizing, and implementing educational and recreational programs for children and young adults."

    • A second line that identifies those skill areas you are promoting. For example: "Top skills include human resource training, educational and recreational program development, and leadership training."

    • A final line that defines your top personality traits or personal assets (those aspects that most work about you). For example: "A creative, outgoing, and supportive facilitator with a proven track record of inspiring initiative, responsibility and team work in others." You may find it helpful here to review those self-defining attributes you identified from the assessment activities in Chapters 3 and 4.

2. Your resume should go on to list carefully selected achievements that reveal how you have success-fully used those transferable skills that you are "showcasing" in your Career Summary. In writing up your achievements, it's a good idea to identify:

    • specific tasks or problems you tackled

    • definite actions you took

    • concrete results you achieved

In this regard, remember two things: first, it's not enough simply to list your top skills; you need to show how you have used them. And, second, in today's job market—*results count*! Your resume, therefore, must show both that you are skilled and results oriented. Later in the chapter we will look at resume samples that pertain more specifically to career changers. Here are some typical kinds of examples a college student might use:

• As assistant camp director and head counselor: developed, organized, conducted, and evaluated a week-long training course for over fifty counselors, which significantly increased staff professional-ism, enhanced client morale, and reduced staff turnover by over fifty percent.

• Organized, implemented, and managed a creative and unique monthly activities program for a youth social club. The program became so successful that paid group memberships doubled over a two-year period.

• As an academic tutor, helped dozens of students clarify their personal goals and develop and implement self-motivating new plans.

• As a fund raiser for the college newspaper, identified sponsors and communicated to them the value of advertising in and/or supporting the paper. Sold advertisements and generated fund donations that produced over $150,000.00 in an eighteen-month period.

3. You'll need to decide whether a functional or chronological resume is the best format for your purposes. Generally, employers prefer the chronological because it's easier to follow work history in that format. An exception might be where particular types of expertise, skills, or personal attributes are more important than work history. In such cases, a well written functional resume might better lay out your expertise. If you are a job seeker, with a work history of experience that directly relates to the kind of work employers might be looking for, you may be well advised to use the chronological format. If, on the other hand, you are just graduating from college with little relevant work experience but a great deal of knowledge and skill to sell, or if you are making a career change, you may be better advised to develop a functional resume.

   In making your choice about which format to use, keep in mind that a chronological resume tends to focus on your past work history while a functional resume addresses those skills and knowledge bases you intend to concentrate upon in the future. In fact, we recommend that you develop both kinds of resumes, beginning with a functional. The reason is that the process of developing a functional resume forces you to clearly define yourself in terms of what you are selling (knowledge, skills, motivations, personal attributes) and to highlight them with relevant achievements.

4. Study the examples for ideas and consult one or more resume writing guides for additional help. See if your local college career planning and placement office offers resume-writing assistance and take full advantage of it. We strongly recommend that you personally write your resume. While most people find this difficult, the process of self-defining is critical to the whole job campaign. You can't play a winning game without engaging in this critical step!

5. Try out your resume with a number of people to obtain feedback and suggestions. Ask friends, faculty members, administrators, work associates, acquaintances, and networking contacts to critique your resume. And don't be afraid to make changes. Think of your resume as a dynamic and ongoing process of career self-definition, rather than as a finished product.

FIGURE 11.2 Sample Resume

Example: One-page functional resume, graduate student applying to a trade association for a training and development position:

ELLEN H. LAWSON

554 South Road, Queens, New York 10578

(212) 533-1208

<u>SUMMARY</u>	An experienced professional development trainer with multi-cultural experience. Top skills include training needs analysis, program design and delivery, and communications. An energetic, creative, self-initiating, results oriented, highly responsive and responsible individual.
<u>EDUCATION</u>	New York University, ASTD Certificate Program, 1994 Queens College, M. S. in Spanish, 1992 B.A. in Education, 1990. NY State Regents Scholarship, 1987

<u>RELATED ACCOMPLISHMENTS</u>

<u>Training</u>
- Trained and supervised ten professionals in educational methodology.
- Organized and conducted training program in elementary English for Hispanic garment workers. Doubled the enrollment by second year.
- Planned and taught college literature to 300 students, primarily adult. Received top evaluation scores.

<u>Needs Analysis</u>
- Initiated, organized, and expanded field work for language majors to meet community needs. Received special Mayoral commendation in 1993.
- Researched, analyzed, and evaluated effects of the open classroom on motivation and achievement. Study resulted in program revision by James Madison High School.

<u>Design and Communication</u>
- Designed program for incorporating audio-visual material into existing courses at Queens Community College. Recommendations were followed by professional staff for three years.
- Organized and supervised overseas study program in England for twenty participants.
- Organized peer-tutoring program, resulting in twenty-five percent increase in standard test scores.

<u>PROFESSIONAL EXPERIENCE</u>

1992–Present	Spanish and Special Education Instructor, Queens Community College.
1990–1992	Spanish Teacher, James Madison High School, Queens, NY.

Adapted from Anne Miller, Finding Career Alternatives for Teachers *(New York: Apple Publishing Company, 1979), p. 53f.*

FIGURE 11.3 Sample Resume

Example: Functional resume, 29-year-old elementary education teacher seeking a media personality or public relations position.

Shawn Medlinger
1791 Sparrow Lane
Shimmering Springs, MD 20908
(301) 774 7464

Summary

An experienced "up-front" communicator with experience in education and public relations that includes working with students grades K-12; teachers; and media personalities, such as journalists, disk jockeys, and television broadcasters. Top skills include public speaking, creative writing, innovative presenting, and acting as a media liaison. A dynamic, creative, well-rounded individual who delights in entertaining and influencing.

Accomplishments

Innovative Presenting

Taught Montessori education for sixth grade students for three years. Developed innovative teaching materials and programs, including subjects like Greek and Roman mythology, Arthurian legend, and basic Latin, which had never been taught in the school before. Used creativity, teaching skills, and love of interacting with youth to successfully prepare sixth graders for junior high.

Created and developed Humane Education program for the Montgomery County Humane Society. Taught students grade K-12 and their teachers about proper animal care, wildlife rehabilitation, and animal-related medicine and legislation.

Public Speaking

Currently serving as Public Relations Director for Montgomery County Humane Society. As the official spokesperson, participate in weekly television interviews and have a permanent time-slot on Channel 23 news. Also, engage in weekly radio interviews to promote the Animal Shelter and animal care. Speak to students, youth groups, and civic organizations on requested topics. Frequently affirmed by broadcasters and television producers to be "a natural" in conducting broadcast interviews.

Creative Writing

Gained valuable writing experience in college as an English major and taught English for three years at the Barrie School. Used writing skills to publish school newsletters and write proposals. Currently serve as chief writer/editor for MCHS: write newsletter ANIMAIL; prepare all correspondence—letters to students, Congressional representatives, sponsors, and celebrities; editor of a bi-weekly column for the *Montgomery Journal;* and prepare all media public service announcements.

Media Liaison

Skilled in working with various forms of media, including radio, television, and print journalism. Track record of success in proposing stories, conducting interviews, and providing public information. Often acknowledged for being "cool under pressure" and diplomatic in handling stressful "on the spot" situations.

Employment History

Montgomery County Humane Society Director of Humane Education and Public Relations	1994–present
Barrie School, Silver Spring, MD Teacher, sixth grade	1990–1993
Barrie Day Camp, Silver Spring, MD Program Director, Summers Work Program	1988–1992
IBM Inc., Rockville, MD Intern, Technical Publications Department	1986–1987

Education

B. A. English, University of Maryland, 1986

This editied version, used by permission, name and address changed

FIGURE 11.4 Sample Resume

Example: Functional resume for career changer—U.S. Naval officer seeking a college counseling/teaching position.

Donald S. Mayport
4401 Anchor Avenue
Annapolis, Maryland 21403
(410) 749-0220

SUMMARY

A seasoned counselor/educator with ten years of experience working with diversified populations in a variety of work places and academic settings. Top skills include educational development, creative problem solving, and personal motivation counseling. Support skills include writing, conceptualizing, and academic research. A personable and resourceful team-player with vision and facility for inspiring individuals and groups to top performance.

ACCOMPLISHMENTS

Educational Development

As a history and government professor at the U.S. Naval Academy, researched and developed course materials, and delivered four different courses for junior and senior year students during a two-year period. Received strong student evaluations in all classes, totaling over five-hundred individuals, in spite of teaching new offerings each semester.

Developed projects and course assignments that resulted in a "love-of-sea" feeling in college students enrolled in a naval operations course that had been considered to be a "dreaded requirement."

Creative Problem Solving

Located and discovered how to use complex training aids and visual graphics to motivate students enrolled in a college navigation course. Result was that while previous classes disliked celestial navigation and acquired techniques through rote memorization of formulas, these students became intrigued with content that they could visualize and mastered techniques through "in-depth" understanding.

Led a team of ten in undertaking a seemingly impossible job to be accomplished within an intolerably short time frame. The task was achieved with sterling results within the allotted time through implementing a number of novel solutions, which in the process significantly boosted team morale and confidence.

Personal Motivation Counseling

In a one-year period, enhanced the morale of a twenty-five person team through individual counseling, publicly affirming individual successes, and establishing a sense of team identity. Resulted in a significant reduction in disciplinary cases and increased utilization of educational development benefits.

Through extensive personal counseling and concerned attention, helped dozens of young men with low self esteem and job performance problems become conscientious self-developers and productive performers.

EMPLOYMENT HISTORY:

U.S. Naval Academy, Annapolis, MD Political Science Instructor	1989–Present
U.S. Navy Manager of 65 man division	1987–1989
University of Minnesota Navigation Instructor and NROTC counselor	1984–1987
Division Officer, U.S. Navy Team leadership and general management	1981–1984

EDUCATION

B.S. in Geology, Colorado State University, Fort Collins, CO 1977.

M.A.T. University of Minnesota, Minneapolis, MN 1987.

Additional training:
- three graduate level courses in human relations training at The George Washington University, Washington, D.C. 1990–1991.
- one week intensive instructor training institute.

FIGURE 11.5 Sample Resume

Example: Chronological resume for career changer—U.S. Naval officer seeking an educational administrative and/or counseling position.

Donald S. Mayport
4401 Anchor Avenue
Annapolis, Maryland 21403
(410) 749-0220

SUMMARY

A seasoned counselor/educator with ten years of experience working with diversified populations in a variety of work places and academic settings. Top skills include human resource development management, educational development, creative problem solving, and personal motivation counseling. Support skills include writing, conceptualizing, and academic research. A personable and resourceful team-player with vision and facility for inspiring individuals and groups to best performance.

PROFESSIONAL EXPERIENCE

Political Science Instructor
U. S. Naval Academy, Annapolis, MD   1989–Present
Teach courses in U.S. Government, Foreign Affairs, History and International Relations. Serve as academic advisor for Midshipmen.

- As a history and government professor at the U.S. Naval Academy, researched and developed course materials, and delivered four different courses for junior and senior year students during a two-year period. Received strong student evaluations in all classes, totaling over five-hundred individuals, in spite of teaching new offerings each semester.

- Developed reading projects and course assignments that resulted in a "love-of-sea" feeling in junior college students enrolled in a naval operations course that had been considered to be a "dreaded requirement."

U.S. Naval Shipboard Division Officer   1987–1989
Managed a 65-person division onboard a U.S. Naval aircraft carrier. Responsibilities included training, evaluating, and directing all activities of a complex and rapidly changing operation.

- Continuously solved complex problems involving the maneuvering of aircraft and equipment on the hangar deck, managing five crews of men, to support flight operations by supplying the aircraft needed, at the time and place needed, and garaging aircraft being removed from the flight deck.

- Safely completed all scheduled operations under duress of intensive operating conditions, while maintaining high crew morale through ongoing personalized attention to the personal and professional development needs of individuals.

<u>Naval ROTC Instructor, University of Minnesota</u>   <u>1984–1987</u>

Taught semester long, college credit courses in navigation and naval operations. Served as the academic and military advisor to sixty junior class level NROTC students.

- Located and discovered how to use complex training aids and visual graphics to motivate students enrolled in a college navigation course. Result was that while previous classes disliked celestial navigation and acquired techniques through rote memorization of formulas, these students became intrigued with content they could visualize and mastered techniques through real understanding.

- Counseled over one-hundred college students, assisting them with academic decision-making within the context of long-term career perspectives.

EDUCATION

B.S. in Geology, Colorado State University, Forth Collins, CO 1977.

M.A.T. University of Minnesota, Minneapolis, MN 1987.

<u>Additional training:</u>
- three graduate level courses in human relations training at The George Washington University, Washington, D.C. 1990–1991.
- one-week intensive instructor training institute.

4th Move—Identifying Your List of Employment Targets (ETs)

Now you're ready to begin the action stage of the game. To do that, you'll need to decide who you're playing the game with—that translates into developing your list of employment targets. We refer to these as your ETs; they are the specific employers you want to contact for a job. Here are a few good resources for developing your ET list.

People: Do you have friends, associates, or acquaintances who might know of employers or employment sites that meet your envisioned job setting and job objective? (Remember, you're looking for employer names for your list rather than known job openings.) Perhaps your acquaintances don't know of specific ETs but know of someone who does.

Information Interviewing/Networking: You've probably already obtained names of ETs while you were doing the information interviews described earlier in the book. When you begin talking with your ETs, if they don't have any potential openings, ask if they can provide additional names for your list.

Yellow Pages Telephone Directories: Although the Yellow Pages are limited by incomplete index headings and incomplete listings, they are a useful directory. Most libraries have Yellow Pages directories for other cities if you're searching for ETs outside your area. Just remember that the size of the ad does not necessarily reflect the size of the employer. In fact, many large organizations do not bother listing themselves in the Yellow Pages.

Classified Advertisements: The classified ads appearing over a period of months are a good source of specific ET names. Look for the organizations that fall into your employment target categories. (They may not be advertising for the position you want, but don't worry about this. You are just compiling an employer list. Many companies never advertise positions they can fill by word of mouth.) For a national or international job search, check the classified ads in appropriate city newspapers or in magazines like *The Economist*.

Chamber of Commerce Offices: Most local Chamber of Commerce offices have listings of employers in their county. Often these lists categorize the employers, list the number of employees, and sometimes include annual sales revenue. Choose the size of employer you seek by consulting such lists.

Magazines, Trade, and Professional Journals: Look through the business news sections of these resources for businesses and organizations engaged in activities of particular interest to you. *Time*, *Newsweek*, *Business Week*, the *Wall Street Journal*, and the *New York Times* are all excellent sources for career-related topics of national scope. Almost every type of business, occupation, trade, profession, or interest area has some kind of a regular publication—professional journal, newsletter, magazine, etc. These are excellent sources of information for ETs. If you aren't familiar with the magazines and journals related to your job interest, look up your field in indexes like the *Magazine Index, Reader's Guide* to *Periodical Literature,* and the *Business Periodicals Index*, to find relevant articles. *The Encyclopedia of Associations* (published by Gale Research Corporation) describes activities and publications of all associations. It provides names, addresses, and phone numbers.

Specialized Directories: These directories provide basic information on business organizations. They include: *Dun and Bradstreet Million Dollar Directory* and *Dun and Bradstreet Middle Market Directory*. The *U.S. Government Manual* describes agencies, programs, and basic job positions. Top managers' names are included, but be careful to assure that you are taking these names from a recently published reference.

College Career Planning and Placement Offices (CPP's): Many of these contain a wealth of information about ETs. University and college CPP's will have information on employers of a national scope, while the community college should have an excellent listing of ETs in the local area. Remember that it doesn't matter whether these ETs have listed current, relevant job openings.

Electronic Networks: Most computer access systems, such as Prodigy, Compu-Serve, and America On-line, have excellent employer data bases. You can search through a wide array of company and organizational data bases through Internet. Developing a computerized resume and placing it on one of the available electronic resume services or computerized skill banks may produce some interesting results, particularly if you have the high-tech skills companies using this service are looking for.

Exercise 11-D. RECORDING YOUR EMPLOYMENT TARGETS

1. Use the above resources to identify an initial list of 50 to 100 ETs.

2. You will have far more success in your job campaign if you are organized. Begin your organization by obtaining 3 x 5 cards and a file box with alphabetical separators. Be sure to record the name, address, telephone number, and potential contact persons for each ET on a separate 3 x 5 card. File your cards in alphabetical order.

5th Move—Designing Your Sales Campaign

Dozens of current books offer their own no-fail variation on the best ways to get a job. If you are perusing these resources, keep this fact in mind—you get job offers only one way. And, like it or not, that way is through effective personal, face-to-face contact. The effectiveness is measured by your ability to sell potential employers on your value to their company or organization. You don't get a job offer through your resume or the "just right" personal appearance, though poor appearance on either may certainly prevent you from getting an offer! And, worst of all, hardly anyone ever gets a good job by being "discovered." The chances of that happening to you are about the same as winning the million dollar lottery. So you might as well concentrate your efforts and energy on kicking off your job campaign, regardless of whether you choose to target the hidden job market or open job market. You might find it worthwhile to enroll in a sales class if you're having difficulty defining yourself as a marketable product or if your feeling awkward about the process of "self-marketing."

The next step in your "getting hired" campaign is to design your sales approach. In addition to the traditional approach of sending a resume with a custom cover letter, consider the following three non-traditional methods for getting job interviews:

Personal Sales Letter. Sending out your personal sales letter to selected employment targets, preferably to a manager with the authority to hire you. This sales letter replaces your resume with cover letter as the initial communication. You present your resume during any interview produced from this approach only if the employer asks for further materials.

Telephoning for Interviews. Calling an appropriate hiring manager with each ET to arrange for information interviews or actual job interviews.

Networking and Job Proposals. Designing a proposal for the job you want to have with a particularly appealing ET. You present your proposal, verbally or in writing, to the person with the authority to hire you for that position. This method is normally used during or after one or more general information gathering sessions or informal interviews, often in combination with other approaches.

In designing your sales campaign, we recommend that you experiment with both traditional and non traditional methods and then concentrate on a combinations of those activities that best fit you. If you are targeting a long-range job campaign to other localities, are a career changer, or are answering a classified ad, you may wish to concentrate your efforts on the personal sales letter and/or telephone methods. If you have developed your telephone skills, you might put most of your effort into this method. If you have narrowed down your employment targets and have significant background information on them, any method can be effective. The job proposal method requires having considerable background information. Become more familiar with the three methods by reading the following descriptions. Then design and kick off your own sales campaign.

Reprinted by permission: Tribune Company Syndicate, Inc.

Your Personal Sales Letter

In writing the sales letter, remember that you will be sending it out to your ETs and that you are writing the letter to show how your skills and qualifications will meet their needs. You want to show in your letter, through your previous accomplishments, in what ways you have the skills, attributes, and experience needed to help solve your ETs' employment problems. However, you don't want to come on too strong or in an arrogant manner by presuming to have instant solutions. Just represent yourself as a motivated candidate with useful, relevant skills and experience. William Cohen identifies these five components of the sales letter.[3]

1. *Opening Attention-Getter.* The task here is to get your ETs' attention and motivate them to read on to discover why you are writing. Examples: (1) (Recent graduate in the communications field) "If your Marketing Department could use award-winning writing and speaking skills, you may be interested in my background." (2) (Recent community college computer programming graduate with volunteer experience but no salaried job experience) "Having worked on professional systems development since my sophomore year in high school, I am ready for a challenging computer-programming position." (3) (Housewife applying for administrative assistant position) "Through fifteen years of experience, I've become an expert on organization, time management, administrative support, and motivation."

2. *Explanation.* Here you answer the question of why you are writing. Example: "I am writing to you directly in case you need someone with my expertise as a computer programmer, administrative assistant, marketing specialist, etc." Be specific in your explanation here. A general statement that implies you are looking for anything or that you can do anything will almost inevitably rule you out.

3. *Motivation.* The task here is to create a strong desire for your service. Cite accomplishments that directly relate to the type of job you are seeking. Examples: (From a homemaker with no previous paid work experience) (1) "In less than two months, I mastered complex IBM and Micro-soft word processing systems through my own self-study and practice. I am now training colleagues in these systems." (2) "In just two weeks of neighborhood canvassing, I collected over $1,500 in contributions to the United Fund." (3) "Over the past five years, I have organized and managed five record-breaking fund raising events for The Sacred Heart Church. My responsibilities included designing a concept; collecting, organizing, and motivating volunteers; promoting the events; and accounting for cash receipts."

4. *Credibility.* The task here is to convince the employer that everything your have said in your letter is true. Incidentally, it is crucial to be honest in your sales letter, just as it is in your resume. The trick is to find the terminology that powerfully reflects what you actually have done and can do. Present facts about your attributes in short, action-packed sentences. Cite only things that relate positively to the kind of job you want, and omit anything else. Find some specific facts of relevance to report. Examples: (1) "I have a B.A. in Business Administration from Ohio State University (1987) specializing in financial management." (2) "I have successfully completed courses at Prince George's Community College and the University of Maryland in Pascal, C++, and Systems Analysis." (3) "I was on the Dean's List for two consecutive years in my Business Administration Program." (List awards, but only if they are relevant.)

5. *Call to Action.* The last part of your sales letter tells the employer what you want him/her to do (invite you in for a meeting/interview). Phrase this in terms of the employer's best interests. Examples: (1) "If you would like a personal meeting to discuss how my background and skills could assist you, please call me at (telephone #) between 9 A.M. and 5 P.M." (2) "I would be happy to demonstrate how I could assist your company. I will call your office within the next two weeks to discuss meeting for that purpose.

FIGURE 11.6 Sample Sales Letter

From Marlene Berg, who is campaigning for a media copywriter's job at a large advertising company.

1822 Malone Drive
Bethesda, Maryland 20815
March 30, 1994

Mr. Robert Blake
Director of Media Sales
Highlights Advertising Agency
1400 Marlow Avenue
Cincinnati, Ohio 54082

Dear Mr. Blake:

As a copywriter I created an ad for radio station WTYK that resulted in a twelve percent product sales increase for the sponsoring agency. This was the greatest response the station had ever had from one of its ads.

Your company may need a creative media copywriter with demonstrated ability to influence through the use of language. If so, you may be interested in some of my other achievements:

• I have a Bachelor of Arts degree in Communications from the University of Ohio (1987).

• I completed 63 hours of course work in marketing and communications, maintaining an "A" average.

• This educational background is supplemented by 14 months of experience writing advertisements for a university and a large advertising firm. During this time I wrote over 50 successful advertisements for the print and broadcast media, including the one described in my opening paragraph.

• I have written two papers on the art of persuasive writing. Both papers have been published by well-known journals in the communications/advertisement fields.

I would like to meet you personally to discuss putting my experience to work for Highlights Advertising Agency. You can reach me at (301) 986-5666 between 9 a.m. and 5 p.m.

Sincerely,

Marlene Berg

Addressing Your Personal Sales Letter

Figure 11.6 shows a sample sales letter. Address these letters to a particular individual and include an accurate title, whenever possible. For impact, send your letter directly to the manager with authority to hire you. You can get this name by calling the organization and asking for the name of the manager who handles the department you are targeting. Just ask the receptionist for the name of the person in charge of marketing, communications, training, computer services, or whatever division fits your job objective best. If you aren't sure, get the name of the general manager of that office. Be sure to get his/her correctly spelled name, title, and address. As standard procedure, you may be transferred to Personnel or asked why you need the information. Just say you're mailing in a proposal, and retain a relaxed, friendly tone. Avoid mailing your letter to Personnel Department unless you seek work in that division. Since the Personnel staff screens out candidates lacking standard credentials, the career changer or recent graduate is often ignored.

Telephoning for Interviews

The objective here is to obtain the name of the person with the power to hire at each ET and then call him/her to arrange a personal meeting (job interview). Your task is to communicate the following: (1) You are interested in that company and the particular mission that this manager's work involves. (2) You feel you have something of real value to contribute to the organization/company and to this mission. (3) You would like to arrange a short meeting to discuss current or future job opportunities. If you get a positive response, arrange a meeting time and place. Record it in your schedule book.

Conducting this kind of telephone campaign is difficult for most people. To prepare for it, you may want to practice making these calls to your career counselor or to friends. Then get out your ET contact cards and start calling. You can expect to hear "no" far more often than "yes" during your telephone requests for meetings. But don't let that discourage you because you will also hear "yes" sooner than in letter writing or resume selling, assuming of course, that you have genuine qualifications and are able to present yourself with confidence and tact. As a motivator in making these calls, you might wish to remember the following:

> ### *The Getting Hired Reality*
> 1. *You get jobs through interviews.*
> 2. *The more calls you make, the more interviews you obtain.*
> 3. *The more interviews, the better your chances of job offers.*
> 4. *The more job offers, the better your chances of a great job.*

Example of a Telephone Approach

Begin by finding out the name of the person with the power to hire for the kind of position you want (obtain his/her title, and phone number). Often you will be able to get this information by calling the organization and asking the receptionist the right questions. You may want to call at a busy time such as a lunch hour when you're less likely to be asked the purpose of your call. (By the way, some employers screen out these calls because they assume you are an executive search specialist trying to offer their managers another job!) If you're asked the purpose of your call, tell them you have a personal matter to discuss.

Your conversation might go something like this: "Hello, my name is Marlene Berg, and I need to get in touch with the person responsible for your radio advertisements. May I have that person's name and title please? . . . Thank you, and how can I get in touch with him?" (Have your ET index card and pen handy to write down the information as you get it.)

Once you get the right name, decide what you want to say and what action you want as a result of your call. Let's assume that you get the information you need and put your call through to Robert Blake, Director of Media Sales. Your first task will be to get the secretary to let you talk with Mr. Blake. You might say something like, "Hello, this is Marlene Berg calling for Robert Blake."

If the secretary puts you through immediately, consider yourself lucky. Most likely the secretary will ask for your company name and the reason you're calling. In response be prepared to say something like, "I have a business proposal that I want to discuss with him." Should she ask if she may help, tell her why you are calling, briefly stressing that you have some useful experience to offer, and ask for the most convenient time to call. Take your ET's secretary into your confidence rather than being terse or hostile. Secretaries are typically asked by busy managers to screen calls, but if they think you are sincere, motivated, and qualified, they just might help. Be positive and gracious.

Once you get through to Mr. Blake, your conversation might proceed something like the following: "Hello, Mr. Blake, this is Marlene Berg. Do you have a moment?" If he says "no," respond, "Fine, when would be a good time to call back. I'd like to talk with you about your new contract with WTYK." If he says "yes," begin with a statement that will get his interest, such as, "I believe that you do all of radio station WTYK's advertisements. Is that correct?" Once you have his attention, be prepared to communicate something about yourself that relates directly to the challenges he has such as, "You may be needing creative copywriters with expertise in promoting commercial products to WTYK's younger listeners. I have had excellent results in similar kinds of work and am very familiar with the preferences of WTYK's listening audience. I would like to meet with you to discuss how I could be of service."

At this point, listen to his response and be prepared to add specific facts about your relevant skills and experience. For example, "I worked for two years with one of the best media experts in Maryland and have substantial knowledge of ad writing and experience with radio advertisements." Close the conversation with a request for a meeting (avoid the use of the word "interview") to talk further. You might say something like, "I think it would make sense to show you some of my work and discuss this in more detail. Are you free tomorrow afternoon or Wednesday morning?"

If Mr. Blake says "okay," then prepare for your meeting (interview). If he indicates that he has nothing available now, say that you understand and would still like to meet him to discuss future opportunities if he anticipates openings within the next six months.

Don't let an ET's initial resistance deter you. Resistance is a natural and expected reaction to a cold telephone call of any kind. Continue communicating enthusiastically the value you can contribute to the company. Your assurance can break through objections and get you an interview.

Once you're in the office, if Mr. Blake likes you, he'll remember you. He may have an opening in a few days or weeks. If he's sufficiently impressed by you, he just might create a position for you. On the other hand, if he says "no" to the meeting, don't take it personally. Just call the next person on your list.

The Job Proposal

The job proposal approach involves using the information interviewing process to meet three goals:

1. Identify and become familiar with potential organizations where you might like to work.

2. Determine current needs and problems of these employers, and match these with your skills and experience.

3. Determine the name of the person who has the power to hire someone for the type of job you want.

Accomplishing these goals involves first conducting numerous information interviews with well qualified people who are doing the kind of work that interests you. As you talk with these individuals, ask them questions designed to acquaint you with how one gets hired for a job like theirs, what they like and don't like about this organization, and what the organization's primary strengths and problem areas are. After you have conducted a sufficient number of these job research interviews, you should know which organizations you prefer, who has the power to hire you for the type of job you want, the organization's unique needs, and how your strengths and assets can be of particular assistance there.

With this knowledge, you then design a specific proposal of how you can be of assistance to that organization. Next, arrange for a personal meeting with the person with actual hiring power. At this meeting you convincingly present your proposal. With this method, you can effectively promote yourself for current or future job openings. You might even find that an employer is so impressed by you that he/she develops a special position for you—it happens! This method is more fully described in Richard Bolles' best-selling book, *What Color Is Your Parachute?* (available in most bookstores and college career planning offices).

Exercise 11-E. KICKING OFF YOUR SALES CAMPAIGN

1. Conduct ten to twenty information interviews with people who are working in a job similar to the kind you think you would like to have. Your task here is to get a better sense of their job and their company. Note: These are to be information interviews and not job interviews. Focus on four areas of inquiry:

   • What it's like to do that job and what the career opportunities are at that organization? Where could an entry-level position lead in the years ahead?

   • What that particular organization is like. What business is it in? What are its strengths and what are its major problems? What kinds of employees succeed at this organization? Who has the power to hire people in that particular field within that company (name of person, title, what he/she is like, a good way to get to meet them, etc.).

   • What other types of related jobs does this person know about that might possibly interest you? You're looking for new job possibilities, too.

   • Can this person refer you to other individuals for information interviews or recommend other organizations as ETs?

2. Out of the companies you have visited for information interviews, pick three you like the best. Develop a two-page written proposal to present to the person with the power to hire at each of these ETs. In your proposal indicate how you could serve that organization/business by helping them capitalize on their strengths and solve their problems. Be sure to show how your service will provide more value to the organization than the cost of your salary.

   Arrange for a meeting with the person with the power to hire you. Your previous information interviews (contacts) within that organization should be of great assistance here. Use your proposal as interview preparation, and be prepared to discuss your ideas, if appropriate. If you get positive response, you may want to leave your written proposal. Ask whether an appropriate job opening will be available during the following few months. Be sure to send a thank-you letter as a follow-up to these proposal presentation meetings and include any details you were asked about but didn't have available at the time.

3. Refine your personal sales letter, and send it out to twenty-five ETs or modify it as a response to current classified ads that appeal to you. (A well-written and targeted sales letter often has a better chance against the classified ad competition just because it stands out.) You are trying to get at least one interview. The experience you have acquired in conducting information interviews and presenting your proposals should help you improve your sales letter. If you get no interviews, you need to assess and revise your letter and your techniques. If you get more than five interviews from this mailing, you have done a terrific job!

4. Select 30 to 50 ETs and telephone for interviews to the people with the power to hire. If this produces three to five job interviews, you're doing great. If less than that, you need to evaluate and revise your approach. Should you obtain ten or more interviews—hire out as a consultant!

Getting Hired Guide

Many factors influence the number of contacts required to get one job interview. These include: your qualifications for the job, availability of the job type in the locality you are exploring, the degree of your assertiveness and salesmanship, the time of year, etc. Nevertheless, here are some rough guidelines to help establish your sales campaign. Use these to play the getting hired game:

10–20 contacts	=	1 job interview
5–10 interviews	=	1 job offer
1–5 job offers	=	1 great job

Evaluating Your Results

Keep assessing the progress of your "getting hired" campaign, and revise your game plan as needed. Use your ET index cards to keep track of your actions and results. Here are some sample entries:

Date	Action Taken/Results Produced	Action Party
4/20/94	Conducted information interview. Harry Owens, Vice President for Sales and Contracts has the power to hire. Phone: (421) 397-2888. His secretary is Sue Hawkins.	Mel Downs, Exec. Dir. for Marketing Phone: (421) 397-2801
4/21/87	Sent Mel a thank-you letter.	
4/29/87	Received letter of no openings now/will keep you on file. Note: Still some promise here. Call Doug P. back about 5/15/87 with a new issue.	Doug Powell, Dir. of Public Relations, Phone: (875) 101-1542
4/30/87	Telephoned for interview. Arranged meeting for 5/3/87 8 A.M. in her office (Rm. 307)	Marge Tower, Managing Editor (310) 572-0893

As you review your entries, stop and take stock of how you're doing. What seems to work the best and why? What causes problems and why? It's always worth the effort to redesign your sales campaign, if needed.

6th Move—Creating a Support Group

The next step in your "getting hired" game is to identify your needs for personal and financial assistance and to set up a support group to help meet these needs, if necessary. Finding the right job may take anywhere from two to six months of full-time, concentrated work. Even if it doesn't take that long, it's a good idea to prepare yourself emotionally and financially for that contingency.

If unemployed, you may need financial help sometime in your job campaign. Plan for it now by developing a realistic estimate of money needed and a list of possible sources. Too many job seekers make abrupt, destructive career decisions because they feel trapped financially. If your ETs and information interview network are substantial, getting a loan from credit card/bank sources or friends may be your best alternative. Otherwise, consider part-time or temporary work to provide some financial security. Career planning offices, classified ads, and state employment services and temporary agencies can assist you here. Just keep enough time and energy free to attain the award you've strived for—a fulfilling job with good pay.

Because the job campaign is psychologically stressful for most people, it's also a good idea to establish a personal support group. Enlist the support of friends, acquaintances, your college counseling staff, or a professional career counselor, if you need it and can afford it. If there is a job club in your area, join it. Inquire at your college career planning office and/or employment service office to see if there is one available.

Once you have obtained your support group, check in with them on a regular basis. Also, call upon them when you are feeling low and need support or when things look promising and you want to celebrate. You will need to be prepared for rejection, even if you are a strong job candidate. By sharing your feelings of disappointment, your support group can help you recharge your energy and motivation.

1. Using the guidelines described above, estimate how long your job campaign may take and determine your financial needs for that period of time. If you will need money, make a list of people who might be able to help. Decide on your best approach and then contact them for assistance. Keep trying until you know your financial needs are adequately addressed.

2. Arrange for personal support from acquaintances, a college career planning and placement office, job club, or professional counselor. Schedule regular times to meet (at least once per week) and make agreements to check in when you need encouragement or have good news to share.

7th Move—Prepare for Job Interviews

You can expect your personal visits, sales letters, and telephone calls to begin paying off in the form of formal and/or informal job interviews about two to three weeks after your "kick-off campaign." You need to prepare for this in several ways. First, develop interviewing skills well before you reach the job interview stage of the game. If you are not experienced with interviews, seek the help of a career counselor, and/or visit your library and read up on the subject, and/or enroll in an interviewing course.

Second, be prepared for the kinds of questions that you are likely to be asked. Below are some examples. Practice answering these until you have concise, confident, enthusiastic responses that are always well-targeted to the job you seek:

1. Tell us something about yourself.

2. What are you looking for in a job?

3. Why do you want to leave your current job?

4. Why are you interested in working with this organization?

5. What background and experience do you have to bring?

6. What are your top strengths?

7. What are your weaknesses?

   (Answer by explaining how you are transforming a former minor weakness into a strength. Don't say that your only weakness is that you work too hard. Employers don't like baloney.)

8. What are your future goals and plans?

9. What salary are you asking for? What did you earn in your last job?

10. What would you like to know about us?
    What questions do you have for us?

    (Be prepared to ask at least three questions that show you know something about the organization and want to know where it's heading.)

Third, have a wardrobe that is appropriate for the interview. Your personal appearance is very important. Ask your friends and/or support group to check you out and give honest feedback. Get into proper attire, and be at the right place at the right time!

Fourth, prepare for the interview. Learn as much as possible about your ET's business. You can usually get information by visiting your ET's personnel office well before the interview. Explain that you're interviewing for a position there and would like to see an annual report, company newsletter, brochures, or any other available information.

Be prepared to ask questions as well as to answer them. Remember, interviews are a two-way proposition: you'll be deciding whether a company is the right place for you just as they assess whether you are the right person for them. Employers are rarely impressed by job candidates who are so passive that they have no questions to ask. On the other hand, don't try to take over the interview. Finally, review the job interviewing "do's and don'ts" listed in Table 11.1 several times to keep an overall perspective.

TABLE 11.1 Job Interviewing Tips

What to do	*What not to do*
• Prepare for the interview.	• Arrive late.
• Know the organization's purpose, strengths, and problems.	• Forget your interviewer's name(s).
• Know how you can be of value.	• Ask what the company does.
• Dress appropriately (the way people dress at that organization).	• Bring and read notes.
• Bring samples of your work.	• Get lost in your own thoughts.
• Know what points you want to make.	• Focus on your need for the job.
• Be prepared to ask insightful questions.	• Pretend to know things you don't.
• Sell your skills, interest, energy, and achievements.	• Indicate that you have all the organization's answers.
• Relate your career goals, skills and achievements to the mission of the organization.	• Just sit and wait for the interviewer(s) to ask questions.
• Listen closely to questions, and respond only to what is asked.	• Answer a question not asked.
• Know your field's salary ranges (the "going rate") for the type of position you want and the minimum salary you're willing to accept.	• Give long meandering responses.
• Answer the real question—Why should they hire you?	• Indicate that your main interests are in salary and benefits.
	• Monopolize the conversation.
	• Be overly concerned about time off
	• Be defensive
	• Be dogmatic
	• Avoid eye contact

Henderson realized that he had chosen the wrong clothes for the interview

---

Exercise 11-G. INTERVIEW PREPARATION

Prepare for each interview by answering questions like these:

1. What business is the employer in?

   - What products/services do they sell and to whom?
   - What is their history?
   - Where are they heading in the future?
   - What thing is the organization noted for and proudest of?

2. What are the three major problems this organization now confronts or will confront?

3. What specific value can you be to the company in solving these problems?

4. Which of your top skills would be most valuable to this company?

5. How do your past achievements and current goals relate to the goals and mission of this company?

6. If you were the interviewer, why would you hire you for the job you want? List ten reasons, but use only the top three or so. Blasting the employer with too many reasons on the spot may make you look over- or under-confident.

7. What is the salary range the company pays for a job like this? (Find this out through information interviews.)

8. What is the minimum salary you will accept and your realistic ideal salary?

8th Move—Get Attractive Job Offers

Your goal in each job interview is to discover whether you really want the job and if so to lead your interviewer(s) to making an attractive offer. To do that, you need to come to each interview prepared to help direct the outcome. That doesn't mean that you aggressively take over the interview. It does mean, however, that you come prepared with information, the right attitude, and a clear goal. A successful interview usually follows these steps:

1. Personal introductions and small talk.

2. Short introduction of yourself and your interest in a job with that organization.

3. Questions and answers to establish your qualifications and interest in the job and to assess how well you would fit in with that organization.

4. Your questions to obtain additional information about the organization, the job, and the career possibilities.

5. Closure involving either a job offer and salary negotiation or clarification of the steps remaining to a job offer.

To get into the right frame of mind for the interview, we recommend that you mentally rehearse an ideal interview two or three times before the actual meeting. Use the envisioning exercise described in Appendix D. Relax, close your eyes, and then run through the whole interview in your mind. See yourself meeting your interviewer(s), knowing his/her/their name(s), and feeling relaxed and assured. Envision yourself doing well and fully enjoying the interview game. Imagine your interviewer(s) asking questions and your responding to them with assurance and enthusiasm. In your mind, establish good eye contact with your interviewer(s), and ask questions that will give you needed information and demonstrate your knowledge and interest in the organization.

Envision your interviewers moving from asking you questions to convincing you of the benefits of working at that organization. Picture the interview coming to a close, with the interviewers offering you the job at a fair salary and your thanking them and asking for a couple of days to think it over. This envisioning process will help you prepare for the interview and generate the personal confidence you'll need to do a terrific job.

Perhaps the best thing that you can do during the interview is to be honest, assured, prepared, energetic and, most of all, to be your best self. During the interview, you will want to stress how your skills/experience relate to the job. Express enthusiasm for the opportunity to provide a valuable service for the organization. Of course, you don't want to be overbearing about your knowledge and skills. Don't pretend to have all of the answers to the organization's needs. That could be a real turn off to an interviewer. Instead, let your personal confidence in your abilities and your enthusiasm for the job shine through.

Be prepared to answer questions honestly, and don't pretend to know something you don't. Be goal oriented during the interview so you and the interviewer stay on track. Remember, you want to get a positive job offer and not just have a nice conversation.

At appropriate times during the interview, be prepared to ask questions like these:

1. What kind of a person would you consider an ideal candidate for this job?
2. What kind of challenges does this job offer?
3. What are the organization's primary goals and plans for the future?
4. What achievements in your division make you the proudest?
5. What kinds of people would I be working with here?
6. How would you describe the management style here?
7. What kind of advancement would be possible for anyone performing this job well?
8. What traits do you appreciate most in an employee?
9. What are the major strengths of the organization?

If you are seriously interested in the position, begin moving the interview towards a job offer. Think of yourself as a salesperson closing the deal. Don't leave the interview without offering your interviewer(s) ample opportunity to purchase your services. Ask questions like: "What do you think? Do we have a possible match here between your requirements and my qualifications?"

If your interviewers show some reluctance, try to discover their real objections. If they have some reservations about a particular aspect of your experience or skill, respond with positive facts and examples to resolve any false concerns. If their objections are legitimate, reconsider whether the position is suitable for you.

SALARY NEGOTIATION

If you are asked salary-related questions early in the interview, answer generally. Just say that your salary requirements are negotiable and depend upon the job description. Once there is strong mutual interest, go ahead and discuss salary. Ask the interviewer what salary range they have for the position. If the range is acceptable, decide what your worth is and why you think so. Base that on your experience and skills and not that you need the money.

However, if the top of their salary range is below the going rate for this position and below your minimum requirements, express some concern. If your qualifications and experience are limited, it may be fair. But if you are well qualified, don't sell yourself short. You may want to stress again the value you bring to the organization. Ask about additional bonuses, special benefits, or significant salary increases after a three- to six-month trial. When you have a firm offer, express your serious interest. Ask the interviewer to put the offer, including any special agreements, in writing. Finally, inquire when they would like your answer.

INTERVIEW FOLLOW-UP

Immediately after each interview (one to three days), send a typed letter thanking the interviewer for meeting with you. Also, use the letter to indicate any additional points to support your value to the organization. If you are seriously interested in the position, say so and express your hope for a favorable agreement. Include your telephone number so they can reach you for further information or discussion.

If you haven't heard anything from your ET within a reasonable amount of time (two weeks), pursue the matter with him/her by telephone. Also, call a company when you have another job offer, but are still interested in them. This confirmation that you are valuable to another employer often results in action. Be sure to express the confidence that you could make a valuable contribution to the company. If you have acquired any new information, skills, or insights related to the position, mention them. Close by asking whether you are still a candidate. If so, ask whether they have any questions that you could answer or if there is anything else that you might do to support your candidacy. This kind of follow-up can increase your chances of success considerably.

9th Move—Assess Your Offers

At some point, after conducting a number of interviews, your efforts will begin paying off in the form of job offers. The ideal situation, of course, is to have several job offers. If you have done a thorough and assertive job campaign, that is very likely to happen.

As you reach this final stage of the job campaign, there are a few important things to consider. The first issue is what to do after you get a job offer. Do you take it? Do you try for others? What if it's close to what you want but not exactly? These, of course, are questions that only you will be able to answer, and they warrant discussion with your support group. Consider the advancement opportunities, management style, work environment, and your gut feelings.

If you have a tentative offer or are being seriously considered for a job you really want, resist the temptation to halt your job campaign. Tentative job offers often do not pan out. Continue your interviewing process until you get a firm, written job offer that really appeals to you.

10th and Final Move—Complete the Game

When you get the right job, it's time to complete the game and enter the winner's circle. An understandable sense of elation goes along with achieving a great job and a desire to get moving with your career. However, it's a good idea to pause and reflect upon what you have done for yourself and what others have done for you. Completing the game means acknowledging yourself and those who contributed to your successful job campaign.

Entering the winner's circle is symbolic of beginning your new job and experiencing the rewards it offers. A great job offers three major rewards: opportunities for contribution, growth, and income. Research studies consistently show that the main reward people want from a job is the opportunity to make a worthwhile contribution. We're unlikely to experience a sense of meaning or purpose in life unless we know that our skills and energies are being used productively.

The second most important reward your job can offer is the chance to grow. Growing means using and developing your skills along with learning and applying new knowledge. Growing means being stimulated to do and be your best. That is far more important than having a comfortable job. You're likely to become bored and unmotivated in a comfortable job.

The third reward, usually over emphasized, is salary. A good salary is important both for a healthy self-concept and as compensation for worthwhile service performed. Being paid a good salary alone, however, is insufficient to provide job satisfaction. It takes all three rewards for that. Surprisingly, your income is likely to be the least important unless it is considerably lower than average. That observation comes as a result of our work with numerous career changers who were earning a good salary but hated their jobs because they lacked the first two greater rewards.

As you enter the winner's circle with your new job, we encourage you to keep your career and life goals in mind. Remember that career development is a life-long process. Your job is the vehicle that enables you to carry out your worthy life goals. Your job, however, is not the end of the line: it's only the beginning. If you have a job where you're performing useful service and growing, you're sure to reach a point where you'll be ready to make a bigger contribution. Then it will be time for you to revise your career goals and get ready to play a bigger game in your life. And as you do, your valuable service will command a greater income. So play the game well, give it all you've got, and exercise your self empowering skills to the fullest. Go for it! Enjoy being a winner.

Job Search Case Study

This chapter has covered most of the available methods for job search in a competitive job market, stressing nontraditional methods. Career changers will find many of these methods helpful to meet the challenges of their job search. However, if you are about to graduate from college and look for your first entry-level career position, following every step of the "getting hired" game will be overwhelming and probably unnecessary. Consider using a simplified version of these methods, sending out a standard resume and custom cover letter to both advertised openings and prospects uncovered by following the methods of this chapter. Use contacts to bolster these traditional written materials, so they get to the right people. Revise you materials when necessary to fit the particular job. Ara, the case study for this chapter, completed a typical job search for a recent college graduate, including both traditional and nontraditional approaches.

Case Study—Ara

Ara graduated from the University of Maryland with a B.A. in radio and television production. Ready to charge out and land his first full-time career position, Ara combed through the classified sections of the *Washington Post*, *New York Times*, and *Baltimore Sun* newspapers. He had decided he wouldn't limit himself to just the Washington, D.C., metropolitan area. Ara followed up on five ads for production technicians by sending his resume with appropriately enthusiastic cover letters. (At this stage of his search, he was using a standard resume with a customized cover letter.)

While Ara waited for results from this traditional approach, he followed a friend's suggestion to look in trade magazines as well as contact cable organizations for more prospective employers. After doing just that, and making a list of some thirty possibilities, he drafted a general all-purpose cover letter and sent it off with his standard resume to the list of possibilities. By now, a couple of months had passed, and Ara had received his first of what would be five rejection letters for the production technician positions. He was discouraged.

Ara's family and close friends encouraged him to continue looking for the kind of job he really wanted. In fact, his father gave Ara the name and phone number of a colleague at work who knew someone at the local cable commission. Before Ara had a chance to make contact with his father's friend, he received one letter expressing mild interest in his resume but lacking the type of position he wanted. Would he come for an interview for a floor manager's position instead? Ara decided to go for the interview. Since this was the first positive step in his job search, Ara went to the interview for practice. Although this interview didn't have any positive ending, Ara soon got another lead from his applications and interviewed for a set designer position and an audio technician position with local county cable stations. Both interviews went better than his first one, and Ara held out some hope for the audio technician position especially.

By now Ara had called his contact at the local cable commission, introduced himself to the woman, told how he had gotten her name, and explained briefly his relevant interests, experience, and degree. Ara was in luck. The woman told him that he had contacted her just two weeks before a production technician position opening was going to be advertised. She encouraged him to watch for the ad and then submit his resume and letter of interest. Most important, his contact told him how to revise his resume so that his skills would focus on the job description.

Now Ara felt he was getting somewhere. Ara's revisions of his resume were more time-consuming than he had anticipated, but through his contact, he had gotten a head start. While he was working on his resume, he received a few more "thanks but no thanks" letters. He did get two more calls for interviews but turned one down, since it was just for a part-time position in New York City. Ara wisely decided to go on the other interview for set design and construction, instead of counting on the cable commission job. Meanwhile, he got another rejection from the earlier interview for audio technician.

Ara finally finished redoing his resume to "fit" the cable commission position of production technician. This position seemed tailor-made for Ara. It called for some writing and producing, even directing some small projects. These were skills Ara excelled in and enjoyed using in his college T.V. classes. He sent in his resume along with cover letter and kept his fingers crossed. In just five days, he was invited to come in for an interview with the same contact he had originally reached on the phone. What an interview it was! Ara was relaxed from his previous interview experience. He felt very good about the way he answered and asked questions. The woman told Ara he would hear from her in two days. On the second day, Ara received a phone call from the cable commission offering him the job. Although he wanted to shout "yes" into the phone, he kept his composure and said he would like to think it over and let them know in twenty-four hours.

Ara did accept the job offer and is still excited about his work after being on the job for six months. As he reflects back over the five months of ups and downs, raised hopes and rejections, he feels it was all worth it.

Notes

1. William A. Cohen, *The Executive's Guide to Finding a Superior Job* (AMACOM, 135 West 50th Street, New York, New York 10020), p. 7.
2. Tom Jackson, *Guerrilla Tactics in the Job Market* (New York: Bantam Books, 1978), p. 120.
3. Cohen, pp. 36–37.

Some Suggested Additional References

Richard Beatly, *The Perfect Cover Letter*. New York: John Wiley and Sons, 1989.

Anne Boe and Bettie B. Youngs, *Is Your "Net" Working: A Complete Guide to Building Contacts and Career Visibility*. New York: John Wiley and Sons, Inc., 1989.

Robbie Miller Kaplan, *Sure-Hire Resumes*. American Management Association, 1989.

Joyce Lane Kennedy and Thomas J. Marrow, *Electronic Resume Revolution: Creating a Winning Resume for the New World of Job Seeking*. New York: John Wiley and Sons, Inc., 1994.

H. Anthony Medley, *Sweaty Palms: The Neglected Art of Being Interviewed*. Revised edition. Ten Speed Press, 1992.

Tom Washington, *Resume Power: Selling Yourself On Paper*. Revised edition. Mount Vernon Press, 1993.

Martin Yate, *Knock Em Dead: The Ultimate Job Seeker's Handbook*. Holbrook, MA: Bob Adam's, Inc., 1994.

Self-Insights

Self-Insights	Acquired From Chapter # _____

Career Possibilities

Occupations of Interest	Holland Code	Occupations of Interest	Holland Code

A^3 Self Profile Summary

A puzzle is composed of many pieces. As each piece is fitted together in its proper place, a picture of the whole puzzle begins to emerge. Similarly, the self-assessment phase of the Career Decision Making Process includes many pieces in the form of independent assessments. Each assessment you complete is a piece of the personal puzzle that becomes a self profile of your career related attributes. A graphic display of your self profile, together with a completed example, is included in the following pages of this Appendix. The directions for completing your self profile are outlined below.

After completing your Functional Skills Assessment in Chapter 2, place your top individual functional skills in priority order under the Information, People, and Things categories. To round out the skills piece of your self profile, add your top three Special Knowledge Skills and your top five Self-Management Skills listed in priority order.

The next assessment is Ned Herrmann's Thinking Style Assessment included in Chapter 3. After completing your Thinking Style Profile, place the number of your preference code (1, 2, or 3) for each quadrant of the Herrmann pictorial above the line provided in each square.

From Chapter 4 place the letters representing your Holland Code in the boxes provided. Under each letter of your code include three characteristics that best describe you from those listed on pages 106 and 108 of Chapter 4.

The final pieces of your self profile come from Chapter 6. List your top five values in priority order in the space provided. Complete your Life Goal/Mission Statement and place it in the rectangle at the bottom of the page.

The result is a profile of your most important career related attributes.

Self Profile

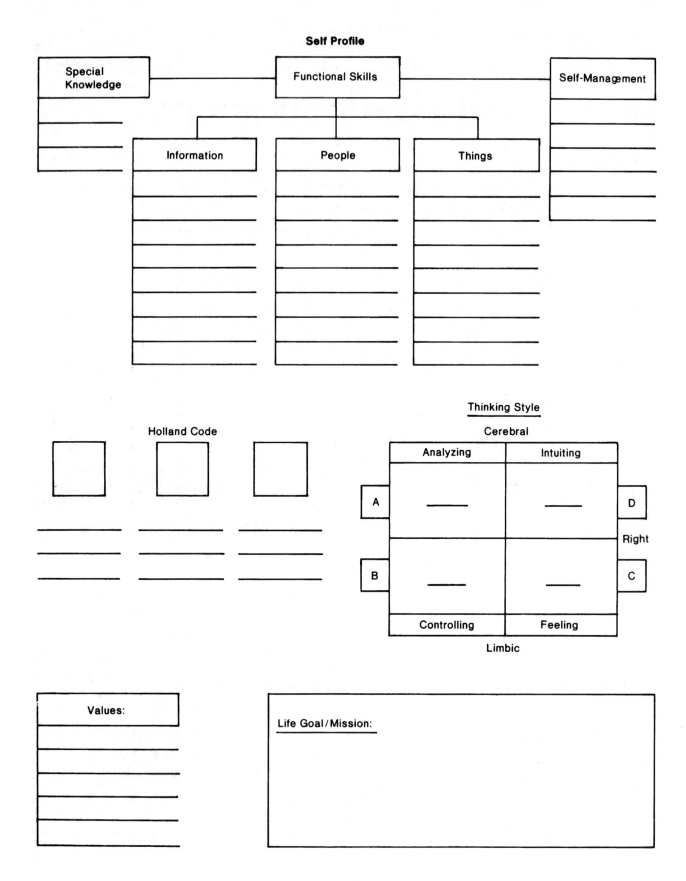

Special Knowledge	Functional Skills			Self-Management

Information	People	Things

Holland Code

Thinking Style

Cerebral

	Analyzing	Intuiting	
A	___	___	D
			Right
B	___	___	C
	Controlling	Feeling	

Limbic

Values:

Life Goal / Mission:

Self Profile Example

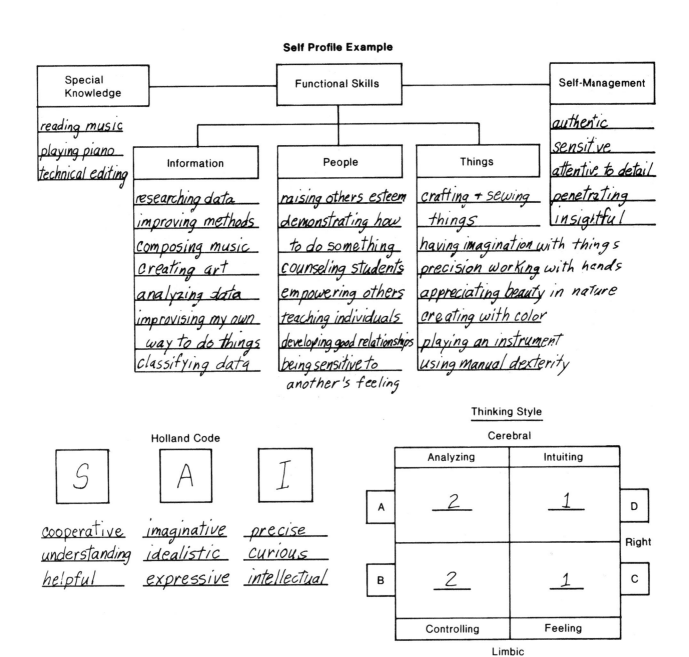

Special Knowledge	Functional Skills			Self-Management
reading music				authentic
playing piano				sensitive
technical editing				attentive to detail
				penetrating
				insightful

Information	People	Things
researching data	raising others esteem	crafting + sewing things
improving methods	demonstrating how to do something	having imagination with things
composing music	counseling students	precision working with hands
creating art	empowering others	appreciating beauty in nature
analyzing data	teaching individuals	creating with color
improvising my own way to do things	developing good relationships	playing an instrument
classifying data	being sensitive to another's feeling	using manual dexterity

Holland Code

S	A	I
cooperative	imaginative	precise
understanding	idealistic	curious
helpful	expressive	intellectual

Thinking Style

Cerebral

	Analyzing	Intuiting	
A	2	1	D
			Right
B	2	1	C
	Controlling	Feeling	

Limbic

Values:

personal development
close relationships
mental challenge
appreciating beauty
empowering others

Life Goal / Mission: By exploring truth and beauty in the arts and physical world, I will strive to grow and find meaning in my own life that I can experience with friends and to improve the lives of others.

APPENDIX B
Personality Style Compatibility Answers

Authors' Answers to Exercise 5-B

1. Since biology is primarily an I curriculum and is opposite E, the E-type person is likely to be very dissatisfied. Types that are opposite each other on the hexagon are very dissimilar. The E type here would probably drop out, flunk out, or wisely change to an academic program that would be compatible with the primary E. The E type, persisting in the I curriculum, would be likely to experience a very low energy level, a tendency to be ill frequently, and a general lack of interest in academics, at least, and probably life in general.

2. Here again, the I type is going into an occupation that is just the opposite. Both salesperson and warehouse manager are E types. The I type is likely to be very dissatisfied on the job and search for ways to experience satisfaction outside of work, if not look for a more compatible occupation.

3. An A person who enrolls in an A curriculum is likely to experience satisfaction. Both personality type and curriculum are compatible. The A person is likely to be very energetic, and enthusiastic about and attentive to his/her studies.

4. The C person is not likely to last very long in an A occupation. The C and A types are opposite on the hexagon. The A environment would be too flexible and frustrating for the C person, who would want structure and a schedule of activities to follow. The C person in this situation would be most likely to channel energy into looking for a new compatible occupation.

5. The energy level of an S person in an R job would be very low. The chances for success and stability would be extremely low, since these types are opposite, and characteristics are very dissimilar. The S person might experience a high absentee rate from work due to illness or lack of interest. Here again, any energy might be directed into seeking a compatible occupation.

C Conducting Career Information Interviews

Talking to people about their work is an effective way to gather information in your occupational exploration. Initially, to get comfortable with the idea of interviewing people, talk to family, friends, or anybody you know well. This should help minimize your anxiety about interviewing.

Conduct information-gathering interviews to find answers to the following questions:

1. How did the person get started in that kind of work?

2. What does the person enjoy about his/her work?

3. What does the person dislike about his/her work?

4. Who else does the person know who is doing similar kinds of work or uses similar skills?

5. What can the person tell you about the employment outlook in his/her occupational field with a particular firm, in a particular locality, or in the nation generally?

In making your initial contact with people, be sure to clarify that you are not interviewing them for a job. Instead, you are considering that line of work and simply trying to learn more about it. At the completion of your interview, ask the person for the names of other people who are doing a similar kind of work or using similar skills. Make every effort to get a specific person's name, so that you have someone definite to contact for an additional information interview. Also, ask the person you are interviewing if you may use his/her name in contacting this other individual.

Conduct additional career information interviews, using the process outlined here. Be sure to send a thank-you letter to the person you have seen within one to three days after the interview. For possible future reference, keep a list of all the people you have interviewed or plan to interview. You may even want to keep a special notebook or cards with interview notes on the five questions covered. Include the main things that you learned from each interview. This file will be a rich source of information as you conduct your occupational exploration.

D Envisioning Process

DAYDREAMING AND FANTASIZING

Daydreaming and fantasizing are commonly considered undesirable, non-productive activities. An individual may be criticized for being "just a dreamer," and we worry about people living in a "fantasy world." Such concern is often justified because both daydreaming and fantasizing are destructive when divorced from reality and action. However, dreaming and fantasizing can be effectively used to reduce stress, conquer fears and phobias, or plan careers and lives.* Specifically, constructive fantasizing can help people develop their inner resources to find imaginative problem solutions, to discover ingenious alternatives, and to invent original goals for career/life planning. By preparing and mentally rehearsing for the future, constructive fantasizing also builds confidence. This is the power of suggestion.

The constructive use of fantasy has been variously called guided fantasy, inner imagery, creative imagining, etc. We refer to productive fantasizing as the envisioning process.

THE LEFT AND RIGHT HEMISPHERES OF THE BRAIN

Recent research has shown that the left and right hemispheres of the human brain perform two completely different functions. In the typical right-handed person, the left hemisphere of the brain is the center of logical thought, language, and mathematical reasoning. The primary functions of the left brain have to do with rational thinking, analytical thought, and intellectual activity such as reading, writing, and classifying. The right hemisphere, in contrast, is the seat of intuition, creativity, holistic thought, and symbolic thinking. It is in the right brain where the power to synthesize, dream, and acquire self-awareness exists. In his book, *The Three Boxes of Life,* Richard Bolles points out that the left side of the brain is the crucial hemisphere for wordsmiths, mathematicians, and scientists. The right side of the brain is crucial for artists, craftspeople, and musicians.** Apparently, the left and right brain functions are reversed for left-handed people.***

USING THE RIGHT HEMISPHERE

While the left hemisphere may work best under pressure, the right operates best in a state of relaxation. To facilitate right-hemisphere use, you need conditions that best enable you to relax while remaining mentally alert. Right-hemisphere functioning is not so much a thinking process as it is a fantasizing process. Right-hemisphere information is experienced as spontaneous awareness or intuition rather than as deliberate or concentrated thoughts. Your right-hemisphere insights are more likely to be images and other sensations than ideas.

Before starting an envisioning process, define your task or problem that would benefit from right-hemisphere insight or resolution. Using the left hemisphere of your brain to define your concern opens the way for a spontaneously acquired right-hemisphere response. This spontaneous insight is the breakthrough that people often have after they have been struggling over some issue or problem for consider-

---

*James Morgan and Thomas Skovalt, "Using Inner Experience: Fantasy and Daydreams in Career Counseling," *Journal of Counseling Psychology,* 24: 391–397, 1977.

**Richard N. Bolles, *The Three Boxes of Life* (Berkeley, California: Ten Speed Press, 1978), p. 96.

***For further information on the two hemispheres of the brain, read Robert E. Ornstein, *The Psychology of Consciousness* (New York: The Viking Press, 1972).

able time without coming to a logical resolution. When you have struggled with some problem until you were about ready to give up, perhaps you then put aside the task. After taking a nap, going for a walk, or engaging in some other low-key activity, did the solution ever suddenly pop into your mind? If so, you have experienced how the right and left hemispheres of the brain function together. This phenomenon is often reported by people who have achieved sudden creative breakthroughs when they shifted from intensive mental concentration to a relaxed state. How or why this happens is a mystery.

Once the creative breakthrough has been achieved, it needs then to be translated into language by the left hemisphere so it will be fully usable and communicable. Einstein is said to have intuitively achieved right- hemisphere understanding of his famous Theory of Relativity before he was able to figure it out logically or communicate it to others.

THE ENVISIONING PROCESS

When using the envisioning process, we suggest you follow these steps:

1. Make arrangements to be quiet and completely uninterrupted for twenty minutes to one hour. That may mean turning down your phone, not answering the doorbell, and ensuring that someone does not walk in on you during the process.

2. Verbalize, write, or ponder (left-hemisphere processes) what you would like to accomplish with the right-hemisphere intuitive process.

3. Sit in a straight back chair or lie on your back on a carpeted floor.

   a. If you sit in a chair, sit erect with your back straight, your feet flat on the floor, head facing straight forward, and shoulders level and relaxed. Sitting this way helps reduce muscle tension and facilitates a general state of relaxation.

   b. If you recline on the floor, lie flat on your back with your feet spread slightly apart and your arms flat on the floor, palms up, about six to twelve inches away from your sides.

4. Close your eyes. While remaining awake:

   a. Relax the muscles between your eyes, and experience the flow of energy released from the previously tensed muscles.

   b. Relax the muscles in your jaw and chin while letting your mouth drop slightly open.

   c. Continue relaxing your body, one part at a time, by concentrating on and then loosening your tensed muscles, letting any tension flow out of your body.

   d. Take deep and even breaths, and consciously relax your body, starting with your toes and feet and working progressively upwards to your head.

      Note: As you relax, you may notice a flowing sensation throughout your body. That is caused by the energy released from tightly held muscles that are now relaxed.

5. In this relaxed state, just let your mind go. Do not consciously think or try to force your thoughts; just let them come freely and spontaneously.

   a. Do not try to figure out the meaning of anything you may be experiencing while in a relaxed state. To do so may result in switching from right to left-hemisphere functioning of your brain.

   b. Remain relaxed and detached from your thoughts and mental imagery. Just let happen what will, and be an observer of your mental processes as if you were viewing a movie of your mind.

6. As you are nearing the end of the process, decide how you want to feel when you finish the process, and then allow yourself to feel that way.

7. When you are finished, come out of your relaxed state gradually. It can be a bit of a shock to your system if you bolt out of a relaxed condition (or are jolted out) too quickly. Begin by moving your feet and/or hands about slowly, recalling your external surroundings. When you are ready, open your eyes.

8. Give yourself a few minutes of detached inactivity as you return to fully conscious thoughts. Then, before doing anything else, begin recording any insights that you acquired during the envisioning process. Do this immediately, so that you will not forget and so that you translate your envisioned insights into language.

   a. Write down what happened in the process, even if you are not aware of any significant insights you had during the process. Sometimes, the process of writing is necessary to make you aware of new insights acquired from envisioning.

   b. By writing, you are likely to more fully understand the insights you had. You also will produce a written record to assist you in career decision making and future planning.

9. You may find it helpful to repeat the same envisioning process over several days, continually building and expanding on previous insights.

10. You may also want to discuss your insights, acquired from envisioning, with an interested listener to develop your understanding further.

Some Additional Resources for Career Assessment and Job Search

PERSONALITY AND INTEREST ASSESSMENTS

California Psychological Inventory (CPI) (Consulting Psychologists Press, 577 College Ave., Palo Alto, CA 94306) The CPI produces a scored report on 20 separate behavioral scales (Dominance, Sociability, Empathy, etc.)

Campbell Interests and Skills Survey (CISS), by David P. Campell: obtained from National Computer Systems, P.O. Box 1294, Minneapolis, MN 55440. Provides a profile of personal interests and relates them to career choices and compares them with self-rated skills.

Deal Me In Question Cards (Career Systems, Inc.) Tel # 800 283-8839. A card sort exercise to help identify your strongest individual interests and arrange them into four categories (data, people, ideas, things).

Myers-Briggs Type Indicator (MBTI) by Isable Briggs Myers and Katherine C. Briggs (Consulting Psychologists Press, Inc.—CPP), 3803 East Bayshore Rd., P.O. Box 10096, Palo Alto, CA 94303. Delineates 16 personality types, each with its own way of understanding the world, each with its own strengths and personal challenges.

Self-Directed Search (SDS) by John L. Holland (Psychological Assessment Resources, Inc.—PAR), P.O. Box 998, Odessa, Fl 33556. The SDS produces a three letter code profiling one's individual interests within six general styles. One's three letter code is then compared to occupations to look for best matches between personal interests and occupational activities.

Strong Interest Inventory (SII), by E.K. Strong, Jr. and Jo-Ida C. Hansen (Consulting Psychologists Press, Inc.—CPP). The SII generates a profile of an individual's personality style and identifies occupations that match interests. Special reports are available for identifying leadership and management potentials and for providing feedback on leisure interests.

Personal Passion Profile (PPP) by David C. Borchard, (Directions for New Realities), 4603 Governor Kent Court, Upper Marlboro, MD. 20772. The PPP survey your strongest personal preference areas and provides information for making intelligent career and life decisions. The PPP provides two graphic profiles that show the magnitude of your personal interests and transferable skills in six areas of basic human interest and relates these to career choices and leisure activities.

SKILL ASSESSMENT

Motivated Skill Card Sort by Richard L. Knowdell, (Career Research & Testing, Inc, 2005 Hamilton Ave. San Jose, CA 95125) Tel # 800 888-4945. A quick and easy way to identify the motivated skills that are central to personal and career satisfaction and success. Use the cards to assess your proficiency and motivation in 48 separate skill area.

Functional Skill Cards, by Fontelle Gilbert Seminars for Personal Growth, 6501 Inwood Drive, Springfield, VA 22150. This deck of cards contains 90 skills to be sorted into categories based on personal preferences and self-rated competencies.

The New Quick Job-Hunting Map by Richard N. Boles (Ten Speed Press, Box 7123, Berkeley, CA 94707). A thorough assessment activity for identifying transferable skills from your personal experience. The Map guides you through processes that help identify, classify, and prioritize your "most preferred skills."

Skill Scan Professional Pack (P.O. Box 587, Orinda, CA 94563 Tel # (510) 254-2705). A card sort exercise to identify which of the indicated skills you want to play a major, secondary, ant minor role in your future work and then sort favorite skills into categories.

BRAIN DOMINANCE AND THINKING STYLES

Learning-Style Inventory by David A. Kolb (McBer & Company Training Resources Group, 173 Newbury Street, Boston MA 02116 Tel # (617) 437-7080). A self-scoring, self-interpreting inventory profiling one's dominant mode of learning in four different styles.

Herrman Brain Dominance Inventory (HBDI), by Ned Herrmann; obtained from Applied Creative Services 2075 Buffalo Creek Rd., Lake Lure, NC 28746. The HBDI generates a personal brain dominance profile showing your thinking-style preferences in four different modes. This information can be very useful in making career choices designed to enhance personal performance.

VALUES CLARIFICATION

Invest in Your Values by Beverly Berstein and Beverly Kaye (Insight Publications, 2252 Beverly Glen Place, Los Angeles, CA 90077 Tel # (310) 474-0959). A prioritization process in which you list your top values from a selection of 35 value choices and use a color code to assess the likely-hood of achieving your values in current situation.

Career Anchors by Edgar H. Schein (Pfeiffer & Company 8517 Production Avenue, San Diego CA 92121 Tel # (619) 578-5900). A self-assessment activity designed for people who have been working for ten years or more to identify their core career related values from eight general categories.

The Values Scale, by Donald E. Super and Dorothy D. Nevill (Consulting Psychologists Press, Inc.—CPP). The Values Scale measures 21 separate values and provide a profile showing your relative degree of strength in each of these.

Career Values Card Sort, by Richard L. Knowdell, Career Research & Testing, 2005 Hamilton Ave., Suite 250, San Jose, CA 95125. A simple card sort device for examining your personal values.

Values Cards, by Fontelle Gilbert, Seminars for Personal Growth, 6501 Inwood Drive, Springfield, VA 22150. A values sort process that helps one prioritize their values and relate there impact on (1) interaction with others and (2) their conflicts or satisfactions both inside and outside the work place.

---

*These are psychological assessment instruments that can be purchased only be certified counselors. Individuals may take them at most agencies that provide career counseling services.

F Small Discussion Groups (Trios)

By sharing your individual achievements with two other people, your functional skill identification can progress far more quickly. Why is this? Most people tend to be too critical about themselves, so they ignore certain talents their achievements reveal. Consequently, it can be very difficult for individuals to identify their own skills completely. However, the process of identifying skills that someone else has used is relatively easy.

Start this process by rounding up two volunteers. Ask friends, classmates, or relatives, making sure that they do not have false preconceived ideas about what your talents are or should be. Your two volunteers might even decide to participate in this process themselves. Once you have selected your group members, decide who will be person A, B, and C. Then follow the remaining steps as outlined.

Step 1: Person A will read a story about one of his or her top satisfying achievements, while persons B and C will listen closely, noting on paper any functional (transferable) skills that they think were used. If the story is not clear, B and C should interrupt by asking the question, *"What did it take for you to do that?"* The purpose for asking this question is to encourage the storyteller to describe the particular situation more completely. It is important for the listeners (now B and C) to keep asking this question until they fully understand the situation and are able to identify the functional skills involved.

Step 2: Person A will next say what functional skills he/she used to make the achievement happen. Person A names and records these skills *before* hearing what B and C have to add.

Step 3: Now, persons B and C will respond to person A's story reading. Person B will identify functional skills that he or she heard in the story. When person B is finished, person C will repeat the process. Person A, meanwhile, is writing down all the skills that B and C have mentioned.

Step 4: If desired, repeat this entire process, now giving person B the opportunity to read a story while persons A and C listen. Continue as above. For maximum benefit, repeat this process over a period of time until you have uncovered skills from all five stories you wrote in Exercise 2-B on page 24.

Murry couldn't decide which discussion group he wanted to attend

G Prioritizing Process

In many situations, you need to choose your top preference or preferences from among numerous options. While it's easy to choose with just two options, that task becomes much more difficult as the number of options increases. A quick and easy process to find your top preference and rank the remaining choices is the prioritizing process.* In this process, you will be choosing between just two items at a time. This greatly facilitates the process of determining overall preferences from a list of items.

To demonstrate how to use this prioritizing process, consider the following list of sample activities for a Saturday night. We have arbitrarily numbered this list without considering preference at this point.

1. roller skating
2. movies
3. supper club
4. Irish pub
5. sports event

6. popular music concert
7. ballet
8. bowling
9. symphony concert
10. dancing

To determine the two most preferred activities you would like to do on Saturday night, you will prioritize the entire list. On page 285, we have copied each activity from the list in the "ITEMS" blanks down the left-hand side of the sample prioritizing grid. Once again, we've recorded them in the random order of the original list.

Each number on the right-hand side of the grid corresponds to the same numbered activity. For example, #1 refers to roller skating, #2 to movies, etc. Starting with items #1 and #2 on the list, ask yourself which of the two—roller skating or attending a movie—would you enjoy doing more this Saturday night. Let's assume you say going to the movies. You would then circle item #2 in the pair $\frac{1}{2}$ on the prioritizing grid (see the sample grid). In this way, you have indicated your preference for item #2 when given a choice between #1 and #2. Continue along the top row of the grid, row A, pairing item #1 in turn with items #3, #4, #5, #6, #7, #8, #9, and #10, circling your preference in each pair. For example, when pairing item #1 with item #5, let's assume you would prefer attending a sports event to roller skating, so you would circle item #5 in the pair $\frac{1}{5}$. Continue this forced choice process in rows B through I. If you have done the process correctly, only one choice will be circled in each pair of items, i.e., $\frac{4}{5}$. Make sure you don't end up with two circled items, i.e., $\frac{4}{5}$.

Once you have completed circling the items on the grid, record in the second column the number of times each item has been circled anywhere on the grid. You will use this total to determine final priority ranking. For example, item #2, circled seven times, will rank ahead of item #3 which was circled only six times. In the event of ties, check the grid to see which item is circled when the two are paired against each other. For instance, items #1 and #6 are tied, both having been circled three times. To determine your preference ranking, you merely need to look at the grid to see which item you preferred

*From *The Three Boxes of Life and How to Get Out of Them,* by Richard N. Bolles, © copyright 1978, by Richard N. Bolles. Used by special permission. Those desiring a copy of the complete book for further reading may procure it from the publisher, Ten Speed Press, P.O. Box 7123, Berkeley, CA 94707.

in your initial assessment. If you look at Row A on the sample grid, you can see that item #1 was chosen over item #6. Therefore, item #1, roller skating, wins out over item #6, attending a popular music concert. Similarly, the tie between item #4 and item #7 is resolved in favor of item #4. When you have finished counting the circled numbers, you can see from the sample grid that the first choice for Saturday night is to go to a symphony concert and second choice is to go to a sports event, etc. The final prioritized list then looks like this:

First choice:	symphony concert
Second choice:	sports event
Third choice:	movies
Fourth choice:	supper club
Fifth choice:	Irish pub
Sixth choice:	ballet
Seventh choice:	roller skating
Eighth choice:	popular music concert
Ninth choice:	bowling
Tenth choice:	dancing

This prioritizing process will be used many times throughout the book. You will be using it to prioritize your preferred transferable skills, achievements, self-management skills, values, and people preferences.

This process is an extremely helpful decision-making tool in any situation where you have to make difficult choices from among competing alternatives.

Prioritizing Grid* — Sample

Items	Number Of Times Circled	Final Prioritized Order
1. roller skating	///	7
2. movies	///// //	3
3. supper club	///// /	4
4. Irish pub	////	5
5. sports event	///// ///	2
6. popular music concert	///	8
7. ballet	////	6
8. bowling	/	9
9. symphony	///// ////	1
10. dancing	0	10

*Adapted from *The Three Boxes of Life and How to Get Out of Them*, by Richard N. Bolles, © copyright 1978, by Richard N. Bolles. Used by special permission. Those desiring a copy of the complete book for further reading may procure it from the publisher, Ten Speed Press, P.O. Box 7123, Berkeley, CA 94707.

Prioritizing Grid*

Grid

Row									
A	1/2	1/3	1/4	1/5	1/6	1/7	1/8	1/9	1/10
B		2/3	2/4	2/5	2/6	2/7	2/8	2/9	2/10
C			3/4	3/5	3/6	3/7	3/8	3/9	3/10
D				4/5	4/6	4/7	4/8	4/9	4/10
E					5/6	5/7	5/8	5/9	5/10
F						6/7	6/8	6/9	6/10
G							7/8	7/9	7/10
H								8/9	8/10
I									9/10

Items

	Items	Number Of Times Circled	Final Prioritized Order
1.			
2.			
3.			
4.			
5.			
6.			
7.			
8.			
9.			
10.			

Prioritizing Grid*

Items	Number Of Times Circled	Final Prioritized Order	Grid									Row
1.	—	—	$\frac{1}{2}$	$\frac{1}{3}$	$\frac{1}{4}$	$\frac{1}{5}$	$\frac{1}{6}$	$\frac{1}{7}$	$\frac{1}{8}$	$\frac{1}{9}$	$\frac{1}{10}$	A
2.	—	—	$\frac{2}{3}$	$\frac{2}{4}$	$\frac{2}{5}$	$\frac{2}{6}$	$\frac{2}{7}$	$\frac{2}{8}$	$\frac{2}{9}$	$\frac{2}{10}$		B
3.	—	—	$\frac{3}{4}$	$\frac{3}{5}$	$\frac{3}{6}$	$\frac{3}{7}$	$\frac{3}{8}$	$\frac{3}{9}$	$\frac{3}{10}$			C
4.	—	—	$\frac{4}{5}$	$\frac{4}{6}$	$\frac{4}{7}$	$\frac{4}{8}$	$\frac{4}{9}$	$\frac{4}{10}$				D
5.	—	—	$\frac{5}{6}$	$\frac{5}{7}$	$\frac{5}{8}$	$\frac{5}{9}$	$\frac{5}{10}$					E
6.	—	—	$\frac{6}{7}$	$\frac{6}{8}$	$\frac{6}{9}$	$\frac{6}{10}$						F
7.	—	—	$\frac{7}{8}$	$\frac{7}{9}$	$\frac{7}{10}$							G
8.	—	—	$\frac{8}{9}$	$\frac{8}{10}$								H
9.	—	—	$\frac{9}{10}$									I
10.	—	—										

Prioritizing Grid*

Items		Number Of Times Circled	Final Prioritized Order	Row			Grid						
1.				A	$\frac{1}{2}$	$\frac{1}{3}$	$\frac{1}{4}$	$\frac{1}{5}$	$\frac{1}{6}$	$\frac{1}{7}$	$\frac{1}{8}$	$\frac{1}{9}$	$\frac{1}{10}$
2.				B		$\frac{2}{3}$	$\frac{2}{4}$	$\frac{2}{5}$	$\frac{2}{6}$	$\frac{2}{7}$	$\frac{2}{8}$	$\frac{2}{9}$	$\frac{2}{10}$
3.				C			$\frac{3}{4}$	$\frac{3}{5}$	$\frac{3}{6}$	$\frac{3}{7}$	$\frac{3}{8}$	$\frac{3}{9}$	$\frac{3}{10}$
4.				D				$\frac{4}{5}$	$\frac{4}{6}$	$\frac{4}{7}$	$\frac{4}{8}$	$\frac{4}{9}$	$\frac{4}{10}$
5.				E					$\frac{5}{6}$	$\frac{5}{7}$	$\frac{5}{8}$	$\frac{5}{9}$	$\frac{5}{10}$
6.				F						$\frac{6}{7}$	$\frac{6}{8}$	$\frac{6}{9}$	$\frac{6}{10}$
7.				G							$\frac{7}{8}$	$\frac{7}{9}$	$\frac{7}{10}$
8.				H								$\frac{8}{9}$	$\frac{8}{10}$
9.				I									$\frac{9}{10}$
10.													

*Adapted from *The Three Boxes of Life and How to Get Out of Them*, by Richard N. Bolles, © copyright 1978, by Richard N. Bolles. Used by special permission. Those desiring a copy of the complete book for further reading may procure it from the publisher, Ten Speed Press, P.O. Box 7123, Berkeley, CA 94707.

Prioritizing Grid*

Grid

Row									
A	1/2	1/3	1/4	1/5	1/6	1/7	1/8	1/9	1/10
B		2/3	2/4	2/5	2/6	2/7	2/8	2/9	2/10
C			3/4	3/5	3/6	3/7	3/8	3/9	3/10
D				4/5	4/6	4/7	4/8	4/9	4/10
E					5/6	5/7	5/8	5/9	5/10
F						6/7	6/8	6/9	6/10
G							7/8	7/9	7/10
H								8/9	8/10
I									9/10

Items	Number Of Times Circled	Final Prioritized Order
1.	_____	_____
2.	_____	_____
3.	_____	_____
4.	_____	_____
5.	_____	_____
6.	_____	_____
7.	_____	_____
8.	_____	_____
9.	_____	_____
10.	_____	_____

*Adapted from *The Three Boxes of Life and How to Get Out of Them,* by Richard N. Bolles, © copyright 1978, by Richard N. Bolles. Used by special permission. Those desiring a copy of the complete book for further reading may procure it from the publisher, Ten Speed Press, P.O. Box 7123, Berkeley, CA 94707.

Prioritizing Grid*

Row	Grid								
A	1/2	1/3	1/4	1/5	1/6	1/7	1/8	1/9	1/10
B		2/3	2/4	2/5	2/6	2/7	2/8	2/9	2/10
C			3/4	3/5	3/6	3/7	3/8	3/9	3/10
D				4/5	4/6	4/7	4/8	4/9	4/10
E					5/6	5/7	5/8	5/9	5/10
F						6/7	6/8	6/9	6/10
G							7/8	7/9	7/10
H								8/9	8/10
I									9/10

Items	Number Of Times Circled	Final Prioritized Order
1.		
2.		
3.		
4.		
5.		
6.		
7.		
8.		
9.		
10.		

Prioritizing Grid*

Items	Number Of Times Circled	Final Prioritized Order	Grid	Row
1.			1/2 1/3 1/4 1/5 1/6 1/7 1/8 1/9 1/10	A
2.			2/3 2/4 2/5 2/6 2/7 2/8 2/9 2/10	B
3.			3/4 3/5 3/6 3/7 3/8 3/9 3/10	C
4.			4/5 4/6 4/7 4/8 4/9 4/10	D
5.			5/6 5/7 5/8 5/9 5/10	E
6.			6/7 6/8 6/9 6/10	F
7.			7/8 7/9 7/10	G
8.			8/9 8/10	H
9.			9/10	I
10.				

*Adapted from *The Three Boxes of Life and How to Get Out of Them*, by Richard N. Bolles, © copyright 1978, by Richard N. Bolles. Used by special permission. Those desiring a copy of the complete book for further reading may procure it from the publisher, Ten Speed Press, P.O. Box 7123, Berkeley, CA 94707.

Prioritizing Grid*

Row	Grid								
A	1/2	1/3	1/4	1/5	1/6	1/7	1/8	1/9	1/10
B		2/3	2/4	2/5	2/6	2/7	2/8	2/9	2/10
C			3/4	3/5	3/6	3/7	3/8	3/9	3/10
D				4/5	4/6	4/7	4/8	4/9	4/10
E					5/6	5/7	5/8	5/9	5/10
F						6/7	6/8	6/9	6/10
G							7/8	7/9	7/10
H								8/9	8/10
I									9/10

Items	Number Of Times Circled	Final Prioritized Order
1.		
2.		
3.		
4.		
5.		
6.		
7.		
8.		
9.		
10.		

*Adapted from *The Three Boxes of Life and How to Get Out of Them*, by Richard N. Bolles. © copyright 1978, by Richard N. Bolles. Used by special permission. Those desiring a copy of the complete book for further reading may procure it from the publisher, Ten Speed Press, P.O. Box 7123, Berkeley, CA 94707.

Prioritizing Grid*

Items — **Number Of Times Circled** — **Final Prioritized Order** — **Grid** — **Row**

1. _____ | ____ | ____

2. _____ | ____ | ____

3. _____ | ____ | ____

4. _____ | ____ | ____

5. _____ | ____ | ____

6. _____ | ____ | ____

7. _____ | ____ | ____

8. _____ | ____ | ____

9. _____ | ____ | ____

10. _____ | ____ | ____

Grid

Row									
A	$\frac{1}{2}$	$\frac{1}{3}$	$\frac{1}{4}$	$\frac{1}{5}$	$\frac{1}{6}$	$\frac{1}{7}$	$\frac{1}{8}$	$\frac{1}{9}$	$\frac{1}{10}$
B		$\frac{2}{3}$	$\frac{2}{4}$	$\frac{2}{5}$	$\frac{2}{6}$	$\frac{2}{7}$	$\frac{2}{8}$	$\frac{2}{9}$	$\frac{2}{10}$
C			$\frac{3}{4}$	$\frac{3}{5}$	$\frac{3}{6}$	$\frac{3}{7}$	$\frac{3}{8}$	$\frac{3}{9}$	$\frac{3}{10}$
D				$\frac{4}{5}$	$\frac{4}{6}$	$\frac{4}{7}$	$\frac{4}{8}$	$\frac{4}{9}$	$\frac{4}{10}$
E					$\frac{5}{6}$	$\frac{5}{7}$	$\frac{5}{8}$	$\frac{5}{9}$	$\frac{5}{10}$
F						$\frac{6}{7}$	$\frac{6}{8}$	$\frac{6}{9}$	$\frac{6}{10}$
G							$\frac{7}{8}$	$\frac{7}{9}$	$\frac{7}{10}$
H								$\frac{8}{9}$	$\frac{8}{10}$
I									$\frac{9}{10}$

*Adapted from *The Three Boxes of Life and How to Get Out of Them*, by Richard N. Bolles, © copyright 1978, by Richard N. Bolles. Used by special permission. Those desiring a copy of the complete book for further reading may procure it from the publisher, Ten Speed Press, P.O. Box 7123, Berkeley, CA 94707.

Prioritizing Grid*

Items	Number Of Times Circled	Final Prioritized Order	Row	Grid
1. _____	___	___	A	$\frac{1}{2}$ $\frac{1}{3}$ $\frac{1}{4}$ $\frac{1}{5}$ $\frac{1}{6}$ $\frac{1}{7}$ $\frac{1}{8}$ $\frac{1}{9}$ $\frac{1}{10}$
2. _____	___	___	B	$\frac{2}{3}$ $\frac{2}{4}$ $\frac{2}{5}$ $\frac{2}{6}$ $\frac{2}{7}$ $\frac{2}{8}$ $\frac{2}{9}$ $\frac{2}{10}$
3. _____	___	___	C	$\frac{3}{4}$ $\frac{3}{5}$ $\frac{3}{6}$ $\frac{3}{7}$ $\frac{3}{8}$ $\frac{3}{9}$ $\frac{3}{10}$
4. _____	___	___	D	$\frac{4}{5}$ $\frac{4}{6}$ $\frac{4}{7}$ $\frac{4}{8}$ $\frac{4}{9}$ $\frac{4}{10}$
5. _____	___	___	E	$\frac{5}{6}$ $\frac{5}{7}$ $\frac{5}{8}$ $\frac{5}{9}$ $\frac{5}{10}$
6. _____	___	___	F	$\frac{6}{7}$ $\frac{6}{8}$ $\frac{6}{9}$ $\frac{6}{10}$
7. _____	___	___	G	$\frac{7}{8}$ $\frac{7}{9}$ $\frac{7}{10}$
8. _____	___	___	H	$\frac{8}{9}$ $\frac{8}{10}$
9. _____	___	___	I	$\frac{9}{10}$
10. _____				

*Adapted from *The Three Boxes of Life and How to Get Out of Them*, by Richard N. Bolles, © copyright 1978, by Richard N. Bolles. Used by special permission. Those desiring a copy of the complete book for further reading may procure it from the publisher, Ten Speed Press, P.O. Box 7123, Berkeley, CA 94707.

Prioritizing Grid*

Row	Grid								
A	1/2	1/3	1/4	1/5	1/6	1/7	1/8	1/9	1/10
B		2/3	2/4	2/5	2/6	2/7	2/8	2/9	2/10
C			3/4	3/5	3/6	3/7	3/8	3/9	3/10
D				4/5	4/6	4/7	4/8	4/9	4/10
E					5/6	5/7	5/8	5/9	5/10
F						6/7	6/8	6/9	6/10
G							7/8	7/9	7/10
H								8/9	8/10
I									9/10

Items	Number Of Times Circled	Final Prioritized Order
1.		
2.		
3.		
4.		
5.		
6.		
7.		
8.		
9.		
10.		

*Adapted from *The Three Boxes of Life and How to Get Out of Them*, by Richard N. Bolles, © copyright 1978, by Richard N. Bolles. Used by special permission. Those desiring a copy of the complete book for further reading may procure it from the publisher, Ten Speed Press, P.O. Box 7123, Berkeley, CA 94707.

Prioritizing Grid*

Items	Number Of Times Circled	Final Prioritized Order	Grid	Row
1.			1/2 1/3 1/4 1/5 1/6 1/7 1/8 1/9 1/10	A
2.			2/3 2/4 2/5 2/6 2/7 2/8 2/9 2/10	B
3.			3/4 3/5 3/6 3/7 3/8 3/9 3/10	C
4.			4/5 4/6 4/7 4/8 4/9 4/10	D
5.			5/6 5/7 5/8 5/9 5/10	E
6.			6/7 6/8 6/9 6/10	F
7.			7/8 7/9 7/10	G
8.			8/9 8/10	H
9.			9/10	I
10.				

Index

Traits table (HBDS), 46–47
Trios (small discussion groups), 281

U

U.S. Government Manual, 232

V

Value Summary Table (HBDS), 50–51
Values
    acquiring and changing, 122
    assessment, life, 119–122
    career goals and objectives compatible with,
       178
    core of your, 127–128
    criteria for, 119–120
    defining and clarifying, 119–120
    discovering hidden, 122–123
    identifying career related, 144
    importance of, 119, 124–126
    listing your, 233–34
    needs and, 46, 109
    needs versus, 118
    strategy, 123–125
Victims, real and self-made, 190
Volunteer work to investigate a field, 207, 236

W

Wants, clarifying your career, 173–176
Wardrobe for job interviews, 255
Work
    conditions, rating, 125
    experiencing satisfaction with, 105
    groups, GOE, 138–140
    purposes, rating, 125
    relationship, rating, 124
    role of, 1–2
    values, 124–126
Work settings
    interviews with several, 148
    relating self-management skills to, 37–38
Work, world of
    bridging the gap between people and, 91
    structure of, 91–94
    understanding, 227–239

Y

Yellow Pages as source of employment targets,
    245